KU-281-870

Easy PC
troubleshooting

R. A. Penfold

Bernard Babani (publishing) Ltd
The Grampians
Shepherds Bush Road
London W6 7NF
England
www.babanibooks.com

Please note

Although every care has been taken with the production of this book to ensure that any projects, designs, modifications, and/or programs, etc., contained herewith, operate in a correct and safe manner and also that any components specified are normally available in Great Britain, the Publisher and Author do not accept responsibility in any way for the failure (including fault in design) of any projects, design, modification, or program to work correctly or to cause damage to any equipment that it may be connected to or used in conjunction with, or in respect of any other damage or injury that may be caused, nor do the Publishers accept responsibility in any way for the failure to obtain specified components.

Notice is also given that if any equipment that is still under warranty is modified in any way or used or connected with home-built equipment then that warranty may be void.

© 2000 BERNARD BABANI (publishing) LTD

First published - March 2000
Reprinted - August 2000
Reprinted - January 2001
Reprinted - May 2001
Reprinted - October 2001
Reprinted - December 2001
Reprinted - April 2002

British Library Cataloguing in Publication Data

A catalogue record for this book is available from the British Library

ISBN 0 85934 484 3

Cover design by Gregor Arthur
Printed and bound in Great Britain by Cox & Wyman Ltd

Preface

Undertaking do-it-yourself repairs on a high-tech product such as a PC may seem to be bordering on the foolhardy, but the modular approach to construction used in these computers makes virtually any repair a relatively simple affair. It is basically just a matter of removing the faulty component and bolting in a new one. There is no need for a vast array of electronic faultfinding equipment, and most faults can actually be fixed without resorting to any test equipment whatever. In fact most PC faults can be repaired using nothing more than a crosshead screwdriver. Even if you should happen to have a vast collection of tools and electronic test equipment it is unlikely that you will need any of it when undertaking PC repairs. There is no need to worry about soldering, because the electrical connections between the components in a PC are made via plugs and sockets rather than soldered joints. The low cost of PC components makes repairs to faulty components uneconomic. Fixing a PC is all about replacing broken parts and not repairing them.

All this does not mean that PC repairs can be undertaken by absolutely anyone. Some experience of using and dealing with PCs is essential, and you need to be reasonably practical. Obviously some technical knowledge is needed in order to locate the fault, buy suitable spare parts, get everything reassembled properly, and undertake any necessary setting up or reinstallation. This book explains in simple terms how to locate faults, replace faulty components, make BIOS adjustments, and reinstall Windows 95 or 98. Whether a problem necessitates a replacement motherboard, or just needs some contacts cleaned, this book explains how to successfully complete the repair. Newcomers to PCs should certainly not attempt their own PC repairs without the aid of an experienced helper, but anyone who is reasonably practical and has at least a couple of years experience at using PCs should be able to tackle most PC repairs with the aid of this publication.

There is a big incentive to do your own PC repairs, which is the high cost of professional repairs. Replacing a £10 floppy disc drive costs £10 if you opt for the do-it-yourself approach, but it would probably cost five to ten times as much to have the drive replaced by a service centre. Obviously there is a slight risk of things not going according to plan if you perform repairs yourself, although for most repairs the risk is very small indeed. If a PC requires major surgery the risks are slightly greater, but are still minimal for someone with some experience of PC servicing. Provided you do not start with a major repair such as replacing a motherboard, processor, and memory, you should not run into any major difficulties.

R.A.Penfold

WARNING

Sensible safety precautions should always be observed when dealing with electrical and electronic equipment, particularly any equipment that connects to the mains supply or operates at high voltages. **Do not open the case of a monitor or a PC power supply unit.** Apart from the fact that both of these are mains powered, they operate using high voltages that can remain on the circuit boards even after the equipment has been switched off for some time. If you use a PC connected to the mains supply as an earth for anti-static purposes, make sure that the power is switched off at the mains outlet so that the PC can not be accidentally switched on. With an AT case and power supply, examine the connections to the on/off switch before connecting the unit to the mains supply. All four connections should be completely covered by plastic insulators. **Do not use the unit if there are any signs at all of problems with the insulation.** Never work on a PC while it is switched on.

Contents

1

PC Versions 1

2

The basics 51

3

Disc drives 105

4

Video and sound 155

5

Motherboard, Memory, Proc 173

6

Other components 209

Trademarks

MS/DOS, Windows 95, Windows 98, and Windows NT are registered trademarks of Microsoft Corporation

Pentium is a registered trademark of Intel Corporation

Athlon is a registered trademark of AMD Corporation

PC types

PC versions

The PCs and compatibles have evolved over a period of several years, and the more up-market systems in use today have specifications that bear little resemblance to the original IBM PC, which was launched in 1981. I would guess that the best modern PCs are around one thousand times faster than the originals, and they certainly have about one thousand times more memory. The original IBM PC had just 64K of memory, a monochrome text only display, and included a cassette port. The PC I am using to produce the text and illustrations for this book has 192 megabytes (192000K) of RAM, a colour graphics board and monitor that can handle up to 1600 by 1200 pixels with 16 million colours, plus a 40X CD-ROM drive and a 13.6 gigabyte fast hard disc. The microprocessor in this PC renders it a few hundred times faster than the original PC. Despite this, it is still highly compatible with the original computer. It can almost certainly run any software written for the original version of the computer, and can take practically any expansion card that is compatible with the original machine.

The opposite is not true though, and there is much software and a lot of expansion cards that will work in my PC, but are unusable with the original computer (and many of the more recent compatibles come to that). In fact most modern software is unusable on an old PC. Also, the old PC standards are gradually being phased out, and compatibility with those standards is then lost. Consequently, a growing percentage of modern PCs are not compatible with some older expansion cards. In the context of PC repairs there is not full hardware compatibility between the old and the new anyway. Motherboards designed to take old processors will not accept more modern types, and the memory used in old and modern computers is also different. In fact memory has undergone several changes in recent years. Many quite recent PCs can not be used with the latest forms of memory.

It is worth briefly considering basic details of the various versions of the IBM PC range. This is not just a matter of historical interest, but because it can be helpful to know how your particular machine fits into the overall scheme of things. In fact it is essential to known this. Unless you do, getting the right parts to repair it could be difficult, and costly mistakes could be made. With PCs that are several years old it is also necessary to make a decision on whether or not it is worthwhile trying to replace a faulty component. In some cases a major upgrade is the most cost-effective method of repair, and in others it might not be worthwhile repairing the faulty PC at all. The current low cost of new and second-hand PCs make it uneconomic to spend money on expensive spare parts, particularly with a PC that is many years old and is unlikely to operate reliably for long once it has been repaired.

Original PCs

The "PC" in IBM PC merely stands for "personal computer". This is a possible cause of confusion since the IBM PCs and compatibles are often referred to simply as "PCs", but this is also a general term for any microcomputer which is primarily intended for business rather than home use. Anyway, in this book the term "PC" will only be used to refer to the IBM PC family of computers and the many compatible machines.

The original PC had relatively limited expansion potential. It had facilities for five full-length expansion slots, but this was not quite as good as it might at first appear. With a maximum of only 256K RAM on the main circuit board, (64K on the earliest PCs), and slots being required for disc controllers, serial and parallel ports, and the display card, some of these slots were required to provide essential functions. To ease the problem, several manufacturers produced multi-function cards, which gave such things as an extra 384K of memory, plus serial and parallel ports all on one card. This was more than a little helpful at the time, but with modern PCs this sort of thing is unnecessary, because the standard interfaces are included on the main board.

I referred previously to full-length expansion slots, and I should perhaps make it clear what this means. This term simply refers to the physical length of an expansion card, which can be any type, ancient or modern. It is the amount of clear space in front of the slot that determines whether or not it is a full-length type. A full-length slot has no obstructions in front of the slot other than the front of the case itself, and any expansion card will fit into these. With some slots there is an obstruction, such as the disc drive bays, and this limits the slot to operation with cards that are (say) half-length. This factor tends to be less of an issue with modern PCs as they are less dependant on expansion cards for standard functions, and few modern expansion cards are of the full-length variety

Fig.1.1 Expansion cards come in a variety of shapes and sizes

anyway. To illustrate the point that not all expansion cards are the same length, Figure 1.1 shows two cards of very different sizes.

The main problem when trying to expand an early PC was often the power supply. This had a rating of 63.5 watts, which is low in comparison to the ratings of around 150 watts for the later versions, and 230 watts for a modern PC. 63.5 watts was actually quite a hefty power supply for a microcomputer of the time, but it nevertheless provided little more power than the basic system required, and little more than many modern microprocessors consume. Anything more than the addition of one or two low power cards required the fitting of a more beefy power supply unit, which usually meant a 150-watt type, as fitted to some later versions of the PC, and most early PC compatibles. Upgrading an early PC is not a worthwhile proposition these days, and the original PCs are now entering the realms of collector's items. Repairing an original PC might be worthwhile if you work on the basis that it is of historic interest and therefore worthwhile keeping in working order regardless of cost, but is otherwise uneconomic.

PC XT

IBM introduced the PC XT in 1983, and it is this model rather than the original PC that tends to be considered as the first "real" PC. The "XT" part of the name is an abbreviation for extended, incidentally. It was an improvement on the original design in a number of ways. One of the improvements was the ability to have up to 640K of socketed RAM on the main circuit board, or "motherboard" as it is usually termed. The original PCs had all the RAM chips soldered directly to the board, making it difficult and expensive to replace a faulty chip. With the ability to have 640K of RAM on the motherboard, which is the maximum that the design of the computer permits, there was no need to take up an expansion slot with a memory board if you need the full complement of RAM.

The expansion slot problem was eased anyway, by the inclusion of no less than eight slots on the motherboard. Even with slots occupied by disc controllers, serial and parallel ports, and a display board, there would still typically be four or five slots left for more exotic peripherals. Two of the slots are only suitable for short expansion boards. It was not inconceivable that users would wish to have seven or eight full-length boards in an XT, but this was a highly unlikely state of affairs. However, some compatibles were capable of taking eight full-length cards. The 135-watt fan cooled power supply (usually 150 watts on clones) enabled plenty of peripherals to be powered without any risk of overloading the supply unit. Originally the XT was supplied complete with a 10-megabyte hard disc drive, but this was later made an optional extra. A 20-megabyte hard drive option was also available

Turbo PCs

The computers in the IBM PC family are all based on microprocessors from the Intel 8086 series of microprocessors. The PC and PC XT computers are based on the 8088, which is a slightly simplified version of the 8086. Whereas the 8086 processor has 16 pins to carry data into and out of the device, the 8088 has only eight pins for this purpose. This means that the 8088 has to take in and put out 16-bit chunks of data or program instructions as two 8 bit chunks ("bytes"), one after the other. This is undesirable as it slows down the computer to a significant degree. Coupled with the relatively slow clock speed used in the PC and PC XT of just 4.77MHz, this meant that the standard PCs had little more computing power than the faster 8-bit computers of the time. It could be argued that the XT class PCs were in fact eight-bit computers and not "real" 16-bit types. By current standards they are very slow computers, and like the original PCs are now collector's items rather than computers for everyday use.

IBM never produced what could really be regarded as a "turbo" version of the PC or PC XT. Most PC clones were and are of this type, although, modern PCs have developed to the point where the "turbo" name is no longer adequate to describe them. In the early days of "turbo" PCs there were three basic routes to obtaining increased speed. These could be used singly or in any combination. Details of the three methods are given below.

Increased speed

The most obvious way of obtaining increased operating speed is to use a higher clock frequency. It is an oversimplification to say that doubling the clock frequency of the processor doubles the speed of the computer, but in practice this is more or less what happens. In order to use a higher clock frequency successfully the microprocessor must obviously be able to run reliably at the higher frequency, as must the memory chips and other circuits in the computer. Alternatively, the processor can operate at full speed, with the other circuits operating more slowly. The processor has so-called "wait states" to slow things down and let the rest of the hardware catch up.

8086 processor

Using the 8086 with its 16-bit data bus might seem an obvious way of getting improved performance, but matters are not as simple as it might at first appear. The early PCs had 8-bit expansion slots, making it difficult to obtain full hardware compatibility with them if the 16-bit 8086 was used. This problem was not insurmountable, and some 8086 based compatibles (notably some Amstrad and Olivetti machines) were produced. This method of performance boosting was a relatively rare one though.

NEC V20

The NEC V20 microprocessor was capable of undertaking all 8088 instructions, and was fully compatible with it. The point about the V20 is that compared with the 8088 it took fewer clock pulses to complete some instructions. This obviously gave a boost in speed, but not a vast one. From my experience and tests I would say that the increase was somewhere in the region of 20% to 30%. There was a V30 microprocessor, which was a streamlined version of the 8086. Although we are now used to PCs fitted with non-Intel processors, for many years the V20 and V30 were the only compatible processors available.

PC AT computers

Rather than trying to speed up the PC and PC XT, IBM produced what was effectively a completely new design, but one which largely maintained software and hardware compatibility with the PC and PC XT. This computer was the PC AT, and the "AT" part of the name stands for "advanced technology." This was based on the Intel 80286 microprocessor, which is an improved version of the 8086. Like the 8086 it has a 16-bit data bus, and the AT was therefore a true 16-bit computer. The AT achieves higher operating speeds than the PC and PC XT because it operates at a higher clock speed. The original AT operated at 6MHz, but the later versions had an 8MHz clock. Comparing the speed of the PC and PC XT computers with the AT models is difficult since the 80286 takes fewer clock cycles per instruction than the 8086 or 8088. Thus, while it might seem as though a 10MHz XT compatible was faster than a 6MHz or 8MHz AT, this is not actually the case. Popular methods of speed testing generally put the AT many times faster than the original 4.77MHz PC and PC XT machines. If you take the clock speed of an AT in MHz, then it is roughly that many times faster than a 4.77MHz XT, according to the popular speed test programs anyway.

The original IBM AT computers were fitted with 512K of RAM on the motherboard, but later compatible machines were able to take the full 640K on the motherboard. In fact most AT computers could take at least 1 megabyte of memory on the main circuit board, and many were equipped to take 4 or 8 megabytes. These large amounts of RAM are made possible by an extra operating mode of the 80286 which takes advantage of extra address lines on the chip. However, when running PC/MS-DOS software the 80286 can not directly use the RAM above the 640K limit. This is not to say that there is no point in having the extra RAM. Some programs can use it in slightly roundabout methods, such as using the RAM for a disc cache or a RAM disc. Also, operating systems such as OS/2 and Windows 95/98 can run programs in the mode that takes full advantage of the whole 16-megabyte address range.

As it was a true 16-bit computer, in order to take full advantage of the 16-bit data bus the AT needed to have 16-bit expansion slots. This obviously raised possibilities with incompatibility between the AT and existing 8-bit PC expansion cards. In order to minimise these problems the 16-bit expansion slots of the AT and subsequent PCs are in the form of standard 8-bit slots plus a second connector which carries the extra lines needed by 16-bit expansion boards. This means that any 8-bit card should work in an AT style computer, with the only exception of boards that are PC or PC XT specific for some other reason. The only common example of this that springs to mind are the PC and PC XT hard disc controller cards. These have their own BIOS, whereas an AT hard disc controller card makes use of routines in the main BIOS on the motherboard. This gives what is really a firmware compatibility problem, rather than what could strictly speaking be termed hardware incompatibility. There were actually some boards, such as certain 16-bit VGA display cards, that would work in either type of computer. They sometimes achieved this by detecting electronically which type computer they were fitted in, and then configuring themselves accordingly. In other cases the user had to set a switch on the card to the appropriate position. In most cases though, 16-bit cards are incompatible with PC and PC XT machines.

AT computers, even those using the faster versions of the 80286 chip, are now well and truly obsolete. If still in good order they will quite happily run contemporary software, but there are no practical upgrades that will bring one of these computers up to a specification that is suitable for running modern software. So much of the original PC would have to be replaced that you would effectively be building a new computer. If you are happy with an 80286 PC and do not require higher performance, it must be tempting to keep it in running order for as long as possible. Why spend money on a new PC when the old one does everything you need perfectly well? On the other hand, spares for PCs as old as this can be difficult to obtain and expensive. The chances of obtaining a hard disc drive that is a direct replacement for the original are slim, and the replacement could easily be older than the one it is replacing! The position is similar for many of the other components. If an 80286 can be repaired cheaply, and you are happy with its performance, it is probably worthwhile fixing it. In most cases one or other of these criteria will not be met, and replacement will be the only sensible course of action.

80386 ATs

When Intel produced an improved version of the 80286 microprocessor, the 80386, it was inevitable that this device would soon be used in a new and faster generation of PCs. However, IBM never produced an 80386-based version of the PC. IBM has produced computers based on this microprocessor, but not in a straightforward PC guise. The IBM "PS/2" range used a different form of expansion bus, and it is discussed in more detail later on in this chapter. This lack of an IBM 80386 based PC to copy meant that the clone manufacturers were left without any standards to follow when producing 80386 PCs. Computers of this type are effectively AT clones, but using the 80386 plus its support chips instead of the 80286 and the relevant devices. Modern PCs are developments of the 80386 AT style computers. Although they have developed almost beyond recognition, modern PCs are still AT class PCs.

Using the 80386 in an AT style computer does have some advantages. The 80386 can operate with clock rates of up to 33MHz, or 40MHz for some 80386 compatible chips. I have often seen it stated that the 80386 performs instructions in fewer clock cycles than the 80286, giving a vast increase in performance. On the other hand, the results of speed tests on various 80286 and 80386 computers would seem to suggest that there is little to choose between the two types of computer when running at the same clock rate. The 80386 is a 32-bit microprocessor, which makes it potentially more powerful in maths intensive applications than the 16-bit 80286. However, to take advantage of this it is necessary to have software that is written specifically for the 32-bit 80386. These days we take 32-bit operating systems and applications software for granted, but when the 80386 first came along there was relatively little software that could fully exploit its potential.

Apart from its ability to access memory 32 bits at a time, the 80386 has other advantages in the way that it handles memory. For straightforward PC/MS-DOS applications it runs in the "real" mode (as does the 80286), and effectively just emulates the 8086. In the "protected virtual" mode (often just called "protected" mode) it is much like the 80286 in its mode which gives a 16 megabyte memory address range. It has some extensions in this mode though; including a memory management unit (MMU) which provides sophisticated memory paging and program switching capabilities. Perhaps of more immediate importance to most users, the 80386 can switch from the protected mode back to the real mode much more simply and quickly than the 80286 can manage. A program running in real mode, but making use of extended memory and protected mode via a RAM disc or whatever, will therefore operate more quickly when accessing the extended memory. This is not purely of academic importance, and some methods of using the extended memory on an 80386 based AT are not worthwhile when implemented on an 80286 based AT as they simply do not work fast enough.

The 80386 has a third mode of operation called "virtual real" mode. The 80286 has no equivalent of this mode. In essence it permits the memory to be split into several sections, with each one running its own operating system and an applications program. Each program is run entirely separately from the others, and if one program should crash then all the others should remain running normally. Only the crashed section of memory needs to have its operating system rebooted and the program reloaded. This solves what has tended to be a big problem with many multi-tasking computers, where programs tend to crash regularly due to one program interfering with another, and with one program crashed the whole system tends to follow suit. The amount of memory that the 80386 can handle is so large (4 gigabytes, or some 4000 megabytes in other words) that even today's PCs can not actually take this much RAM.

There is a sort of cut down version of the 80386, the 80386SX. This has a 16-bit bus like the 80286, but internally it has all the 80386 registers. This enables it to run 80386 specific software as well as standard PC software, albeit somewhat more slowly than on an 80386 based computer. The reduced speed is the result of the 32-bit pieces of data or instructions having to be loaded as two 16-bit chunks rather than being loaded simultaneously.

80386 based PCs are now well and truly out of date, and in most cases are probably not worth repairing or upgrading. There are exceptions though, and if a PC of this type has been kept up to date with new peripherals such as multi-media add-ons it might be worth upgrading to a modern specification. In order to do this it will be necessary to renew much of the computer though. Like an 80286 based PC, if it can be repaired cheaply and you are happy with the performance obtained, then it is probably worthwhile keeping it going. Otherwise it is time to move on to a newer and better PC.

PS/2 computers

When IBM ceased making the PC range of computers they were replaced with the PS/2 range. This should perhaps be considered as two ranges, since it consists of relatively simple machines that could reasonably be regarded as PC compatibles, and a more advanced range which are still basically PCs, but which depart from the previous standards in some quite radical ways.

The most basic of the PS/2 range were the Model 25 and the Model 30. These were 8MHz 8086 based computers which used standard ISA expansion slots of the 8-bit variety. They differed from earlier PCs in that they had a number of functions (such as the display generator circuitry) on the motherboard rather than requiring these functions to be provided by cards fitted in expansion slots. There was also a Model 30 286 computer, which was a 10MHz 80286 based computer having 16-bit ISA expansion slots. ISA (industry standard architecture) slots are the ordinary 8-bit and 16-bit PC expansion slots incidentally. The Model 25/30 and Model 30 286 computers were effectively more modern equivalents of the XT and AT computers, and PCs in the generally accepted sense of the term.

The Model 50, 60, 70, and 80 computers were more advanced computers which used a different form of expansion bus called "micro channel architecture", or just "MCA" as it is much better known. This is not really the place for a discussion of this expansion bus standard, since the subject of this book is the expansion of what for the want of a better term we will call the traditional PC. The subject of MCA will therefore not be considered any further here.

80486

The 80486DX is essentially a more efficient version of the 80386 that requires fewer clock cycles per instruction, and has some extra instructions. It departed from the 80386 and previous processors in this series by having the maths-coprocessor built-in, rather than as a separate chip. The maths-coprocessor is a microprocessor that is designed to handle complex mathematics, and is mainly intended as a means of speeding up floating-point calculations. Virtually all PCs using an 80386 or earlier processor had a socket on the motherboard for a maths-coprocessor, but it was normally an optional extra and not fitted as standard. Most software did not require the coprocessor, and few PC users actually bothered to add one. The 80486DX encouraged software authors to make use of the maths-coprocessor by making it a standard feature instead of an expensive add-on. The 80486DX version of the coprocessor was more efficient than its predecessors, giving a useful increase in performance. There was a cut-down version of the 80486DX, the 80486SX, which lacked the built-in coprocessor. Like the earlier PC processors, the maths coprocessor was available as an optional extra.

The original 80486DX operated at a clock frequency of 33MHz, but some of the 80486SX chips were slower than this. Faster versions were developed over the years though, including some non-Intel alternatives to the 80486DX. I think I am right in stating that the fastest genuine Intel 80486DX operated at 100MHz, but non-Intel chips operating at up to about 133MHz were produced. The faster 80486DX based PCs are powerful computers, and if fitted with adequate RAM they can run a fair percentage of modern software. On the other hand, new software releases seem to place ever-higher demands on the hardware, and there is an increasing amount of software that will not operate on an 80486DX-based PC. If you are happy with the performance of an 80486 based PC it is almost certainly worth repairing it. Unless you are very unlucky it will be possible to obtain suitable spare parts. If a boost in performance is required there are processor upgrade kits that can be used to boost the performance of these PCs. In many cases it is worthwhile spending money on a major upgrade to replace the processor, motherboard, and memory with modern components.

Pentiums

All modern PCs are based on an Intel Pentium processor, or a compatible processor from another manufacturer. Pentium processors have additional instructions, but are basically just faster and more efficient versions of the 80486DX. The original chips ran at 60MHz and 66MHz, and in most speed tests did not perform significantly better than the faster 80486 chips. Later versions used higher clock rates, fitted into a different socket, and had improved motherboards. In particular, the motherboards had chipsets that were specifically designed to produce optimum performance from a Pentium processor. This provided a boost in performance and much better results than any 80486DX PCs could achieve. The clock frequencies for these "classic" Pentium processors are 75, 90, 100, 120, 133, 150, 166, and 200MHz. Figures 1.2 and 1.3 respectively show the topside and underside of a 133MHz Pentium.

Although relatively recent, these processors are now obsolete and are not used in new PCs any more. Pentium processors with MMX (multimedia extension) technology replaced them. The MMX technology is actually an additional 57 processor instructions that are designed to speed up multimedia applications, but can also be used to good effect in other applications such as voice recognition. There were also some general improvements that produced an increase in performance by around 10 or 15 percent when using non-MMX specific software. These MMX Pentium processors were produced in 166MHz, 200MHz, and 233MHz versions.

These are now obsolete and have been replaced by Pentium II processors. At the time of writing this, Pentium II processors are available with clock frequencies of 233, 266, 300, 333, 350, 400MHz, and 450MHz.

Fig.1.2 Top view on an Intel Pentium

The original Pentium processors fitted onto the motherboard via a conventional integrated circuit holder known as Socket 4. Those operating at 75MHz and above used an improved version called Socket 7. Pentium II processors look nothing like conventional processors, and in physical appearance they are like a cross between a videocassette and a memory module. They fit into a holder that is more like a PC expansion slot or holder for a memory module than an integrated circuit holder. Figure 1.4 shows a Slot 1 motherboard, and the slot for the microprocessor is the one in the upper right-hand side of the board.

One reason for this change in style is that it potentially enables higher clock speeds to be utilized. Another reason for this change in style is that Pentium II chips are so complex that it is not possible to put the processor and cache memory on the same chip. Cache memory is high-speed memory that is used to store recently processed data. It is likely that this data will need to be accessed again, and having it available in high-speed memory ensures that it can be processed very efficiently when it is needed. In virtually all practical applications this significantly speeds up the rate at which data can be processed. Previous Pentium processors had some cache memory (typically 32K) on the chip, with a much larger cache of about 256 to 512K on the motherboard. These are known as level 1 and level 2 cache respectively. Level 1 cache is faster, but there are practical limits on the amount of cache memory that can be included in the processor. With the Pentium II chips it had to be omitted altogether, but a "piggy-

Fig.1.3 The pins on the underside of a Pentium processor

Fig.1.4 A Slot 1 motherboard lacks a conventional processor socket

back" memory chip included in the processor module provides a 512K cache.

The Pentium II is really a development of the Pentium Pro processor. This relatively unsuccessful processor was an improved version of the "classic" Pentium design, but when running Windows 95 software it often failed to provide much improvement over an ordinary Pentium chip. The Pentium Pro became overshadowed by the MMX Pentium processors, which proved to be an immediate hit with PC buyers. The Pentium II has the additional MMX instructions, and slightly improved performance compared to an ordinary MMX Pentium processor. The 350 and 400MHz versions are designed to operate on motherboards that operate at a 100MHz clock frequency and use fast memory modules. The slower Pentium processors operate with 66MHz motherboards and relatively slow RAM. This gives the 350 and 400MHz chips a greater speed advantage over the slower versions than a comparison of the clock frequencies would suggest.

Pentium III

The Pentium II chips are now being phased out in favour of the Pentium III. This processor requires Slot 1 motherboards and is similar in general appearance to the Pentium II. Most modern Slot 1 motherboards can be used with Pentium II or Pentium III processors. The Pentium III processor seems likely to take over from the Pentium II before too long, and the difference in price between the two is relatively small these days. The Pentium III has SIMD (single-instruction multiple data) technology, which is 70 new instructions designed to speed up certain types of software. These instructions are mainly aimed at high-speed 3D graphics and applications that include voice recognition. They are only of use with software that is written to take advantage of them. Like the Pentium II processors, the Pentium III has 512K of cache memory running at half the clock speed. At the time of writing this there are 450, 500, and 550MHz Pentium III processors, with 600MHz chips just starting to find their way into the shops. Faster versions should arrive soon.

Celeron

Intel has now abandoned Socket 7 technology in favour of the Slot 1 technology used for the Pentium II processors, and even higher tech Slot 2 processors are planned. The Intel processor for entry-level PCs is the Celeron, and in its original form it is basically just a Pentium II with the add-on cache omitted. This saves on manufacturing costs, but clearly gives a reduction in performance. The original Celeron did not exactly receive universal praise from the reviewers, and the absence of any on-board cache gives it a tough time keeping up with the latest budget processors from other manufacturers. Its performance is actually quite respectable, being around 15 to 30 percent faster than an Intel 233MHz MMX Pentium chip, depending on the type of software being run. Its performance is still well short of the slower Pentium II chips though.

The original Celeron processors were soon dropped in favour of a 300MHz version with 128K of on-chip cache running at the full processor clock speed. A 333MHz version and a succession of even faster chips soon followed this. At the time of writing this, the fastest Celeron chips run at 500MHz. Although at 128K the cache is only one quarter of the size of the cache fitted to Pentium II and III processors, the fact that it is on the same chip as the processor and operating at the same clock speed to some extent makes up for the smaller size. In fact with much software there is remarkably little difference in performance between a Pentium II processor and a Celeron operating at the same clock frequency.

The original Celeron processors used the same Slot 1 technology as Pentium II processors, and could be used in Pentium II motherboards.

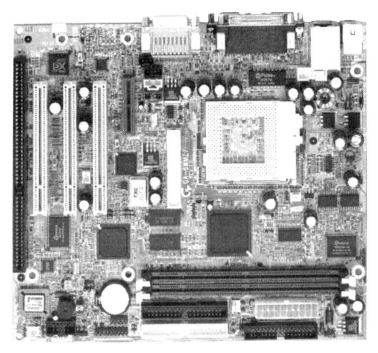

Fig.1.5 A modern Celeron fits in a conventional socket

The current Celeron processors look very much like classic Pentium processors and are designed to fit Socket 370 motherboards (Figure 1.5). This reversion to old-style processor technology apparently helps to keep down the cost of these budget processors. The new Celerons will not fit directly onto a Slot 1 Pentium II motherboard, but it is possible to fit them onto this type of motherboard by way of an adapter. As far as I am aware, Socket 7 motherboards and Socket 370 chips are totally incompatible, as are Socket 7 chips and Socket 370 motherboards.

Xeon

The Xeon is a form of Pentium II processor, and it is available with various cache options and clock speeds of 400MHz and upwards. Some previous Pentium processors can be used in dual processor systems, which, with the right software support, give significantly higher performance than equivalent single processor systems. The Xeon takes things further, and can be used in four processor systems, with eight processor computers planned for the future. It uses Socket 2 technology, and is therefore physically and electrically incompatible with Slot 1 motherboards. With its larger and faster cache than earlier Pentium processors, together with a 100MHz system bus, this processor is substantially faster than ordinary Pentium II chips. It is really intended for use in expensive network servers and not desktop PCs. It is beyond the budgets of most PC users and is not a processor that we will consider further in this book.

Non-Intel inside

The manufacturers of compatible processors have been reluctant to shift over to Slot 1 technology or their own version of Slot technology. Until recently they have instead opted to develop Socket 7 technology as far as possible. The front runners in compatible chips are AMD and Cyrix. At the time of writing this Cyrix has been sold by National Semiconductors and is now owned by VIA, the PC support chip manufacturer. Development of these processors should therefore continue.

The first AMD processor for PCs was the K5, which was produced in 75, 90, 133, 150, and 166MHz versions. This chip was an alternative to the "classic" Pentium processor. It was replaced by the K6, which has the MMX instructions, and clock frequencies of 166, 200, 233, 266, and 300MHz. This was replaced by the K6-2, which was in turn superseded by the K6-2 3D Now! chip. This is a Pentium style processor that includes the MMX instructions, but it also has its own set of instructions that, together with the later versions of Microsoft's Direct X system, enable 3-D games to run at increased speeds. This processor requires a motherboard that can operate at 100MHz and fast memory modules. It is available with clock speeds of up to 475MHz.

The K6-2 has now been joined by the K6-3, which is basically just a K6-2 with 256K of on-chip cache operating at the full processor clock speed. The cache on the motherboard operates as a level three cache incidentally. Versions having clock speeds of 400, 450, 475, and 500MHz are available. With a substantial amount of on-chip cache memory running at the full clock speed the K6-3 provides a high level of performance. It is no longer the fastest AMD processor though, and that title goes to the Athlon (formerly known as the K7). This uses a slot rather than a socket and looks similar to a Pentium II or III (Figure 1.6), but it does not utilize Intel's Slot 1 technology. Instead it uses what AMD have dubbed Slot A technology. The Athlon is available with clock speeds of 500, 550, and 600MHz, has 512K of level two cache, and operates with a system bus frequency of 200MHz.

The Cyrix equivalent of the AMD K6 is the 6X86 processor. This was produced in 90, 120, 133, 150, 166, and 200MHz versions. These chips cause a certain amount of confusion, because their speed ratings are not their actual clock frequencies. For instance, a 200MHz 6X86 processor is a 200MHz chip in the sense

Fig.1.6 An AMD Athlon processor

that it offers performance that is broadly similar to an Intel 200MHz Pentium. The actual clock frequency is somewhat less, and is actually 166MHz in this case. It has to be pointed out that how well (or otherwise) one make of processor compares to another depends on the type of software being run. Intel chips traditionally do well on floating point mathematics, but perform less well in other areas. If you are running a reasonably wide range of applications software, overall you are unlikely to notice much difference between equivalent chips from different manufacturers.

The original Cyrix processors are now obsolete, and they now produce processors that have the MMX instructions and these are the M2 series. These have nominal clock frequencies of 166, 200, 233, 266, 300, and 333MHz, but only the two faster chips are currently available. Like the 6X86 processors, the speed ratings of M2 chips are their equivalent clock frequencies, and the actual clock frequencies are lower (225MHz or 233MHz for the 300MHz chip for example). As far as I can ascertain, at the time of writing this, Cyrix has released nothing beyond the 333MHz M2. Always handle Socket 7 and 370 chips with due care as they will not fit into the holder if any of the numerous pins are buckled.

IDT and its Winchip are relative newcomers to the world of PC processors. The Winchip is intended to be a low cost processor for entry level PCs. It has the MMX instructions, and is produced in 150, 180, 200, 225, and 240MHz versions. At the time of writing this piece the rights to the Winchip are up for sale, and the future of these processors is uncertain.

There are other PC processors, but these are non-standard devices that integrate functions such as video and sound onto the processor chip.

These require special motherboards that do not seem to be generally available. Some of these chips are intended for use in low cost PCs, but others are for use in embedded applications. In other words, for use in household gadgets, etc., that include a basic PC for Internet connection, or something of this type. This includes things like Internet television sets and the well-publicised Internet connected "smart fridge".

With any PC based on a Pentium class processor it should be possible to effect most repairs quite easily and at reasonable cost. Unless something pretty catastrophic happens, such as dropping the PC from a second floor window, it should be economic and worthwhile repairing this type of PC. Rather than opting for a straightforward repair you may decide to undertake a major upgrade instead. This will inevitably cost more than simply replacing the faulty part with a new one, but for the extra money you may well obtain a vast improvement in performance. The best choice depends on the particular PC you have, and how badly (or otherwise) you require an increase in performance. It also depends on the nature of the fault. There is little point in opting for a major upgrade if a replacement floppy drive is all that is needed. On the other hand, if a motherboard becomes faulty it would probably be worthwhile replacing the processor and memory as well, to bring the PC up to a more modern specification.

System Make Up

Before undertaking PC repairs it is essential to understand the general makeup of a PC. A traditional PC is a so-called three-unit style computer. These three separate units are the keyboard, the main computer unit, and the monitor. They are connected together by cables, with the familiar curly type normally being used for the keyboard. This is a convenient set-up in that it makes it easy to accommodate everything on practically any computer desk. The main unit is comprised of several sub-units. The main ones are the case, power supply unit, motherboard, and one or more disc drives. Additionally, certain expansion cards must be present on the main board for the system to function. In the past it was necessary to have a hard/floppy disc controller card, plus a card or cards to provide standard interfaces such as serial and parallel ports. The current practice is for these functions to be provided by the motherboard, and the only essential expansion card is a video type to drive the monitor. In fact a few motherboards have an on-board display generator as well. This is not a common feature, but it seems to be gaining in popularity. Although a sound card is not essential, a sound card and speakers has become a standard PC feature. The sound card usually includes a game port for joysticks, etc. This doubles as a MIDI port that enables the PC to be connected to synthesisers and other musical instruments or gadgets that have a MIDI port. Some PCs now have the soundcard integrated with the motherboard, and it is increasingly common for both the sound and graphics circuits to be included on the motherboard. A basic multimedia PC would consist of something like the following list of main parts.

Keyboard and mouse

Case

Motherboard fitted with BIOS and memory nodules

14/15 inch colour monitor

SVGA display card with 4 megabytes of RAM

Floppy disc drive

Hard disc drive

CD-ROM

Sound card and speakers

A more up-market PC might have the following set of main components.

Keyboard and mouse

Case

Motherboard fitted with BIOS and memory modules

17/19 inch colour monitor

2-D/3-D display card with 8/16 megabytes of RAM

Floppy disc drives

Hard disc drive

DVD drive

CD-ROM writer

Sound card and speakers

Modem for Internet connection

Some of these constituent parts, plus more specialised forms of expansion are discussed in later chapters, but there are a few aspects of these main parts that we will take the opportunity to discuss here.

Keyboards

The original PC keyboard was an 83-key type. At least, it was in its native (U.S.A.) form. The U.K. version had a slightly different layout plus an extra key in order to accommodate the pound sign ("£"), which was absent on the U.S.A. keyboard. The U.K. version was therefore generally known as the 84-key layout PC keyboard. This had ten function keys in two vertical rows of five, positioned to the left of the main QWERTY keys, and is now obsolete. 83/84-key keyboards were replaced by the enhanced layout that was introduced by IBM in 1986. This has 101 keys in its original U.S.A. version, or 102 keys in the case of the U.K. version. Twelve function keys on the enhanced layout replace the ten function keys of the original design. These keys are relocated to a single row above the main QWERTY keyboard (which is where the "Esc" key is also to be found). The numeric keypad/cursor key arrangement is retained, but only for those who are used to the original scheme of things and wish to go on using it. This keypad is moved over to the right in order to make room for a separate cursor cluster, etc.

The 102-key layout has now been replaced by the 105-key Windows 95/ 98 layout (Figure 1.7). This is basically the same as the 102-key layout, but there are three additional keys next to the spacebar. These bring up Windows 95/98 menus, and two of the keys have the same effect as operating the "Start" button on the Windows desktop. The third is equivalent to right "clicking" the mouse. As the additional keys are simply duplicating functions provided by the mouse, it is not essential to have a 105-key keyboard in order to use Windows 95/98. All current keyboards seem to have the 105-key layout.

If you look at the keyboards in a computer shop you can not miss the "ergonomic" variety, which have the two sides of the keyboard at different angles. They are designed to make touch-typing easier and less fatiguing, and seem to be liked by many touch-typists. Two-finger typists should stick to the traditional style PC keyboard.

The enhanced keyboards retain the original method of interfacing, and it is quite possible, for instance, to use a 105-key keyboard as a replacement for a 102-key, or even an old 84-key type type. This will not necessarily give perfect results though, since the BIOS in the computer may not be equipped to deal with a modern keyboard. Although most of the keys are merely duplicating those of the old 83/84-key layout, there are obviously a few additional ones that might have no effect when used with an old PC, or could produce the wrong characters. Any problems when using a new keyboard on an old PC are usually quite

Fig.1.7 A standard 105-key PC keyboard

minor, and most users can live with them. Note that XT class PCs have the same type of keyboard connector as later PCs, but are nevertheless incompatible with modern PC keyboards. If the keyboard of an XT class PC fails, it must be replaced with a proper XT keyboard and not a modern one. The chances of finding a suitable replacement keyboard are quite small, since XT computers are now obsolete, and have been for some years. In the past it was normal for PC keyboards to have an XT/AT switch so that they could accommodate both types of computer. Others had automatic detection and switching circuits. Modern PC keyboards lack either of these features and will not work with an old XT type PC.

A PC keyboard is a quite sophisticated piece of electronics in its own right, and is actually based on an 8048 single chip microprocessor (or "microcontroller" as these devices are alternatively known). This controller provides "debouncing", which prevents multiple characters being generated if the keyboard switches open and close something less than completely cleanly (which is always the case in practice). The keyboard controller also performs simple diagnostic tests, and can detect a key that is stuck in the "on" position for example. It also contains a 20 byte buffer, which is simply a small amount of memory that is used to store characters if one key is pressed before the character from the previous one has been read by the computer.

The keyboard also has multi-character rollover. In other words, if you press one key, and then another while still holding down the first one, the second key will be read correctly. In fact you can hold down several keys and the next one that is operated will still be read correctly. I do not know how many keys can be pressed before this system breaks down, but attempts to overload the keyboard on my computers proved to be

Fig.1.8 PS/2 (left) and DIN (right) keyboard connectors

fruitless. Of course, like most computer keyboards and electric typewriters, the keyboard includes an auto-repeat function (i.e. holding down any character key results in that character being produced once initially, and then after a short delay it is repeated for as long as the key is pressed).

Connection to the computer is mostly via a 5-way cable fitted with a 5-way 180-degree DIN plug. There is an alternative form of connector (the PS/2 type), which is a sort of miniature version of the standard type. This is becoming much more common, and when buying a replacement keyboard you must ensure that it has the right type of connector for your PC. Both types of connector are shown in Figure 1.8. The connector used would seem to be the only difference between the two types of keyboard, and some keyboards are equipped with both types of plug. Others are supplied with one plug and an adapter so that they can be used with DIN or PS/2 keyboard ports.

Motherboards

The motherboard, which is also known as the main board, carries the processor, memory, support chips, BIOS, and the expansion cards. In fact everything else in the PC is either mounted on the motherboard or connects to it via a multi-way cable. The motherboard is very much at the centre of things. At one time there were two main motherboard categories: the XT type, and the AT variety. However, the original XT and AT style motherboards are now well and truly obsolete, although modern motherboards are actually developments of the AT layout. I suppose that if you look at things in broad terms there are still two forms of motherboard, which are the AT and ATX varieties. The AT boards use what is basically the original AT layout, although modern AT boards are generally much smaller than the original design. Hence they are sometimes referred to as "baby AT" boards (Figure 1.9). ATX motherboards have a modified layout that puts the processor to one side of the expansion slots. Modern processors, when complete with heatsinks and cooling fans, tend to be quite tall and can obstruct several

Fig.1.9 A "baby" Socket 7 AT motherboard

of the expansion slots. This prevents the slots from being used with the longer expansion cards. By moving the processor to one side this problem is avoided, and it is possible to use long expansion cards in any of the expansion slots.

There are other differences between the two types of board, such as the different power supply requirements and the on-board serial and parallel port connectors of ATX boards. The practical consequence of these is that the two types of board require different styles of power supply and case. When replacing a motherboard you must therefore be careful to replace it with one that has the same form factor. The board shown previously in Figure 1.5 is an ATX type.

AT and ATX boards can be further subdivided according to the processors that they support. When buying a replacement motherboard you must therefore make sure that it has the correct form factor and that it supports the processor you are using. Obtaining a motherboard to suit an early Pentium processor or any pre-Pentium processor can be difficult and expensive. Similarly, obtaining a replacement for an early

Pentium processor or an 80X86 series processor can be time consuming and costly. If a fault occurs in the motherboard or processor of a PC that is something less than up-to-date it is often better to upgrade it to a more modern specification rather than try to do a straightforward repair job. With older PCs it is often worthwhile checking local computer fairs to see if suitable parts can be obtained cheaply, but if not a simple repair is probably not a practical proposition.

Chipsets

When looking at the specifications for Pentium based PCs and Pentium motherboards you will inevitably come across references to chipsets. These are the integrated circuits that provide various essential functions that are not included in the processor itself. In the original PCs these functions were provided by dozens of ordinary logic integrated circuits. Even though a modern PC requires much more help from the supporting electronics, there are normally just two support chips. Intel has manufactured various Pentium support chipsets, and these seem to be used on most motherboards. However, other manufacturers make support Pentium chips. Here are brief details of the Intel chipsets.

FX   Early and basic Pentium chipset.

HX   Early chipset that is in many ways basic but is also fast. Provides dual processor support. Used for both Socket 7 and early Slot 1 motherboards.

VX   Early and basic chipset for Socket 7 motherboards giving SDRAM support.

TX   Improved chipset for Socket 7 motherboards which provides support for SDRAM, USB, and UDMA33 hard disc interface.

LX   First chipset specifically for Pentium II processors and Slot 1 motherboards. Provides dual processor, SDRAM, USB, UDMA33 and AGP support. Maximum memory of 512MB SDRAM, or 1GB EDO RAM.

BX   Effectively an improved LX chipset that supports 100MHz system bus and fast SDRAM. Up to 1GB or SDRAM or EDO RAM. Also supports 66MHz system bus for compatibility with 333MHz and slower Pentium II processors.

EX   Optimised for Celeron processor. Up to 256MB of SDRAM or EDO RAM. No dual processor support.

GX   Optimised for the Pentium II Xeon processors (i.e. 100MHz system bus processors) with no support or 66MHz bus.

NX   Support for up to four Pentium II Xeon processors and 8GB of SDRAM or EDO RAM. No AGP support.

810   The first of a new generation, this particular chipset is for budget PCs and has integrated sound and graphics.

820   This is the up-market chipset in the new generation of Intel chips. It supports high-speed operation with a 133MHz bus, Ultra DMA66, and a 4x AGP slot. Also designed for improved security with Pentium III processors.

Configuration

For the computer to function properly it must know a few basic facts about itself, such as the type of display card and amount of memory fitted. This ensures that it produces an initial display properly, that it does not try to access memory it does not have, or ignore memory that it does have available. On the original PCs some switches on the motherboard were used for configuration purposes. AT class computers, from the originals to the latest super-fast PCs, have some low-power CMOS memory that is powered from a battery when the main power source is switched off. This memory circuit is actually part of a built-in clock/calendar circuit, which the operating system uses to set its clock and calendar during the booting process. It is also used by applications software, such as a word processor when it automatically adds the date into a letter or other document. If a PC keeps failing to boot-up correctly, and takes you into the BIOS Setup program instead, it is likely that the back-up battery for the CMOS memory has failed. Most modern motherboards have a lithium battery that should last about five years or so. Older motherboards often have a rechargeable battery that is trickle-charged while the computer is switched on. If the PC is not used for a week or two the battery can run flat, but if the computer is reconfigured using the BIOS Setup program and left running for a few hours it should then boot-up properly again.

Various aspects of configuring motherboards using the BIOS Setup program is dealt with in subsequent chapters of this book.

Maths coprocessor

A maths co-processor is an integrated circuit, which looks very much like the main microprocessor in most cases. It is not normally fitted via an expansion card, but instead fits into a socket on the motherboard. Any PC processor from the full 80486DX onwards has the maths coprocessor built-in, and not as an add-on chip. Therefore, provided you are using a reasonably modern PC it should be able to run any software that requires a maths coprocessor without having to resort to an upgrade. If you have an old PC that requires a maths coprocessor upgrade you are probably out of luck, because these chips are now obsolete.

Ports

While it is not inconceivable that a computer could be put to good use without the aid of printers, modems, and other peripheral devices, few people can utilize one in this way. Unless you are using a computer for an application where there will be no need to produce any hard copy, or transfer data via means other than swapping floppy discs, at least one parallel or serial port will be required. Modern PCs have two serial ports and a parallel port built-in, with the necessary hardware included on the motherboard. Connection to the outside world is via sockets mounted on the rear of the casing (most cases have holes for standard D-type connectors ready cut), or mounted on expansion slot blanking plates. With ATX motherboards the connectors are mounted on the motherboard, and are accessed via cutouts in the rear of the case, rather like the keyboard connector of an AT style motherboard and case.

Probably for many users the serial and parallel ports supplied as standard with the PC will suffice. Most computers are connected to a printer, usually via a parallel port. This is the only parallel port peripheral used with many computer systems although parallel port scanners are now quite popular, as are various types of external add-on disc drive such as Zip drives. These all normally have a connector for a printer so that you can use one printer port to drive both a printer and a scanner or drive. If you should need an extra printer port, it is just a matter of adding a printer port card into one of the expansion slots. At present, parallel port cards invariably seem to be ordinary ISA types, and not the more modern PCI variety.

A mouse (or other pointing device such as a digitising tablet or tracker ball) is now a standard PC peripheral, and these can be of either the mouse port (PS/2) or serial varieties. There is also a third type known as a bus mouse, which is supplied complete with an expansion card that interfaces the mouse to the computer. However, the built-in mouse port of most modern PCs has led to the demise of this type of mouse. A serial mouse connects to a standard serial port, and on the face of it a mouse port mouse is the better option, as it leaves the serial port free for other purposes. In practice there is a slight risk of a mouse port mouse conflicting with other hardware, but it should be possible to sort out any hardware conflict that occurs.

Even with a printer and a serial mouse connected to the computer, the ports supplied as part of the standard system will almost certainly suffice. It is only if you need to add a second printer, a plotter, a modem, or some more exotic piece of equipment that further ports might be needed. You need to bear in mind that there is a limit to the number of serial and parallel ports that can be added to a PC. You can have up to three parallel ports ("LPT1" to "LPT3"), and up to four serial ports ("COM1" to "COM4"). Software supports for anything beyond LPT2 and COM2, used to be something less than universal. In fact some software, rather unhelpfully, seems reluctant to recognise anything beyond LPT1 and (possibly) COM1. Windows has eased this problem, and if Windows recognises a serial or parallel port it should be usable with any Windows applications software.

When buying parallel and serial port cards you need to ensure that the card will provide the particular port you require. Most cards of this type now have configuration switches or jumper blocks so that they can be set to act as at least port 1 or port 2, and possibly as port 3 or 4. You may still find some cards that have the port number or numbers preset. This is most common with single parallel and serial port cards, where the port is often preset as port 1. With twin serial port cards you sometimes find that the port is preset at port 1, with some optional components providing a second port that acts as port 2. However, with most modern serial and parallel port cards you have a large amount of control over the port numbering.

When expanding a system, what you will almost certainly need is a card to provide port 2 or beyond. Expansion cards that do not allow you to set the port number via configuration switches or jumper blocks are probably best avoided. Although you might be able to reconfigure one of the existing ports to operate as port 2, so that the new port can operate as port 1, these older often lack the capabilities of modern cards. For example, modern parallel ports have bi-directional modes that enable them to receive parallel data as well as send it. This capability is exploited by many modern peripherals that utilize a parallel port, including printers, scanners, and external disc drives of various types. Where possible it is preferable to leave the existing ports operating under their original numbers, and to have any new ports as port 2, port 3, or whatever. If you do need to reconfigure the built-in ports, it will be necessary to do so via the BIOS Setup program.

When configuring serial and parallel ports you do not normally set them as LPT1, COM2, or whatever. Instead you set the port base address. In the case of a parallel port (and possibly a serial port) an interrupt number as well. Port addressing works much like ordinary memory addressing, and it enables the processor to "talk" to the appropriate register in a selected piece of hardware. A hardware interrupt is where a peripheral device or a piece of built in hardware activates an input line of the processor to indicate that it has produced data that requires processing. Every time you move the mouse, for instance, it generates an interrupt. The processor then fetches and processes the new data, moves the cursor to the appropriate new screen position, and then carries on where it left off. This avoids having the processor waste large amounts of time repeatedly monitoring hardware devices that are idle.

This table shows the usual addresses and (where appropriate) interrupt numbers for COM1, to COM4, LPT1, and LPT2 (the addresses are in hexadecimal and are the base addresses. If a parallel port has a base address of 3BC (interrupt 7) it will probably be set as LPT1 by the operating system, and the other printer ports are moved one number higher.

PORT	ADDRESS	INTERRUPT
LPT1	378	IRQ7
LPT2	278	IRQ5
COM1	3F8	IRQ4
COM2	2F8	IRQ3
COM3	3E8	
COM4	2E8	

USB, etc.

Although USB ports have been around for some time, and most modern motherboards include two USB ports, they have not been used a great deal in practice due to a lack of proper support from the Windows operating system. This has been rectified with the release of Windows 98, and USB seems likely to play an increasingly important role in the PC world. USB is a form of serial interface, but it is much faster than a conventional RS232C serial port. An ordinary PC serial port can, at best, operate up to about 115000 bits per second, whereas a USB port can operate at up to 10 million bits per second. In fact a USB port is potentially faster than a parallel port. Another advantage of a USB port is its ability to operate with more than peripheral device.

Some scanners and other devices interface to the computer via a SCSI port (small computers systems interface and pronounced "scuzzy"), which is a form of high-speed bi-directional parallel port. A few motherboards have a built-in SCSI interface, but this is something of a rarity. There are numerous ISA and PCI expansion cards that provide SCSI ports, and many peripherals that require this type of interface are supplied complete with a suitable card and connecting cable (or they are offered as an optional extra). The card should be supplied with any necessary driver software to integrate it with the common operating systems. SCSI is sometimes used for high performance hard disc and CD-ROM drives, but with modern PCs having high speed UDMA33 hard disc interfaces built-in, it is probably not worth bothering with SCSI drives for a stand-alone PC.

There are other types of input and output port that can be fitted to a PC, such as analogue types. These are only needed for specialist applications such as scientific and medical research. Being specialised items they do not operate under any true standards. Most hardware of this type is fitted into the part of the input/output map reserved for "prototype cards". The exact address range is sometimes adjustable so that more than one card of this type can be used in the computer. However, when purchasing this type of hardware you need to make detailed enquiries in order to ensure that it will fulfil your requirements. You need to be especially careful that it is compatible with any software you will wish to use with it, or that any information you need in order to exploit the interface with your own software is provided by the vendor.

Digitising tablets

Digitising tablets are absolute pointing devices, rather than relative types (like mice). In other words, whereas a mouse can only be used to indicate movement in a certain direction, a digitising tablet deals in definite screen positions. If you lift a mouse from its mat, move it to a new position, and then replace it on the mat, the on-screen pointer will not move. With a digitising tablet, if you raise the "pen" or puck from the tablet, and then move it, the on-screen pointer will not move. However, as soon as you lower the "pen" or puck down onto the tablet the pointer will immediately jump to the appropriate point on the screen.

Most software is no easier to use with a digitising tablet, and they then offer no real advantages. As they are several times more expensive than a mouse, this has led to them being far less popular. Where a program does properly support a digitising tablet, it might be well worthwhile paying the extra money for one. Some CAD programs only use part of the digitiser for controlling the on-screen pointer, with the rest being given over to menus that are used instead of on-screen menus. This leaves virtually the whole screen free to act as the drawing area. Usually the digitising tablet can accommodate a large number of menus, and user defined menus incorporating macros (a series of commands) can be used. This enables quite complex tasks to be performed with a minimum of effort, and is one of the most efficient ways of working.

A tablet is very useful for use with illustration programs, etc. where it is often necessary to trace existing artwork into the computer, and to do freehand drawing work. The ability of a tablet to operate using a "pen", or "stylus" as it is more correctly termed, makes it more suitable for applications where free-hand drawing is involved. Most people, even after gaining much experience with a mouse, find it difficult to use for freehand drawing. A stylus is much better for this type of thing, being very much like using an ordinary pen or pencil. Modern tablets are quite sophisticated, often using a lead-free stylus, and offering pressure sensitivity when used with suitable software. Pressure sensitivity is very useful when a tablet is used with software such as paint and photo-editing programs. The pressure of the stylus can be used to control line width, colour strength, etc., making it possible to accurately simulate real painting and drawing media. With the increasing use of PCs in graphics applications, digitising tablets are becoming more and more popular.

In the past there could be difficulties in using graphics tablets due to a lack of support in the applications programs. This problem has been eased to a large extent by the popularity of Windows 95/98. Any graphics tablet should be supplied complete with a Windows 95/98 driver, and with this installed it will operate as the pointing device for any Windows applications. Support for pressure sensitivity is not guaranteed, but this feature is supported by many Windows graphics applications. With most graphics tablets you can also have a mouse connected to the computer, and can move freely from one to the other. This is a useful feature, because some software is difficult to control using a tablet and stylus. Of course, separate ports are required for the mouse and the tablet, but as most PCs have two serial ports and a mouse port this should not be a problem.

Soundcards

PCs have a built-in loudspeaker, but this is driven by some very basic hardware that is really intended to do nothing more than produce a few simple "beep" sounds. For anything more than this a proper sound card and a pair of active speakers is needed. Most soundcards do actually have built-in amplifiers, but they only provide low output powers and generally provide quite modest volume levels when used with passive speakers (i.e. speakers that do not have built-in amplifiers). The simplest soundcards only offer synthesised sounds, almost invariably produced using FM (frequency modulation) synthesis. This gives adequate sound quality for many purposes, but wavetable synthesis is better for music making. This method uses standard analogue synthesis techniques, but the basic sounds are short bursts of recorded instrument sounds rather than simple waveforms from oscillator circuits. This gives much more realistic results, although all wavetable sound cards seem to produce variable results. There are usually a few hundred different sounds available, and I suppose it is inevitable that some will sound more convincing than others. Modern soundcards can typically produce 32 or 64 different sounds at once, and they are capable of reproducing quite complex music sequences. Even the cheapest cards have the ability to record and play back in high quality stereo, and to play back pre-recorded sound samples (.WAV files).

Apart from three or four audio input and output sockets, soundcards normally have a 15-way connector that is a combined MIDI port and game port. When used as a game port it takes standard PC joysticks and similar devices. When used as a MIDI port it enables music programs to operate with MIDI synthesisers, keyboards, sound modules, etc. However, note that standard MIDI cables have 5-way (180 degree) DIN plugs at both ends, and are therefore incompatible with the 15-way D connector of a PC soundcard. A special MIDI cable is needed to connect a PC soundcard to MIDI devices.

PC soundcards are often equipped with an interface for a CD-ROM drive. The reason for this is simply that many peopled added a CD-ROM drive to their PC at the same time as they added a soundcard, since both of these items are required in order to run multimedia applications. Several CD-ROM interfaces have been used in the past, but only the ATAPI interface is currently used for low cost drives (the SCSI interface is used for some up-market CD-ROM drives). The ATAPI interface is the same as the !DE interface used for normal PC hard disc drives, and modern motherboards have two ports of this type, each of which is capable of supporting two drives. Any IDE port fitted on a soundcard is therefore of no value when the card is used in a reasonably modern PC, and if possible it should be switched off. Otherwise it is simply ignored.

Floppy drives

The original PCs were equipped with a single 5.25-inch 360-kilobyte floppy drive, and could take a second drive of this type. When the PC AT was introduced it was given a new floppy disc drive of higher capacity (1.2-megabytes), which could also read 360-kilobyte discs. This type of drive can, after a fashion, write to 360-kilobyte discs, but they are normally only readable on a 1.2-megabyte drive. Next it was decided that 3.5-inch floppy disc drives should be the standard, and both types of 5.25-inch disc drive were phased out. There are actually plenty of PCs still around today that have a high-density 5.25-inch drive, but this is usually in addition to a 3.5-inch type so that data can be read from old 5.25-inch discs. The original 3.5-inch drives had a capacity of 720-kilobytes, but these were gradually replaced by 1.44-megabyte drives. An attempt was made to introduce 2.88-megabyte drives, but due to initial "teething troubles" and the relatively high cost of the discs they never really caught on in a big way. The 3.5-inch 1.44-megabyte drives remain the standard for PCs, and are the only type fitted to most PCs.

Replacing a standard 1.44-megabyte drive should be simple and inexpensive. 5.25-inch 1.2-megabyte drives are still available, but are increasingly difficult to obtain. They are sometimes to be found quite cheaply at computer fairs, but are otherwise likely to be an expensive spare part. Finding replacement floppy disc drives of other types could be difficult or impossible.

Modern PCs have the floppy disc interface included on the motherboard. With older PCs the floppy disc controller is normally in the form of an expansion card, but this card is normally a multi-function type that includes other facilities such as serial and parallel ports. Spare cards of this type are becoming increasingly difficult to obtain.

Hard drives

Hard disc drives on early PCs had the disc controller circuit on an expansion card. In fact there was some control electronics in the drive itself, and this was augmented by the circuitry on the controller card. This method of handling things is little used these days. The up-market approach to handling hard disc drives is to have a SCSI interface card (or a SCSI interface built onto the motherboard), and a SCSI hard disc drive. SCSI is actually a general-purpose high-speed parallel interface, and not one intended specifically for use with hard drives. If you require the ultimate in PC hard disc performance a SCSI drive is probably still the best option, although improvements in other types of drive have eroded their advantage in recent years.

Modern PCs, and most middle-aged ones come to that, use some form of IDE interface. This more or less connects straight on the computer's buses and does not require a controller card. The control electronics is all included within the hard disc drive. With modern PCs the IDE interface is included on the motherboard, and in most cases there are actually two of them. Each interface can accommodate two IDE devices (the "master" and "slave", or "primary" and "secondary" devices), and most PCs can therefore have up to four IDE devices. This type of interface is also used for most CD-ROM drives, some CD writers and rewriters, and other types of drive such as Zip drives, etc. Even so, a capacity of four drives is adequate for most users. Some older PCs have a multifunction controller card that has the floppy disc drive controller and one or two IDE ports on the same card. Some other functions such as the serial and parallel ports may be included on the card as well. Replacement multi-function cards of this type are increasingly difficult to track down, as are simple IDE-only interface cards.

Which type?

If you are not sure whether or not your PC has an IDE hard disc drive, how do you find out? If you do not still have the specification sheet for the PC, the easiest way to find out is to open the PC and look at the cables that connect to the hard disc drive. If it is an IDE type there will be a small multi-coloured power supply cable, and one "ribbon" data type having 40 leads. If there are two data cables, or one that has more than 40 leads, the disc drive interface is an older type such as a ST506 interface.

Memory

Memory is a potentially confusing subject, since there are now several types of memory in common use. PCs prior to the 80386 processor had their memory in the form of integrated circuits that plugged into rows of holders on the motherboard. In some cases there were about three dozen of these sockets. If you ran out of sockets it was possible to increase the RAM further using expansion cards, but this gave rather poor performance due to the relatively low operating speed of the ISA expansion bus. Memory expansion cards are now totally obsolete, but you can still obtain the chips for on-board memory upgrades or for replacement purposes. Memory in this form is quite expensive though, and upgrading an old PC is unlikely to be worth the expense involved. Replacing a faulty memory chip should not be very expensive, but locating the faulty chip can be time consuming, particularly if the PC is fitted with a large number of memory chips. In this chapter we will only deal with memory upgrades to reasonably modern PCs that use some form of memory module.

Memory map

Memory that comes within the normal 640K MS/DOS allocation is usually termed "base memory". Unless you have a "collectors item" PC there will be no need to expand the base memory, as the computer will have been supplied with the full 640K of RAM as standard. RAM, incidentally, stands for "random access memory", and is the form of memory used for storing application programs and data. The contents of the RAM in a PC are lost when the computer is switched off, and are, for all practical purposes, lost if the computer is reset (whether a hardware or software reset is used). ROM (read only memory) is used for programs that must not be lost when the computer is switched off, which in the case of a PC means its BIOS program. The 8088 series of microprocessors can address 1 megabyte (1024 kilobytes or 1024K) of memory, but in a PC only 640K of this is allocated to RAM for program and data storage. The rest is set aside for purposes such as the ROM BIOS and the video RAM. Figure 1.10 shows the memory map for a PC.

Modern processors can operate in modes that permit large amounts of RAM to be accessed. Even on the most modern of PCs the maximum RAM limit is usually imposed by the motherboard design and not the processor, with an upper limit that is usually around 256 to 1024 megabytes. This is far more than is needed for most modern applications, the majority of which will run under Windows 95/98 with about 16 to 32 megabytes of RAM. This is not to say that these programs will not run better with more RAM. Probably the most frequently asked of frequently asked PC questions is "how much RAM do I need." This is very much a "how long is a piece of string" style question, and it is entirely dependent on the applications software that you will be running. The software manuals should give details of the minimum requirements, but the minimum is the bare minimum needed to run the software at all. Most programs can run in a relatively small amount of RAM by using the hard disc for temporary storage space. This usually works quite well, but gives noticeably slower results than when using RAM as the temporary data store. With complex graphics oriented programs the operating speed can be

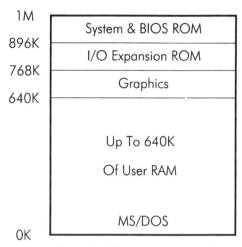

Fig.1.10 PC memory map for the base memory

painfully slow unless the PC is equipped with large amounts of RAM. There will probably be a recommended minimum system to run the software, a typical system, or something of this type. I tend to regard the amount of RAM recommended for a typical system as the minimum that will really be usable in practice.

For most software at present, 32 megabytes of RAM is quite sufficient. A few applications require much more than this, and programs that handle photographic images or other large bitmaps are particularly demanding in this respect. When handling large bitmap images in PhotoShop for example, it is recommended that the amount of RAM in the PC should be at least double the size of the bitmap. In order to handle scanned bitmaps of around 25 to 30 megabytes at least 60 megabytes of RAM would therefore be required. Fitting the PC with 64 megabytes of RAM should therefore give workable results, but 96 or 128 megabytes would probably give noticeably quicker and smoother running. Bear in mind that large amounts of RAM can be needed in order to run several programs at once. In theory you do not need (say) 48 megabytes of RAM to multitask with two programs that require 16 and 32 megabytes of RAM. Somewhat less than 48 megabytes should suffice, because you are only running one copy of the operating system, and the two programs will share some resources. However, practical experience would suggest that 48 megabytes would actually represent a realistic minimum in this situation.

Although memory has been very expensive in the past, it is currently quite cheap and putting large amounts of RAM into a PC is likely to be well worth the modest cost involved. Memory is like you-know-what and hard disk space: you can never have too much of it. You do not hear people claiming that they have wasted money putting too much memory in their computers, but you do hear people expressing regret for not having specified more RAM when buying their PC.

SIMMs

Until recently virtually all new PCs had their memory in the form of SIMMs (single in-line memory modules). A memory module of this type is a small printed circuit board, which is fitted with miniature DRAM chips of the surface-mount variety. This board plugs into a socket on the motherboard, and this set-up is like a sort of miniature version of the standard expansion slot system. 80386 and 80486 based PCs mostly use 30-pin SIMMs. These modules are available with normal eight-bit wide memory, and nine-bit wide memory. It is the nine-bit variety that is needed for most 80386 and 80486 PCs, but before buying any memory you should check this point in the manual for the computer or the motherboard. The additional bit, incidentally, is used for a method of error checking known as parity checking. These modules come in 256K, 1 megabyte, and 4 megabyte varieties, reflecting the type of DRAM chip they use. Only the 4-megabyte version is readily available now, but this is probably the only type you would require anyway. These modules are also available in a variety of speed ratings, again reflecting the type of DRAM chip they utilize. These days only the fastest (70ns) version seems to be readily available. With 80386 based PCs the modules normally have to be used in pairs or even in sets of four, but some 80486 can use odd numbers of these modules. There may also be restrictions on using SIMMs of different sizes. With many 80386 motherboards it is not permissible to use two 256K SIMMs in one pair of sockets and two 4 megabyte SIMMs in the other pair. Again, it is a matter of checking with the relevant instruction manual to determine what limitations apply to your PC.

There are some computers that have motherboards, which do not take either DRAM chips or SIMMs directly. Instead they have special plug-in memory cards, which in turn take either DRAMs and (or) SIMMs. I am not quite sure what advantages (if any) that this system brings, and it never caught on in a big way. This system has not been used on PCs built within the last few years. Note that the memory board slots on computers of this type are not standard memory expansion cards, but seem to be one-offs designed specifically for each computer. Unlike the old method of adding memory via ordinary expansion slots, no additional wait states are introduced when using these add-in memory cards, or when using SIMMs fitted directly onto the motherboard.

Bigger and better

30-pin SIMMs are now obsolete, and have not been used in new computers for some years. They were superseded by 72-pin SIMMs, which provide capacities of more than 4 megabytes per module. 72-pin SIMMs are available in 4, 8, 16, 32, and 64 megabyte versions. Like the 30-pin variety they are available with or without the parity bit. Unlike the 30-pin SIMMs, it is the modules that lack the parity bit that are normally used in PCs. Some motherboards can actually accommodate either type, but where you have the choice it is better to opt for the non-parity variety. These are significantly cheaper than the modules that have the parity bit.

Two types of memory are available in 72-pin SIMM form. The original modules of this type were fitted with fast page memory (FPM), which is basically just ordinary DRAM chips. More recently an alternative form of memory called extended data output (EDO) RAM became available. This usually gives somewhat faster performance than fast page memory, although the improvement obtained is unlikely to be more than about 10 percent or so. On the other hand, EDO memory no longer costs significantly more than the fast page variety, and is often significantly cheaper. It therefore makes sense to use EDO memory where possible, but it is not compatible with early Pentium motherboards, or any PCs of the pre-Pentium era. If in doubt, it is again a matter of checking the manual for the computer or the motherboard to determine which type or types of memory module are supported.

Although SIMMs are not exactly obsolete, they have largely been replaced by DIMMs (dual in-line memory modules), and are not normally found in new PCs. DIMMs look like outsize SIMMs, and have 168 terminals. SIMMs operate from a 5 volt supply, but the DIMMs used in PCs operate from 3.3 volts (like the input/output terminals of a Pentium processor). However, 5 volt DIMMs are produced. Fast page and EDO DIMMs are available, but it is SDRAM (synchronous dynamic random access memory) DIMMs that are normally used in PCs. Many PC motherboards will actually operate with fast page and EDO DIMMs, but as these are more difficult to obtain, slower, and usually more expensive than SDRAM, there would seem to be no point in using them. Buffered and unbuffered SDRAM DIMMs are available, but it is the unbuffered variety that is normally required for use in PCs. SDRAM DIMMs are available with capacities of 16, 32, 64, and 128 megabytes, but many of the early Pentium motherboards that accept this type of memory are incompatible with the larger sizes. In fact some of the first boards to accept DIMMs will only take the 16-megabyte type.

SDRAM is available in various speeds. For ordinary socket 7 and Pentium II computers the 12ns variety is sufficient, but the faster 10ns DIMMs are also suitable. PCs which use super-fast motherboards which operate at 100MHz, such as 350MHz and faster Pentium II and III systems, require 10ns SDRAM, but it seems that not all 10ns SDRAM DIMMs will work properly on these fast motherboards. They require memory modules that are usually referred to as "PC100" DIMMs in the advertisements. Even faster DIMMs such as the 133MHz PC133 type are now starting to appear.

There is a trend for motherboards to only have sockets for DIMMs, but there are still a few new boards that can take either type. A typical Socket 7 motherboard has sockets for two DIMMs and four 72-pin SIMMs. Some PC upgraders get into difficulty because they assume that it is possible to utilize all six sockets. Using a mixture of DIMMs and SIMMs is not a good idea, and is strictly prohibited with many motherboards. Even where the manufacturer of the motherboard does not ban this practice, I would certainly advise against it. The problem in using a mixture of the two memory types seems to stem from the fact that they operate at different supply voltages rather than any differences in their timing. Whatever the cause, I have never managed to get satisfactory results when using a mixture of these two types of memory module. If you read the "fine print" in the motherboard's manual you will almost certainly discover that one bank of SIMM sockets is connected to use the same address space as the DIMM sockets. Regardless of any other considerations, it is not possible to use both of these sets of sockets, as there would be a hardware conflict.

The right memory

When purchasing memory for a modern PC it is clearly imperative to proceed carefully, as it would be very easy to buy the wrong type. There is really no alternative to reading the relevant section of the computer's manual, or the manual for the motherboard if that is what was supplied with the PC, to discover what type or types of memory module are usable.

Do not use more than one type of memory. If the PC already has two fast page SIMMs, use two more fast page SIMMs to increase its memory and not a couple of EDO SIMMs. If you have to replace a memory module, replace it with one of exactly the same type. With very few exceptions, SIMMs must be used in pairs in Pentium PCs, but DIMMs can be used in multiples of one. It will sometimes be necessary to remove one or more of the existing memory modules in order to increase the memory capacity of the computer. With only a few memory sockets on the motherboard, you can not go on increasing the amount of memory fitted by simply adding more and more memory modules. It therefore pays to think ahead and fit large memory modules, rather than working your way up to high capacity modules, wasting a lot of smaller ones along the way.

Identifying memory

If you are not sure of the way in which the memory of your PC is made up, one solution is to simply look inside to see which memory sockets are occupied. This may not be necessary, because the BIOS start-up routine usually produces a screen that gives this sort of information about the system hardware. The BIOS will probably report the amount of memory in each bank of sockets, and the type of RAM fitted. It is best to be prudent and check this type of thing before the PC develops a fault. If a memory fault occurs you will presumably get an error message and not details of the memory present in the PC! Older types of memory tend to be more expensive than newer types, presumably because the older types of memory module no longer sell in large quantities. If your PC will take a more up-to-date form of memory than the type currently fitted, it might actually be cheaper to dump the original memory and start "from scratch" with more modern memory modules. Apart from being cheaper, changing to a more modern form of memory will probably provide a modest increase in performance.

If you are unsure of the physical memory type you PC uses (chips, SIMMs, or DIMMs), a quick look inside should provide an answer. With an old PC (80286 or earlier) there will probably be no SIMM or DIMM sockets, and instead there will be rows of integrated circuit holders on the motherboard. Depending on the amount of memory fitted to the PC, these sockets may all be occupied or some of them may be empty. If the PC is quite old but does have SIMM sockets, these will almost certainly be of the smaller 30-pin variety. These are easily distinguished from 72-pin SIMMs as they are much smaller with a length of about 90 millimetres

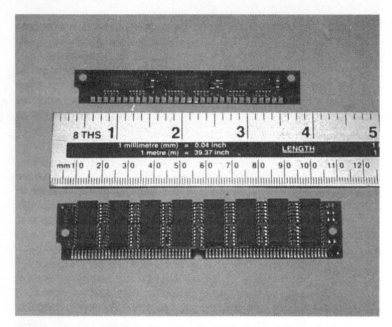

Fig.1.11 30-pin SIMMs are much smaller than the 72-pin variety

rather than 108 millimetres (Figure 1.11). Also, the two types can obviously be distinguished by counting the number of "pins" on a module itself or the number of connectors in one of the sockets. In the case of SIMMs it might be possible to determine whether they contain EDO or fast page memory by looking at the markings. If not, as explained previously, the manual for your PC or the BIOS Setup program should be able to provide an answer. DIMMs are much larger than either type of SIMM (Figure 1.12), having an overall length of about 133 millimetres. Again, if you wish to do things the hard way a DIMM can be identified by counting the number of "pins" or the connectors in one of the holders.

It is only fair to point out that some PCs utilize non-standard memory, and upgrades and repairs are then only possible if you can obtain the correct proprietary memory modules, or a true equivalent to "the real thing". Proprietary memory for a PC up to about five years old should still be available, but is likely to be much more expensive than the same amount of memory in standard "off the shelf" form. The PC's manual should have details of memory requirements if some unusual form of memory is used.

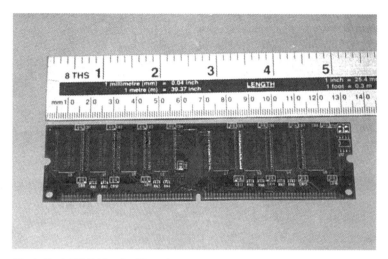

Fig.1.12 A DIMM is significantly larger than either type of SIMM

Video cards

PC expansion slots have evolved over the years, and the expansion cards have had to evolve with them. The search for better video performance was behind many of these developments. Early PCs only had ISA expansion slots in either their original eight-bit form, or a mixture of eight and sixteen-bit slots. The faster PCI expansion slots have

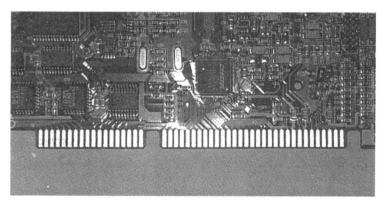

Fig.1.13 The connector on an ISA expansion card

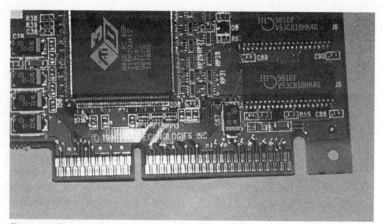

Fig.1.14 The connector on an AGP card is more complex than that of
         an ISA or PCI card

gradually replaced these, although most PCs still have at least a couple
of ISA expansion slots.   Most recent PCs also have an AGP expansion
slot, which is specifically designed for use with video cards. Video cards
for all four types of expansion port have been produced, and you
therefore have to be careful to obtain a suitable replacement.   There
should be no room for confusion as to the type of card already fitted to
a PC.   The old ISA cards have the terminals on the edge at 0.1-inch
(2.54-millimetre) intervals and are relatively chunky (Figure 1.13). PCI
cards have a lot of terminals crammed into a small space, but are relatively
simple when compared to AGP cards (Figure 1.14).

There is actually a fifth type of expansion card in the form of VESA cards.
This was a general-purpose expansion slot but it was mainly used for
video cards.   At one time it looked as though VESA would replace ISA
expansion slots and become the new "standard", but it eventually lost
the war against PCI slots and is now completely obsolete. Consequently,
obtaining a replacement for any form of VESA expansion card can be
difficult or even impossible.

Overall construction

The best way to learn about the overall layout of a PC is to remove the
outer casing from one or two or them and take a careful look inside.
There are actually some PCs that do not conform to any of the standard

layouts, and it is mainly the smaller desktop PCs that fall into this category. Before doing any work on a PC of this type you have to undertake a visual inspection and carefully note how everything fits together. In general, PCs of this type are relatively awkward to deal with. Assuming you will be working on PCs that use some form of standard case type, the general layout is much the same. There are minor differences between desktop and tower cases, but tower cases are

Fig.1.15 Mains input and output connectors

basically just desktop cases stood on-end. Apart from this the general placing of the major components is much the same.

Towards one end of the case, or at the top of a tower case, the power supply will be found. This is mounted on the rear panel of the case and invariably has its own cooling fan. Next to the mains inlet most power supply units have a mains outlet that can be used to power the monitor (Figure 1.15). With an AT power supply this outlet is switched on and off via the PC's on/off switch, but with an ATX power supply it is either absent or always active when the PC is connected to the mains supply. Modern monitors go into a low power standby mode when there is no video signal from the PC, and effectively switch themselves off when the PC is switched off. This factor is presumably deemed to render any switching of the mains outlet unnecessary.

With an AT power supply there are two multi-coloured cables that connect to the motherboard, but an ATX case has just one power lead for the motherboard. There are typically five or six other cables that provide

Fig.1.16 The connectors of an ATX style PC

power to the disc drives. One or two of these cables are fitted with small connectors that match the power connectors of 3.5-inch floppy disc drives. The other cables are fitted with larger connectors that match those fitted to virtually all other drives, including 3.5-inch hard disc drives. The disc drives themselves fit into metal bays in front of the power supply. Modern PCs have bays that take the drives directly, but some 80386 and most earlier PCs require the drives to be fitted with plastic guide rails. The drives and rails then slip into the bays and are fixed using screws that fit into the guide rails. Although 5.25-inch floppy drives are now almost extinct, all standard PC cases have two or more 5.25-inch drive bays. In a modern PC these are used for CD-ROM drives, tape backup devices, etc.

The motherboard is mounted on the base panel of the case (or on one side panel for a tower case) in the space beside the drives and power supply unit. The processor and memory are mounted on the motherboard, as are any expansion cards. As already pointed out, the motherboard connects to the power supply, but it also connects to most other components in the PC. Except for older PCs. the motherboard connects to the drives via large data cables. With older PCs the drives connect to a controller card or cards instead. The motherboard also connects to various items on the case, such as indicator lights and switches. The on/off switch of an AT power supply is a conventional type connected in the mains supply. The on/off switch for an ATX power supply is a simple pushbutton type that connects to the power supply via the motherboard. It does not directly control the mains supply, but instead sends a signal to the supply that toggles it on and off by way of its electronic control circuitry. This may seem like an "over the top" way of doing things, but it enables automatic on/off switching via sophisticated modems and other gadgets. Also, a modern operating system can automatically switch off the PC at shutdown.

An ATX motherboard has the connectors for two serial and two USB ports, a parallel type, plus PS/2 style mouse and keyboard ports included

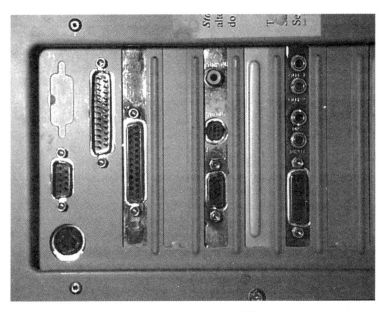

Fig.1.17 The port connectors for an AT style PC

on the board. These are accessed through a cutout in the rear of the case (Figure 1.16), rather like the keyboard port on an AT motherboard. There will be some other ports included in this cluster if the board has integrated sound and (or) video facilities. Things are less tidy with AT motherboards as they have the port connectors mounted on the rear of the case, or on blanking plates that fit into the case behind vacant expansion slots (Figure 1.17). These connectors are fitted with leads that attach to connectors on the motherboard, which adds significantly to the large amount of cabling already present.

A PC is a complex piece of equipment, but a base unit breaks down into what is typically less than a dozen items, as listed here:

Case

Power supply

Hard disc drive

Floppy disc drive

CD-ROM drive

Motherboard fitted with:

> Processor and heatsink/fan
>
> Memory
>
> Video card
>
> Soundcard
>
> Modem card

Add a keyboard, a mouse, and a monitor and you have a complete PC. Most PC faults require one of these major components to be replaced. Simply discarding a faulty component and replacing it with a new one might seem wasteful, and in a way I suppose it is. However, such is the efficiency of modern production methods in the electronics industry that the cost or repairing (say) a 50 pound video card is likely to be around 100 pounds. Production of computer components is largely automated, but repairing these components requires the time of highly skilled technicians and expensive equipment. This mostly makes the cost so high as to be uneconomic. It is usually worthwhile having an expensive monitor repaired provided it is no more than a few years old, but with other computer components replacement is the only viable option. Where possible make a virtue of a necessity, and take the opportunity to upgrade to a better component rather than simply trying to replace the original with the same item. With something like a video card it will probably be possible to obtain a better card at quite low cost and the original card will probably be unobtainable anyway. This is the down side of the pace at which much of modern computing moves forward. Ever better computers cost less and less, but parts become out of date and disappear from the market quicker and quicker. As a result of this, upgrading is often the only way of effecting a repair.

Shortcut

Never try to repair a PC until you are sure that you know exactly what hardware is present. Some basic information on such things as the floppy disc drive and keyboard types can be gleaned by looking at the outside of the computer, but for most information it is essential to look inside the case. What sort of interface does the hard disc drive use, is its interface on the motherboard or an expansion card, does the CD-ROM drive use an IDE interface, and what sort of memory is fitted? All this type of thing must be determined by inspecting the interior of the base unit and looking at the BIOS settings.

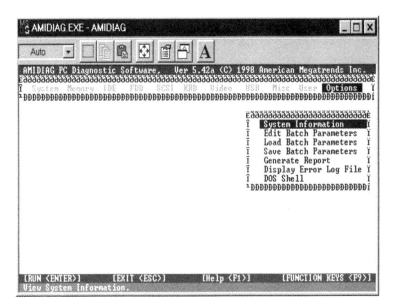

Fig.1.18 The opening screen of the AMIDIAG 5.4 diagnostics program

There is actually an alternative, and this is to use diagnostics software. Programs of this type are primarily for checking the hardware for faults, but a section of the program that can report on the hardware detected seems to be a standard feature. Figure 1.18 shows the main screen of AMIDIAG 5.4, and this offers a "System Information" option that provides quite detailed information on the hardware present. In common with some other programs of this type it must be run under MS/DOS to avoid conflicts with Windows. The Windows MS/DOS prompt is not suitable because it runs within Windows, and with Windows running in the background the diagnostics software program will crash. These days most diagnostics programs will run under Windows, and Figure 1.19 shows the System Summary screen for the popular Checkit program. This screen gives information about the amount of memory, the drive types and (where appropriate) sizes, the expansion cards fitted, and so on.

If a PC is running Windows 98 it should be possible to find some useful information about the hardware using the built-in system information utility. Left-clicking on the Start button and then selecting Programs, Accessories, System Tools, and System Tools will run this program. The

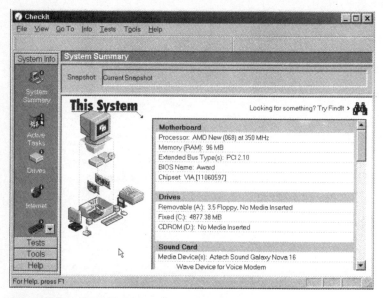

Fig.1.19 The Checkit System Summary screen

initial screen gives some basic information such as the amount of memory fitted (Figure 1.20). There are numerous additional screens available, and quite detailed information is available if you need it, as in the example screen of Figure 1.21.

It is only fair to point out that programs of this type are not perfect. In general the information is correct, but there can be problems if the software is older than the hardware it is testing. The software will then have the task of analysing hardware that it may not be equipped to handle. This can give the odd spurious figure, such as a processor with a reported clock speed of about 2000MHz! The amount of memory fitted to the motherboard should be reported accurately, but it is unlikely that the program will give details about the number of memory modules, or their size and type. In order to obtain really detailed information about the computer's hardware it will still be necessary to do a certain amount of delving into the PC's interior and the BIOS Setup program. A diagnostics program is still useful for providing an almost instant listing of a computer's hardware. Unfortunately, programs of this type are not particularly cheap, and are probably not a practical proposition for the occasional PC repairer. However, it is worthwhile checking through the software supplied with your PCs. Manufacturers sometimes supply some useful utilities including diagnostics software.

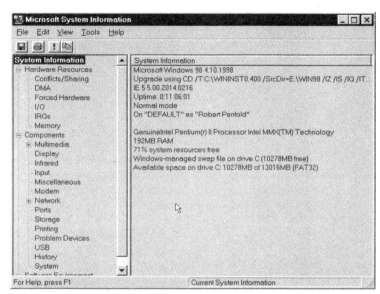

Fig.1.20 A screen of basic information provided by the Windows System Information program

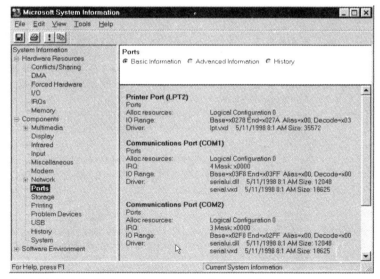

Fig.1.21 Detailed information from the System Information program

Finally

Once you know the complete specification of the PC, how everything fits together including the function of every cable, you are ready to think seriously about servicing the PC. If you jump straight in without knowing this information, expect to buy unsuitable spare parts and waste a lot of time and money.

The basics

Protection racket

This chapter deals with the general principles of PC faultfinding, and will help you to locate the nature of practically any PC problem quickly and accurately. It also provides some general information that will help you to deal with faults, such as handling the BIOS Setup program. Last and by no means least, this chapter will help you to avoid doing more harm than good when faultfinding! In this chapter things are dealt with in broad terms, and it is primarily about locating faults. Methods for dealing with the more simple faults are covered, but subsequent chapters deal with the finer points of replacing disc drives, memory modules, etc.

When dealing with modern electronic components it is not just a matter of handling the components carefully to avoid physical damage. There are hidden dangers that can cause a lot of expensive damage if you do not take suitable precautions. Those readers who are used to dealing with electronic components will no doubt be aware that many modern semiconductors are vulnerable to damage by static electricity, as is any equipment that incorporates these devices. They will also be used to handling static-sensitive components and taking the necessary precautions to protect them from damage. Probably most readers are not familiar with these precautions, and I will therefore outline the basic steps necessary to ensure that no components are accidentally "zapped".

I think it is worth making the point that it does not take a large static charge complete with sparks and "cracking" sounds to damage sensitive electronic components. Large static discharges of that type are sufficient to damage most semiconductor components, and not just the more sensitive ones. Many of the components used in computing are so sensitive to static charges that they can be damaged by relatively small voltages. In this context "small" still means a potential of a hundred volts or so, but by static standards this is not particularly large. Charges of this order will not generate noticeable sparks or make your hair stand on end, but they are nevertheless harmful to many electronic components. Hence you can "zap" these components simply by touching them, and in most cases would not be aware that anything had happened.

I think it is also worth making the point that it is not just the processor and memory modules that are vulnerable. Completed circuit boards such as video and soundcards are often vulnerable to static damage, as is the motherboard itself. In fact most modern expansion cards and all motherboards are vulnerable to damage from static charges. Even components such as the hard disc drive and CD-ROM drive can be damaged by static charges. Anything that contains a static sensitive component has to be regarded as vulnerable. The case and power supply assembly plus any heatsinks and cooling fans represent the only major components that you can assume to be zap-proof. Everything else should be regarded as potentially at risk and handled accordingly.

When handling any vulnerable computer components you should always keep well away from any known or likely sources of static electricity. These includes such things as computer monitors, television sets, any carpets or furnishings that are known to be prone to static generation, and even any pets that are known to get charged-up fur coats. Also avoid wearing any clothes that are known to give problems with static charges. This seems to be less of a problem than it once was, because few clothes these days are made from a cloth that consists entirely of man-made fibres. There is normally a significant content of natural fibres, and this seems to be sufficient to prevent any significant build-up of static charges. However, if you should have any garments that might give problems, make sure that you do not wear them when handling any computer equipment or components.

Anti-static equipment

Electronics and computing professionals often use quite expensive equipment to ensure that static charges are kept at bay. Most of these are not practical propositions for amateur computer enthusiasts or those who only deal with computers professionally on a very part-time basis. If you will only be working on computers from time to time, some very simple anti-static equipment is all that you need to ensure that there are no expensive accidents. When working on a motherboard it is essential to have some form of conductive worktop that is earthed. These can be purchased from the larger electronic component suppliers, but something as basic as a large sheet of aluminium cooking foil laid out on the workbench will do the job very well (Figure 2.1). The only slight problem is that some way of earthing the foil must be devised. The

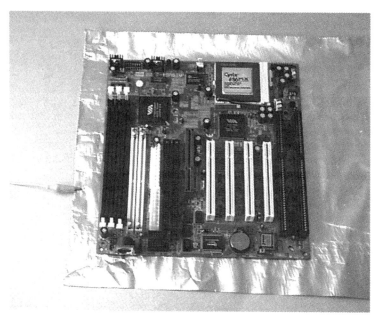

Fig.2.1 An improvised conductive work surface

method I generally adopt is to connect the foil to the metal chassis of a computer using a crocodile clip lead (Figure 2.2). Crocodile clips are available from electronic component suppliers, as are sets of made-up leads. The ready-made leads are often quite short, but when necessary several can be clipped together to make up a longer lead. The computer that acts as the earth must be plugged into the mains supply so that it is earthed via the mains earth lead. The computer should be switched off, and the supply should also be switched off at the mains socket. The earth lead is never switched, and the case will remain earthed even when it is switched off.

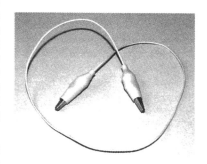

If you wish to make quite sure that your body remains static-free, you can earth yourself to the computer

Fig.2.2 A crocodile clip lead

by way of a proper earthing wristband. This is basically just a wristband made from electrically conductive material that connects to the earth via a lead and a high value resistor. The resistor does not prevent any static build-up in your body from leaking away to earth, but it will protect you from a significant shock if a fault should result in the earthing point becoming "live". If you do not want to go to the expense of buying a wristband, a simple but effective alternative is to touch the conductive worktop or the metal chassis of the computer from time to time. This will leak away any gradual build-up of static electricity before it has time to reach dangerous proportions. Again, the computer must be connected to the mains supply, but it should be switched off and the mains supply should be switched off at the mains outlet.

That is really all there is to it. Simply having a large chunk of earthed metal (in the form of the computer case) near the work area helps to discourage the build-up of any static charges in the first place. The few simple precautions outlined previously are then sufficient to ensure that there is no significant risk to the components. Do not be tempted to simply ignore the dangers of static electricity when handling computer components. When building electronic gadgets I often ignore static precautions, but I am dealing with components that cost a matter of pence each. If one or two of the components should be zapped by a static charge, no great harm is done. The cost would be minimal and I have plenty of spares available. The same is not true when dealing with computer components, some of which could cost in excess of a hundred pounds. The computer would remain out of commission until a suitable replacement spare part was obtained.

Anti-static packing

One final point is that any static sensitive components will be supplied in some form of anti-static packaging. This is usually nothing more than a plastic bag that is made from a special plastic that is slightly conductive. Processors and memory modules are often supplied in something more elaborate, such as conductive plastic clips and boxes. There is quite a range of anti-static packaging currently in use, and Figure 2.3 shows a couple of examples.

Although it is tempting to remove the components from the packing to have a good look at them, try to keep this type of thing to a minimum. When you do remove the components from the bags make sure that you and the bags are earthed first. Simply touching the earthed chassis of a computer while holding the component in its bag should ensure

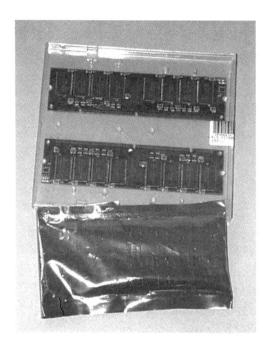

that everything is charge-free. Make sure that you always handle the components in an environment that is free from any likely sources of static charges. There will then be a minimal risk of any damage occurring.

It is worthwhile keeping some of the anti-static packing that you get with spare parts or components bought for upgrading. Repairing a PC often involves partially dismantling the base unit, and it is useful to have some anti-static

Fig.2.3 Two forms of anti-static packing

packing to keep components safe until they are reinstalled in the computer. Some types of anti-static packing are available from some of the larger electronic component retailers incidentally.

Worth repairing?

There is an old joke about the woman who was amazed that her old broom had lasted thirty years - and it only needed two new handles and seven new heads! I suppose that the modular construction of PCs leaves them open to the same sort of claim. Over the years you can put in a new display card here, a replacement disc drive there, and maybe even a new motherboard in the fullness of time. Five or six years later the computer will still be going strong, and will probably have a specification well above that of the original machine, but the case might be the only survivor from the original hardware! If you regularly update a PC it can be kept in working order for many years, but eventually things tend to move on so far that such a major upgrade is needed that you are not really upgrading the PC at all. You are building a new PC using a few parts from the old PC. If a PC is not regularly updated it soon starts to fall behind the times and after a few years it is well and truly out of date.

It is when this happens that you have to think long and hard before repairing a PC. Each case has to be taken on its own merits, and if you can find suitable spare parts at reasonable prices it is probably worthwhile repairing an old PC. The problem with old PCs is that spare parts are generally in short supply, and modern equivalents are not always suitable. When spare parts are available they tend to be offered at high prices when compared to modern components that offer much higher levels of performance. If an old motherboard develops a fault it is not possible to simply replace it with a modern one. The modern motherboard will not accept the old processor, the memory modules or chips, and may not even take the expansion cards from the old PC. It is mainly this factor that brings bit by bit upgrading to a halt. Upgrading one part of the system necessitates upgrades to several others, and you end up with what is virtually a new PC.

Upgrading your way out of trouble is certainly a valid approach where a simple repair is not possible, and the extra performance obtained will be useful. It is not likely to be a cheap solution, but you end up with a much better and largely new PC.

Whether or not a PC should be repaired is really a matter of economics. You first have to ascertain whether or not it is possible to obtain the spare part required, and then assess the viability of the repair. Even if the cost of the spare is slightly outlandish it is still likely to be far less than the cost of a new budget priced PC. However, unlike the new PC the repaired computer is unlikely to offer many years of trouble-free service. A new PC would also have greater scope for running modern applications software. Do not overlook the second-hand option. With new PCs on offer at low prices the second-hand market has prices that are pitched even lower. You could well find that a second-hand base unit having a better specification than you existing PC costs about the same price as the replacement part for your current PC. Paying "through the nose" for old parts is almost invariably the wrong decision.

With any reasonably modern PC things are much clearer cut, and it should certainly be worth effecting a repair yourself. With professional repairs the higher costs mean that in some cases a repair would be barely worth it, but with do-it-yourself fixes the lower cost means that it should always be economically viable with any modern PC. Spare parts for modern computers should be much easier to obtain and prices should be quite low. If you can not obtain an exact replacement for the original there will almost certainly be a more modern equivalent that will give improved performance. A faulty component often makes the perfect excuse to upgrade to something better.

Diagnosis

Diagnosing a fault is sometimes very easy, while in other cases it will take quite a lot of effort to track down the precise nature of the fault. When undertaking any form of servicing it is essential to make reasoned deductions rather than jumping to conclusions. The cause of the problem may seem to be obvious, but all might not be as it seems. If a floppy disc drive fails to work, the obvious conclusion is that the drive is faulty. However, a fully working floppy disc drive is dependent on more than just the drive being in full working order. The drive will not work unless it is receiving power from the power supply, and it is also dependent on the floppy disc controller operating properly. It also requires the ROM BIOS to have the correct settings, and it will only work with undamaged discs that are of adequate quality. Most components in a PC are dependent on at least one other component. Even with something like the memory modules, a fault in the memory could just as easily be due to a problem with the motherboard or a holder as it could with a memory module.

So how do you determine whether the fault is the obvious one or something in the background that has failed? There is more than one way of tackling the problem, and to some extent the way you go about things depends on the particular component that is giving problems. Where a problem might be due to corrupted settings in the BIOS, the obvious first check is to go into the BIOS Setup program and see if the settings are correct. There are programs available that test various items of hardware in the computer, and in some cases these can narrow down a fault to (say) a disc controller rather than the disc itself. Such programs rarely claim to be 100 percent reliable, but they usually provide accurate results.

The best way of checking the nature of a fault is to use component substitution. This method can be rather time consuming, but it should leave no doubt as to the exact cause of a problem. Unfortunately, substitution testing is only possible if you have some spare parts that can be used as substitutes for suspected faulty parts, or if you can borrow parts from another PC. If you undertake computer upgrades it is a good idea to store the old parts in case they can be used for testing purposes.

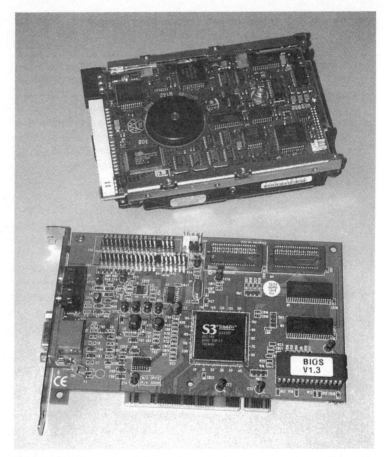

*Fig.2.4 Keep old disc drives, video cards, etc. They can be invaluable
when things go wrong*

If an old PC is scrapped it is also a good idea to keep at lest some of the
parts, and all of them if possible. Things like old floppy disc drives, hard
drives, and video cards are particularly useful for substitution testing
(Figure 2.4).

This method of testing simply involves removing a part that is suspected
of being faulty, and replacing it with one that it known to be fully working.
In our floppy disc example, if a replacement disc drive fails to work, then
the problem is almost certainly due to the controller and not the drive

itself. If on the other hand, the replacement drive works, the old drive is almost certainly faulty. In this situation I tend to try the old drive again in order to make sure that it is genuinely faulty. In a lot of cases the replaced "faulty" component works perfectly.

With substitution testing you can also do things the other way round, with the component that is thought to be faulty being tried in another PC. If the "faulty" component works properly in the other PC, clearly it is not the real cause of the problem. If, on the other hand, it does fail to work in the other PC, it is virtually certain that the component is genuinely broken. The advantage of this method is that no spare parts to act as substitutes are required, but you do obviously need a second PC. When buying a new PC it is usually well worthwhile hanging on to the old computer for use as an emergency standby, and as a test-bed when trying to locate faults in other PCs.

Bad connections

As pointed out previously, when a component that appeared to be faulty is removed from a PC and then installed again, frequently the problem seems to miraculously disappear. The reason for this is not divine intervention. A fair proportion of PC faults are caused by bad connections rather than faulty components. The modular method of construction used in PCs gives tremendous versatility. Using standard components you can have the most basic of PCs, one having all the latest "bells and whistles", or anything in-between. The price that has to be paid for this versatility is a mass of connections between the various components. Over a period of time some of the connectors tend to corrode or oxidise slightly, and connections that were once fine start to fail. The corrosion tends to be scraped off when the components are swapped around, and normal operation is restored.

The obvious lesson to learn from this is that the connectors are the place to start when any component seems to fail. In the case of something like disc drives check that both ends of the data cables are connected properly. Disconnect and reconnect each end of the cable a couple of times in an attempt to remove any corrosion that could be causing problems. Do not forget to do the same with the power cables. Most cables in a PC are polarised, and can only be fitted the right way round. However, it is sensible to note the original orientation so that you can be sure of reconnecting each lead correctly.

Bad connections can also be problematic with expansion cards, which mostly rely on a large number of interconnections between the card and the PC. In days gone by I found that a high percentage of PC faults were due to expansion cards that did not connect to the expansion slot correctly. Many advised removing the expansion cards, cleaning all the contacts, and then reinstalling all the cards about every six months. This might seem to be slightly "over the top" advice, but in those days at any rate, it certainly eliminated a lot of PC breakdowns.

These days expansion cards seem to be less prone to problems with bad connections. In part this is probably due to improvements in the materials used for both the card connectors and the expansion slots. Another major factor is certainly the integration of most ports onto the motherboard, and in some cases other functions are included on the motherboard as well. Even though modern PCs are more sophisticated than those of ten or so years ago, they generally have fewer expansion cards. This leaves less scope for things to go wrong. Obviously there can still be occasional problems with expansion cards, and removing and refitting them may effect a cure with a PC that is causing problems. Contact cleaning sprays and similar items are available from the larger electronic component retailers, but in most cases simply removing and reinstalling a card will clean away any offending dirt and corrosion and restore normal operation.

Alignment

With modern PCs and expansion cards the problem of bad connections giving problems with expansion cards seems to be less prevalent than it once was, but alignment problems seem to be as common as ever. Even with an old ISA expansion card there are numerous closely spaced contacts on each connector, and unless the card and the slot are fitted together with a high degree of precision there is a likelihood of problems occurring. These problems can take several forms. In days gone by it was not uncommon for some expansion slots and cards to be made to rather low standards. As a result, some combinations of card and slot failed to make contact properly. In fact the lack of accuracy often resulted in the card short-circuiting many of the terminals on the expansion slot, bringing the entire computer to a halt. Fortunately, this type of problem is virtually unheard of these days, and if an expansion card is properly seated in its slot, all should be well.

A more common problem with current PCs is that of the expansion card tending to ride up at the rear. Sometimes this happens as soon as the card is bolted into place, but it does sometimes happen that the card is all right for some time, and then it pops up out of place. The usual

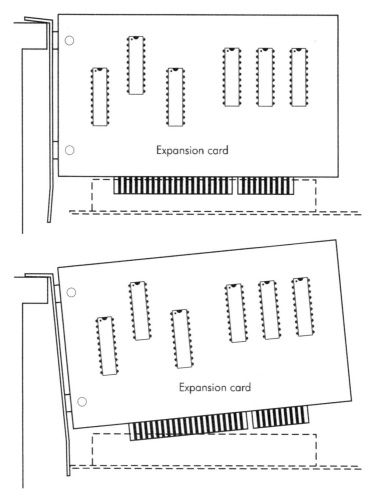

Fig.2.5 A mounting bracket can cause problems if it does not have the correct right-angled bend

cause of the problem is the mounting bracket not having the proper right-angle fold at the top. Initially the card fits down into the slot correctly, as in the upper diagram of Figure 2.5, but when the fixing bolt is tightened the card tends to go out of alignment, as in the lower diagram of Figure 2.5. With the expansion card in the slot at an angle, the terminals of the slot tend to be short-circuited by the expansion card, bringing the whole computer to a halt. A visual inspection of the expansion cards will usually reveal this problem. It is also worthwhile pressing on the expansion cards to see if any of them will push down further into the expansion slots. If a card pushes further into place but almost immediately pops back up again, there is almost certainly a problem with the mounting bracket. The cure is to carefully bend the mounting bracket to the correct shape.

A similar problem can result is a card that looks as though it is properly seated in its expansion socket, whereas it is in fact too high up and not making electrical contact with the slot. Although this is difficult to spot visually, because you can not see how much of the card is within the expansion slot, it should be revealed by firmly pressing down on the expansion cards one by one. If a card presses down into the slot, but springs back up again when you take your hand away, it is not properly seated in its slot. This problem is another one that usually stems from distortions in the card's mounting bracket. The expansion card will normally fit into the slot properly if the mounting bracket is carefully formed into the correct shape. Some expansion cards are fixed to the mounting bracket via flanges on the bracket and a couple of mounting bolts. In order to get the card to fit into the computer reliably it is sometimes necessary to loosen the two fixing nuts, adjust the position of the bracket slightly, and then retighten the nuts.

The BIOS

The BIOS is something that most PC users never need to get involved with, but for anyone undertaking PC servicing it is likely that some involvement will be needed from time to time. Even if you do not undertake work that requires some of the settings to be altered, it will occasionally be necessary to check that the existing settings are correct. Things like memory and disc failures can be due to incorrect settings in the BIOS. In days gone by it was necessary to have a utility program to make changes to the BIOS settings, but this program is built into a modern PC BIOS. A modern BIOS Setup program enables dozens of parameters to be controlled, many of which are highly technical. This tends to make the BIOS intimidating for those who are new to PC servicing, and even to those who have some experience of dealing with PC problems. However, most of the BIOS settings are not the type of thing the user will need to bother with. In general it is only the standard settings that control the disc drives that you will need to check, plus settings that relate to the type of memory used, and possibly one or two others. It is these parameters that we will consider here.

Fig.2.6 The BIOS is a program stored in a ROM chip

BIOS basics

Before looking at the BIOS Setup program, it would perhaps be as well to consider the function of the BIOS. BIOS is a acronym and it stands for basic input/out system. Its primary function is to help the operating system handle the input and output devices, such as the drives, and ports, and also the memory circuits. It is a program that is stored in a ROM on the motherboard. These days the chip is usually quite small and sports a holographic label to prove that it is the genuine article (Figure 2.6). The old style ROM is a standard ROM chip, as in Figure 2.7. Either way its function is the same. Because the BIOS program is in a ROM on the motherboard it can be run immediately at start-up without the need for any form of booting process.

The BIOS can provide software routines that help the operating system to utilize the hardware effectively, and it can also store information about the hardware for use by the operating system, and possibly other software. It is this second role that makes it necessary to have the Setup program. The BIOS can actually detect much of the system hardware and store the relevant technical information in memory. Also, a modern BIOS is customised to suit the particular hardware it is dealing with, and

Fig.2.7 An older style ROM BIOS chip

the defaults should be sensible ones for the hardware on the motherboard. However, some parameters have to be set manually, such as the time and date, and the user may wish to override some of the default settings.

The Setup program enables the user to control the settings that the BIOS stores away in its memory. A backup battery powers this memory when the PC is switched off, so its contents are available each time the PC is turned on. Once the correct parameters have been set it should not be necessary to change them unless the hardware is altered, such as a new floppy drive being added or the hard disc being upgraded. In practice the BIOS settings can sometimes be scrambled by a software or hardware glitch, although this is not a common problem with modern PCs. If the settings do become corrupted, there is no option but to use the BIOS Setup program to put things right again.

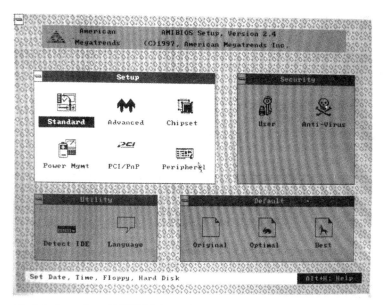

Fig.2.8 A modern AMI BIOS has a form of WIMP environment

Entry

In the past there has been several common means of getting into the BIOS Setup program, but with modern motherboards there is only one method in common use. This is to press the Delete key at the appropriate point during the initial testing phase just after switch-on. The BIOS will display a message, usually in the bottom left-hand corner of the screen, telling you to press the "Del" key to enter the Setup program. The instruction manual should provide details if the motherboard you are using has a different method of entering the Setup program. The most common alternative is to press the "Escape" key rather than the "Del" key, but numerous alternatives have been used over the years.

Every PC should be supplied with a manual that has a section dealing with the BIOS. Actually a lot of PCs are supplied with only a very simple "Getting Started" style manual, but this is usually augmented by the manufacturers' manuals for the main components. It is then the motherboard manual that will deal with the BIOS. It is worth looking through the BIOS section to determine which features can be controlled via the BIOS.

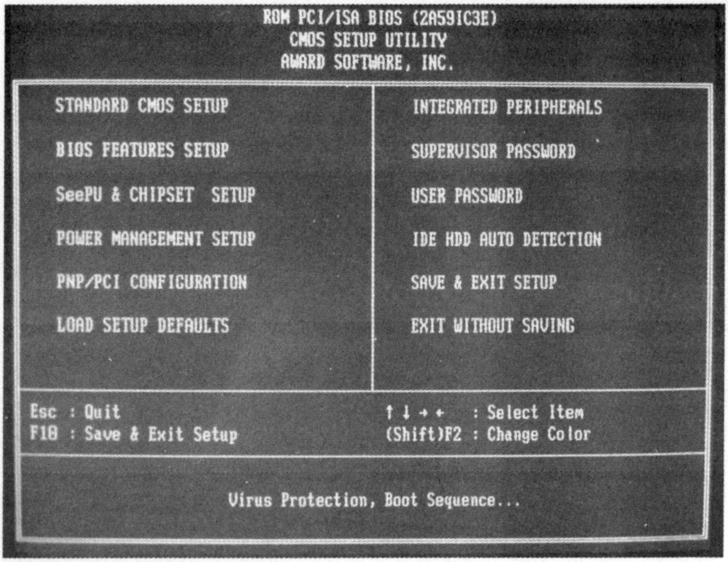

```
                    ROM PCI/ISA BIOS (2A59IC3E)
                         CMOS SETUP UTILITY
                        AWARD SOFTWARE, INC.

     STANDARD CMOS SETUP              INTEGRATED PERIPHERALS

     BIOS FEATURES SETUP              SUPERVISOR PASSWORD

     SeePU & CHIPSET  SETUP           USER PASSWORD

     POWER MANAGEMENT SETUP           IDE HDD AUTO DETECTION

     PNP/PCI CONFIGURATION            SAVE & EXIT SETUP

     LOAD SETUP DEFAULTS              EXIT WITHOUT SAVING


   Esc : Quit                        ↑ ↓ → ←   : Select Item
   F10 : Save & Exit Setup           (Shift)F2 : Change Color


              Virus Protection, Boot Sequence...
```

Fig.2.9 The AWARD BIOS uses keyboard control

Unfortunately, most motherboard instruction manuals assume the user is familiar with all the BIOS features, and there will be few detailed explanations. In fact there will probably just be a list of the available options and no real explanations at all. However, a quick read through this section of the manual will give you a good idea of what the BIOS is all about. Surprisingly large numbers of PC users who are quite expert in other aspects of PC operation have no real idea what the BIOS and the BIOS Setup program actually do. If you fall into this category the section of the manual that deals with the BIOS should definitely be given at least a quick read through.

There are several BIOS manufacturers and their BIOS Setup programs each work in a slightly different fashion. The Award BIOS and AMI BIOS are two common examples, and although they control the same basic functions, they are organised in somewhat different ways. A modern AMI BIOS has a Setup program that will detect any reasonably standard mouse connected to the PC, and offers a simple form of WIMP environment (Figure 2.8). It can still be controlled via the keyboard if preferred, or if the BIOS does not operate with the mouse you are using. The Award BIOS is probably the most common (Figure 2.9), and as far as I am aware it only uses keyboard control.

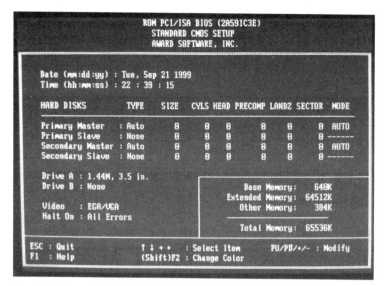

Fig.2.10 An example of a standard CMOS Setup screen

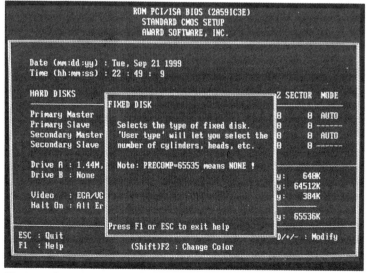

Fig.2.11 Pressing F1 will usually bring up a brief help screen

Apart from variations in the BIOS due to different manufacturers, the BIOS will vary slightly from one motherboard to another. This is simply due to the fact that features available on one motherboard may be absent or different on another motherboard. Also, the world of PCs in general is developing at an amazing rate, and this is reflected in frequent BIOS updates. The description of the BIOS provided here has to be a representative one, and the BIOS in your PC will inevitably be slightly different. In particular, if you are servicing an old PC there will be a much more limited range of parameters that can be controlled via the BIOS Setup program. The important features should be present in any BIOS, and it is only the more minor and obscure features that are likely to be different. The motherboard's instruction manual should at the least give some basic information on setting up and using any unusual features.

Standard CMOS

There are so many parameters that can be controlled via the BIOS Setup program that they are normally divided into half a dozen or so groups. The most important of these is the "Standard CMOS Setup" (Figure 2.10), which is basically the same as the BIOS Setup in the original AT style PCs. The first parameters in the list are the time and date. These can usually be set via an operating system utility these days, but you can alter them via the Setup program if you prefer. There are on-screen instructions that tell you how to alter and select options. One slight oddity to watch out for is that you often have to use the Page Up key to decrement values, and the Page Down key to increment them.

With virtually any modern BIOS a help screen can be brought up by pressing F1, and this will usually be context sensitive (Figure 2.11). In other words, if the cursor is in the section that deals with the hard drives, the help screen produced by pressing F1 will tell you about the hard disc parameters. It would be unreasonable to expect long explanations from a simple on-line help system, and a couple of brief and to the point sentences are all that will normally be provided.

Drive settings

The next section is used to set the operating parameters for the devices on the IDE ports. The hard disc is normally the master device on the primary IDE channel (IDE1), and the CD-ROM is usually the master device on the secondary IDE channel (IDE2). However, to avoid the need for a second data cable the CD-ROM drive is sometimes the slave device on the primary IDE interface. In the early days there were about 40 standard types of hard disc drive, and a it was just a matter of selecting the appropriate type number for the drive in use. The BIOS would then supply the appropriate parameters for that drive. This system was unable to cope with the ever increasing range of drives available, and something more flexible had to be devised. The original 40 plus preset drive settings are normally still available from a modern BIOS, but there is an additional option that enables the drive parameters to be specified by the user. This is the method used with all modern PCs and their high capacity hard disc drives.

The drive table parameters basically just tell the operating system the size of drive, and the way that the disc is organised. Although we refer to a hard disc as a singular disc, most of these units use both sides of two or more discs. Each side of the disc is divided into cylinders (tracks), and each cylinder is subdivided into several sectors. There are usually other parameters that enable the operating system to use the disc quickly and efficiently. You do not really need to understand these parameters, and just need to check that the correct figures are present. The manual for the hard drive should provide the correct figures for the BIOS. If you do not have the manual, it can probably be downloaded from the disc manufacturer's web site.

A modern BIOS makes life easy for you by offering an "Auto" option. If this is selected, the BIOS examines the hardware during the start-up routine and enters the correct figures automatically. This usually works very well, but with some drives it can take a while, which extends the boot-up time. If the PC has been set up with this option enabled, the drive table will be blank.

There is an alternative method of automatic detection that avoids the boot-up delay, and any reasonably modern BIOS should have this facility. If you go back to the initial menu you will find a section called "IDE HDD Auto Detection" (Figure 2.12), and this offers a similar auto-detection facility. When this option is selected the Setup program examines the hardware on each IDE channel, and offers suggested settings for each of the four possible IDE devices. If you accept the suggested settings for the hard disc drive (or drives) they will be entered into the CMOS RAM. There may actually be several alternatives offered per IDE device, but the default suggestion is almost invariably the correct one. If you do not know the correct settings for a drive, this facility should find them for you.

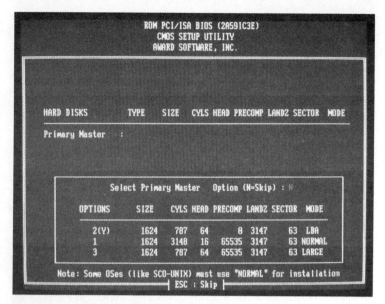

Fig.2.12 An IDE automatic detection screen in operation

It is perhaps worth mentioning that with an IDE drive the figures in the drive table do not usually have to match the drive's physical characteristics. Indeed, they rarely if ever do so. The electronics in the drive enable it to mimic any valid physical arrangement that does not exceed the capacity of the drive. In practice it is advisable to use the figures recommended by the drive manufacturer, as these are tried and tested, and should guarantee perfect results. Other figures can sometimes give odd problems such as unreliable booting, even though they are within the acceptable limits.

The last parameter for each IDE drive is usually something like Auto, Normal, LBA (large block addressing), and Large. Normal is for drives under 528MB, while LBA and Large are alternative modes for drives having a capacity of more than 528MB. Modern drives have capacities of well in excess of 528MB, and mostly require the LBA mode. The manual for the hard drive should give the correct setting, but everything should work fine with "Auto" selected.

Some users get confused because they think a hard drive that will be partitioned should have separate entries in the BIOS for each partition.

This is not the case, and as far as the BIOS is concerned each physical hard disc is a single drive, and has just one entry in the CMOS RAM table. The partitioning of hard discs is handled by the operating system, and so is the assignment of drive letters. The BIOS is only concerned with the physical characteristics of the drives, and not how data will be arranged and stored on the discs.

Floppy drives

The next section in the "Standard CMOS Setup" is used to select the floppy disc drive type or types. Provided the PC is not a virtual museum piece, all the normal types of floppy drive should be supported, from the old 5.25-inch 360K drives to the rare 2.88M 3.5-inch type. You simply check that the appropriate type is set for drives A and B. "None" should be selected for drive B if the computer has only one floppy drive. This bottom section of the screen also deals with the amount of memory fitted to the motherboard. In days gone by you had to enter the amount of memory

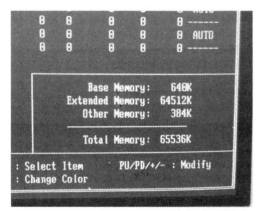

Fig.2.13 The BIOS reports the memory it finds. The user can not alter these settings

fitted, but a modern BIOS automatically detects the memory and enters the correct figures into the CMOS RAM. The "Standard CMOS Setup" screen will report the amount of memory fitted, and will display something like Figure 2.13.

Note that there is no way of altering the memory settings if they are wrong. If the BIOS reports the wrong amount of RAM there is a fault in the memory circuits, and the correct amount will be reported if the fault is rectified. Sometimes what appears to be an error is just the way the amount of memory is reported by the BIOS. For those who are new to computing the way in which the amount of memory is reported can seem rather strange. It should look very familiar to those who can remember the early days of IBM compatible PCs. The original PCs had relatively simple processors that could only address one megabyte of RAM, but only the lower 640K of the address range were actually used for RAM. The upper 384K of the address range was used for the BIOS ROM, video ROM, and that sort of thing.

Modern PCs can address hundreds of megabytes of RAM, but the lowest one megabyte is still arranged in much the same way that it was in the original PCs. The BIOS therefore reports that there is 640K of normal (base) memory, so many kilobytes of RAM above the original one megabyte of RAM (extended memory), and 384K of other memory. This "other" memory is the RAM in the address space used by the BIOS, etc.

The final section of the standard set up enables the type of video card to be specified, and the degree of error trapping to be selected. The BIOS will probably detect the video card and set the appropriate type, which for a modern PC will presumably be a EGA/VGA type. It is possible to select the old CGA and mono adapters, but these are obsolete and not used in modern PCs.

The error trapping controls the way in which the computer responds to errors that are found during the BIOS self-testing routine at switch-on. The default of halt on all errors is probably the best choice, particularly when you are having problems with the PC. Once the PC has been fully serviced and is running properly again you may prefer to alter this setting, but I would not bother. You can alter this setting if you wish to have the computer continue with the start-up routine despite a major error being detected by the BIOS. In theory this might enable the nature of the fault to be investigated more thoroughly, but in practice the PC might simply crash during the start-up routine, or on exiting it.

The BIOS, especially if it is a modern type, is likely to have several pages of additional parameters that can be adjusted. Most of these are not of any great relevance when faultfinding, and "playing" around with most of these settings is likely to do more harm than good. There may be some settings that govern the memory timing, and these will often be found in the section called something like Chipset Setup. If the PC is suffering from a general lack of reliability, with things occasionally coming to an abrupt halt, it is certainly worthwhile checking the memory settings. The memory speed shown in the BIOS Setup program must match that of the memory fitted on the motherboard, and where appropriate the memory type must also match. If the BIOS gives the memory as 60ns EDO DRAM and the board is fitted with 80ns fast page DRAM, it is unlikely that the PC will work properly.

In some cases there is more than one set of timing values given for each type of memory. The choice is usually between a relatively slow but safe option, and one that is faster but may not give good reliability. If the computer lacks good reliability and the faster memory timing is set, it makes sense to use the more conservative setting. In this context larger figures normally correspond to slower memory timing.

Some of the standard ports are integrated with the motherboard of any reasonably modern PC. Typically there are two serial ports, one parallel type, and two USB ports on the motherboard. There will be a page in the BIOS Setup program that deals with these ports, and this will normally be under a heading called something like Integrated Peripherals. If there are problems with one of the built-in ports it clearly makes sense to look at the relevant BIOS settings to ensure that the faulty port is actually switched on, and that any other settings are correct. With modern PCs the CPU settings are often controlled via the BIOS rather than using jumpers or DIP switches. If a PC is proving troublesome it will not do any harm to check the CPU settings, but if the correct CPU is reported during the start-up routine, it is unlikely that any errors will be found here.

In one of the BIOS Setup screens you should be able to choose between various boot options (Figure 2.14). In other words, it should be possible to select which drives the computer tries to boot from, and the order in which it tries them. With some PCs you can select any drive as the first, second, and third boot drives. Others are less accommodating and you have to select from a list of available boot options. This is an important part of the BIOS when servicing PCs, because it is often necessary to change the boot options. For example, you may need to reinstall the operating system by booting from a CD-ROM, but by default most PCs are not set to use this method of booting.

You may need to boot from a floppy disc drive to run anti-virus software or a disc-partitioning program. By default a modern PC may not be set to boot from the floppy disc. It is worthwhile looking at this part of the BIOS Setup program to see what the current settings are, and determine what alternatives are available. Ideally when booting from a floppy disc or CD-ROM drive, that drive should be set as the first boot drive. If the BIOS checks for an operating system on the hard disc drive first, and it finds a faulty operating system, it might bring things to a halt there rather than proceeding to other boot drives.

It is worth noting that no settings are actually altered unless you select the Save and exit option from the main menu. If you accidentally change some settings and do not know how to restore the correct ones, simply

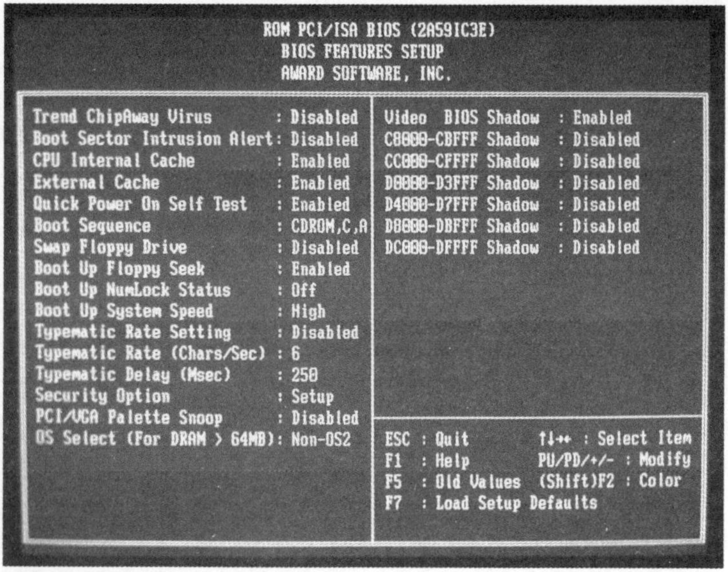

```
                    ROM PCI/ISA BIOS (2A59IC3E)
                        BIOS FEATURES SETUP
                       AWARD SOFTWARE, INC.

Trend ChipAway Virus      : Disabled   Video  BIOS Shadow  : Enabled
Boot Sector Intrusion Alert: Disabled  C8000-CBFFF Shadow  : Disabled
CPU Internal Cache        : Enabled    CC000-CFFFF Shadow  : Disabled
External Cache            : Enabled    D0000-D3FFF Shadow  : Disabled
Quick Power On Self Test  : Enabled    D4000-D7FFF Shadow  : Disabled
Boot Sequence             : CDROM,C,A  D8000-DBFFF Shadow  : Disabled
Swap Floppy Drive         : Disabled   DC000-DFFFF Shadow  : Disabled
Boot Up Floppy Seek       : Enabled
Boot Up NumLock Status    : Off
Boot Up System Speed      : High
Typematic Rate Setting    : Disabled
Typematic Rate (Chars/Sec) : 6
Typematic Delay (Msec)    : 250
Security Option           : Setup
PCI/VGA Palette Snoop     : Disabled
OS Select (For DRAM > 64MB): Non-OS2   ESC : Quit       ↑↓←→ : Select Item
                                       F1  : Help       PU/PD/+/- : Modify
                                       F5  : Old Values  (Shift)F2 : Color
                                       F7  : Load Setup Defaults
```

Fig.2.14 Amongst other things, this screen controls the boot options

exiting without saving the new settings will leave everything untouched. You can then enter the Setup program again and have another try. It is also worth noting that the main menu usually has a couple of useful options such as reverting to the previously saved settings, or loading the Setup defaults. If disaster should·strike, it might therefore be possible to go back one step to some workable settings, or to simply use the defaults and then do any necessary "fine tuning".

Cables

The average PC contains around a dozen cables, including such things as data cables for the disc drives, power cables for the motherboard, processor cooling fan, and the drives, and an audio cable to connect the CD-ROM drive to the audio card. From time to time you will inevitably end up in a situation where you need to know whether it is a cable that is faulty, or the electronics at one end of the cable. If you have spare cables it is possible to use substitution testing to determine if the cable is faulty, but with something as basic as this many people prefer to make electrical checks on the cable. This does not require any advanced test equipment, and it is just a matter of testing to determine whether or not each terminal at one end of the lead is connected to the corresponding terminal at the other end. Sometimes this type of testing is superfluous because there is clear evidence of physical damage to the lead. In most cases though, faulty cables show little or no outward sign of damage.

Any test meter, or "multimeter" as they are generally known, should have a resistance range that can be used for checking cables. In fact virtually all of these test meters have a continuity tester range that is specifically designed for this type of thing. When set to this range the unit emits a "beep" sound if there is a short-circuit or very low resistance across the test prods. This audible indication is better than having some form of visual indication, since it avoids the need to look away from the test prods. Looking away from the test prods is usually followed by one of the test prods slipping out of position about a millisecond later! However, the "beep" is usually in addition to a visual indication rather than instead of it.

A digital multimeter (Figure 2.15) is well suited to this type of testing, but is somewhat over-specified. However, if you can obtain one at a good price it should work well for many years. A basic analogue multimeter (Figure 2.16) is likely to be much cheaper and will do the job well. In fact something much more basic is adequate for testing leads, and even an old torch bulb and battery style continuity checker (Figure 2.17) will do the job perfectly well. The test prods and leads can be the "real thing", but they need consist of nothing more than two pieces of single-strand insulated wire with a few millimetres of the insulation stripped away to produce the prods. This is admittedly a bit crude, but when testing computer leads it is often necessary to get the prods into tiny holes in the connectors. With the improvised prods there is no difficulty in doing so because they are so narrow, but with proper prods they are often too thick to fit into the connectors.

Fig.2.15 A digital multimeter is overspecified for much basic PC checking

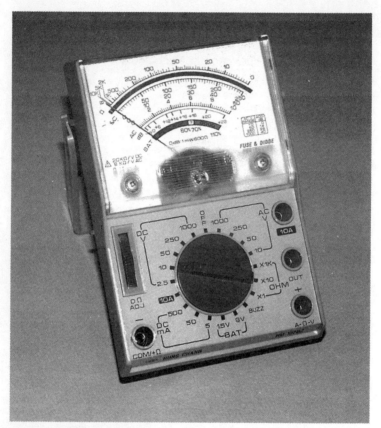

Fig.2.16 An analogue multimeter is adequate for basic PC tests

Testing cables is often rather awkward because you need four hands! One hand per test prod and another hand per connector. The easy way to tackle the problem is to fix both connectors to the workbench using clamps, or something like Bostik Blu-Tack or Plasticine will often do the job quite well (Figure 2.18). With heavier cables such as printer types it is better to clamp the connectors in place, because Blu-Tack and the like may not have sufficient sticking power to keep everything in place. With the connectors fixed to the bench and the metal terminals facing towards you it is easy to check for continuity because you then have both hands free to hold the test prods. Provided the workbench is well

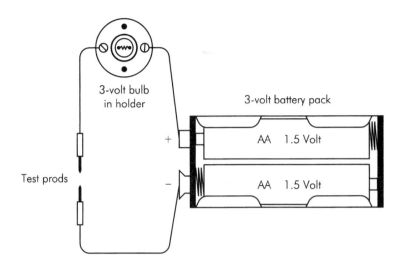

Fig.2.17 A simple continuity checker for testing leads

lit you can also see exactly what you are doing, which should help to avoid errors.

Incidentally, if you use a test meter for cable testing, on the face of it the meter is also suitable for checking the supply levels on the motherboard and other simple voltage checks. I would definitely advise against prodding around on the motherboard or an expansion card using a test meter. With the intricacy of modern boards it is quite tricky to do this, and there is a high risk of the test prods causing accidental short circuits. These could in turn ruin expensive items of hardware. The meter can be used to check for the correct voltages on a disc drive power cable, and for simple continuity tests on cables that have been totally removed from the PC, but it is advisable to go no further with it than that.

Sleuthing

Most PC faults are self-evident, and do not require much investigative work. If a floppy disc drive reads data but fails to write to discs properly, there is no point in looking for faults in the IDE devices or the processor. The fault is probably in the floppy drive itself, but could be in the floppy's data cable or the interface on the motherboard. Some simple testing

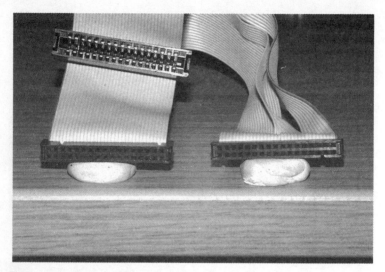

Fig.2.18 Testing is easier with both connectors fixed to the worktop

should soon ascertain the precise nature of the fault. In general, the more of the PC that works, the easier it is to find a fault. With only one section of the computer failing to work, it is very unlikely that the fault lays in any other part of the PC.

Things are more difficult when the PC is totally or largely inoperative. There is a temptation to assume that any major failure is due to a central part of the PC, such as the processor or memory. Unfortunately, a major fault in practically any part of the PC can "gum up" the computer's buses and bring the entire computer to a halt. Finding the cause of the problem when a computer simply "plays dead", or something close to a complete failure, is likely to be quite time consuming. The obvious assumption is that the power supply has failed, but you have to bear in mind that a PC power supply is a complex piece of circuitry that includes comprehensive protection circuits. An overload on one of the power supply's outputs is often sufficient to cause the whole supply to shut down. The problem could indeed be due to a problem with the power supply, but it could just as easily be due to something causing an overload on the supply. Since the power supply unit feeds power to everything in the system, the fault could therefore be anywhere in the PC!

Opinions differ as to the best course of action when faced with a "dead" PC. Assuming you do not go for the popular "give up a buy and new PC option", I would suggest starting by simplifying the PC as much as possible. In other words, disconnect from the power supply and the motherboard anything that is not essential, so that you end up with a basic single floppy PC with a minimal amount of RAM. Exactly how much can be removed will obviously vary from one PC to another. The vast majority of computers that use SIMMs can only use them in pairs, so there is no scope for removing any memory if the PC only has two SIMMs. On the other hand, DIMMs can normally be used singly, so some can be removed if there are two or more of these in the original configuration.

Having reduced the PC to a very basic computer with no hard drive, CD-ROM drive, one floppy disc drive, and no soundcard, modem or other "frills", does it work? With luck it will, and the cause of the fault is then one of the components that have been removed. Try reinstating these components, one by one, until the computer fails to work. The last component to be reinstated is then the one that is faulty. This tends to be quite time consuming, because the PC must be switched off each time another component is refitted. Do not be tempted to take shortcuts and reinstall anything while the computer is switched on. To do so would more or less guarantee the addition of further faults into the computer.

The problems deepen if the ultra-basic PC fails to work. It is virtually certain that the fault lies in a major component such as the motherboard, processor, or power supply unit. You can try a different floppy drive and keyboard to ensure that these are not the cause of the fault, and if possible fit a different memory module or modules. If these fail to bring results, I would suggest testing the power supply unit next. This is made slightly awkward by the fact that the supply will probably not activate unless it is connected to a motherboard that is working properly, or is at least sending the right messages to the power supply. If you have an old motherboard, preferably complete with an old processor and memory, perch it on the case, using some card or paper to ensure that the connections on the underside do not short circuit to anything. You can then connect it to the power supply, and can even connect it to the floppy drive to produce an ultra-basic PC based on the old motherboard.

Eventually you may be faced with a PC where everything has been tested and worked apart from the motherboard and processor. Where possible, try the processor in another PC or try another processor in the faulty PC. If the processor is faulty it is not too difficult to fit another one. The same is not true of the motherboard, and if by a process of elimination you are left with nothing else that can be faulty, you have a major repair on your hands. Replacing a motherboard is not really that difficult, and an experienced service engineer can do this type of thing in an hour or two.

Someone new to PC servicing might reasonably take the view that it is not something they feel competent to tackle. You have to make up your own mind about this, but provided you go about things carefully and methodically there should be no major problems when replacing a motherboard.

With an older PC the real problem is likely to be obtaining a suitable replacement. Replacing an old motherboard with a modern one will probably require a new processor and memory as well. With current prices this sort of repair with built-in upgrade need not cost a proverbial "arm and leg", and you end up with a better PC.

The alternative to the stripped down PC approach is to simply opt for substitution testing right from the start. With no way of knowing where the fault is likely to be, this type of testing becomes a series of "shots in the dark" until you get lucky. You might find the faulty component first time, or it could take a large amount of time. If you methodically work through the PC component by component, you should eventually track down the fault.

Getting the message

Fortunately, most major PC faults do not simply result in the computer failing to do anything at all. It is more usual for the PC to start up normally, but then falter somewhere during the initial testing or boot-up processes. Sometimes the computer fails to boot because the error brings things to a halt before the boot-up phase is reached. In other cases the error message will include a phrase like "boot failure", which means that the BIOS has tried to boot the PC but has failed to find a valid operating system. We will consider pre-boot failures first.

If the computer seems to be starting up normally, but there is no video signal, the obvious first check is to see whether or not the video card is installed correctly. In my experience it is the video card that is most likely to give problems if there is a problem with physical alignment of the cards. A contributory factor here is the heavyweight signal cables used for many monitors. The weight of the cable is often great enough to gradually wrench the video card slightly out of position. Also check that the signal lead for the monitor is connected properly to the video card, and at the monitor if it is detachable at this end as well. If none of the monitor's indicator lights switch on it is likely that the problem is a complete lack of power to the monitor rather than an absence of video output from the computer. There is normally an indicator light switched on even if a modern monitor is receiving no video signal. Either another light switches on or the light changes colour when a video signal is received. If the monitor is completely "dead", it is not receiving power and the power lead and plug must be checked.

Where the monitor is powered via the PC's power supply unit, try powering it directly from the mains supply. This will require a different power lead, but monitors can normally use a standard mains lead of the type used with most modern electrical and electronic gadgets. If necessary, borrow the computer's power lead and try using the monitor on its own. Obviously you will not get any response from the screen, but an indicator light should switch on if power is getting through to the monitor. If this results in it working, either the original power lead is faulty or the power supply unit is faulty and is not providing any power on the mains output socket.

It is possible for the computer to simply grind to a halt during the initial start up routine, but a more likely cause of the problem is that the BIOS has detected a problem and brought things to a halt. The screen may display a message along the lines "Press F1 to continue", but there is probably no point in trying to continue with the boot process if there is a major fault present in the system. The error message may be rather cryptic, giving nothing more than a number for the error. The computer may also do a certain number of "beeps" from the internal loudspeaker over and over again, which is another way of indicating the nature of the fault. Unfortunately, motherboard instruction manuals do not usually give any information about the exact meaning of the error messages, but this information might be available at the web site of the BIOS manufacturer. It is worthwhile looking in the manual to see if it gives any guidance. Some instruction manuals are much more comprehensive than others.

These days the error message usually gives some indication of what is causing the problem, with an error message along the lines "keyboard error or no keyboard present". With the BIOS telling you the cause of the problem you can obviously go straight to the component that has failed to work properly. It is then a matter of checking that the keyboard is connected correctly, the memory modules are seated correctly in their holders, or whatever.

Once again, the substitution method can be used to nail down the exact nature of the fault. It the BIOS reports something like a memory or keyboard problem and everything seems to be plugged in correctly, there is a tendency to jump to the conclusion that the keyboard or a memory module is faulty. This could well be the case, but it is also possible that the problem is due to a fault in the motherboard. If the keyboard is not functioning, try swapping over the keyboard with that of another PC. If the new PC fails to work with the replacement keyboard, but the other PC works perfectly well with the keyboard from the newly constructed PC, it is clearly the motherboard that is faulty. On the other hand, if the new PC works with the replacement keyboard and the other PC fails to work with the keyboard from the new PC, it is clearly the keyboard that is faulty. As always, try to reach reasoned explanations rather than jumping to conclusions.

Motherboard messages

Most error messages are quite straightforward, and will clearly point to the hardware that it at fault. Where the message gives a brief description of the fault, that part of the message may seem like gobbledegook. This is of no practical importance, since you only need to know which piece of hardware is faulty so that it can be replaced. Exactly what is wrong with the faulty hardware is purely academic. Sometimes the error message may refer to a piece of hardware that is not one of the major components in the system. Messages such as "DMA error" or "no timer tick interrupt" are the type of thing we are concerned with here. These messages mostly refer to circuitry on the motherboard, and in most cases the only cure is to replace the motherboard.

There are one or two exceptions, such as "CMOS checksum failure". This means that the system has detected a change in the contents of the CMOS RAM used by the BIOS. Using the BIOS Setup program to put the right parameters back into the CMOS RAM will rectify the problem, but if it keeps returning the backup battery for this RAM has run flat or has leaked. In most cases a new battery can be obtained and fitted. A "Real time clock failure" message may also be due to a faulty backup battery rather than the clock chip on the motherboard. If there is a problem with the cache memory on the motherboard it should be possible to obtain and fit a new memory module provided the faulty module fits onto the motherboard via a socket. Note that error messages concerning memory normally refer to software problems if they occur once the boot up process has started. These messages are usually something like "not enough memory" or "internal stack overflow".

Boot problems

It is by no means unknown for a PC to go through the initial start-up routine and then hang up when the boot process begins. This is not necessarily due to a hardware fault and with modern PCs the majority of boot problems are probably caused by corrupt operating system files rather than hardware problems. As a general rule, it is unlikely that the problem is in the hardware if the computer gets well into the boot-up process before things come to a halt. It is possible that the operating system is crashing while looking for hardware which it fails to find due to a problem with the hardware. However, in the majority of cases the hardware is fine, and things are brought to a halt by one of the hardware drivers being corrupt or missing.

If the boot process never actually gets underway, it could be that the boot files have been seriously damaged or erased, but this is usually indicative of a hardware fault. Does the BIOS recognise the boot drive, which will presumably be the primary hard disc drive, during the initial start up routine? If it fails to find the hard disc drive there is certainly a hardware problem. Check that the data and power cables are connected to the drive properly, and that the BIOS settings that relate to the hard drive are correct. If the hard drive remains "invisible" to the rest of the system it is almost certainly faulty, but it is as well to do some substitution testing to make quite sure.

In my experience of hard disc failures the most common form it takes is with the hard disc drive reported correctly by the BIOS, but with the operating system refusing to commence the boot process. There may be an error message on the screen to say that there is some form of boot failure, or the computer may simply lockup as soon as it tries to boot from the hard disc. Presumably what is happening is that the hard disc interface within the hard disc unit is still functioning normally, and it is able to tell the BIOS that it is present and correct. Unfortunately, the disc drive mechanism is faulty and data can not be read from or written to the drive. Thus, as soon as the boot process commences the computer grinds to a halt because the required files can not be read. In fact none of the files on the disc will be readable if this happens, which highlights the importance of making backup copies of important files.

With the BIOS finding the hard drive correctly it is unlikely that the problem is due to a bad connection in the data cable or something of this nature, but it does no harm to check. The more likely explanation is that the hard drive is faulty and needs to be replaced, but at this stage it is not possible to totally rule out the possibility that the problem is due to corrupted files. In this situation I always try booting the computer from a floppy disc, and then try reading the hard disc drive once the system has booted. If the hard disc is available to the system, try reading the contents of some directories, and carry out some simple operations such as copying files and then deleting the copies. If the hard drive can be accessed normally when it is not used as the boot drive, it is almost certainly serviceable. It is possible that a minor fault has put the boot sectors "out of limits" but left the rest of the drive fully operational, but this is very unlikely.

With the drive apparently working, but booting from that drive failing immediately or almost as soon as the process begins, trying to repair the operating system is probably not going to be worth the effort. The exception to this is if you use software that takes backup copies of the important system files, and can be used to replace damaged files. Where software of this type is in use it clearly makes sense to try it before going on to more drastic solutions. The obvious solution is to simply reinstall Windows 85/98. If you boot up from a Windows 98 recovery disc it should be possible to run the Windows 98 installation disc and reinstall the system. With the Windows 98 disc in the CD-ROM drive, simply typing "setup" should run the Setup program and start the installation process. During installation the program will check the hard disc drive for installed software, and this software should still run once the operating system has been reinstalled.

It does sometimes happen that Windows will have problems installing itself onto a hard disc drive that contains corrupted files and other problems. The Scandisk program will be run during the initial stages of installation, but this basic version of the program will not be able to sort out major problems with the disc drive. If there are any serious problems with reinstallation I would recommend wiping the disc clean and starting from scratch. With the disc totally or largely readable you can backup any important files before clearing everything off the disc. To wipe the disc simply use the MS/DOS FORMAT command to reformat the disc. The operating system, applications software, and data files are then reinstalled, and with a blank disc to start with there should be no major problems. If problems do persist, it seems likely that there is an obscure hardware problem with the disc drive, and it will have to be replaced.

Oddities

There can be occasional problems that some refer to as "out of computer experiences". In other words, what happens seems to be impossible. I had one PC that developed hard disc problems, and it became apparent when listing a directory that something odd had occurred. The computer was fitted with two hard disc drives having capacities of about 850 and 250 megabytes. However, the reported sizes of the discs had changed to around 700 and 500 megabytes. Seemingly, the system had taken some disc space from one drive and allocated it to the other drive, although the total amount of reported disc space had actually increased by about ten percent! Clearly there had been some corruption of the partition table, but the cause was far from obvious. Viruses tend to get the blame for this type of thing, but virus-checking programs failed to reveal a culprit in this case.

Where this type of low level disc corruption occurs I always go right back to the beginning and use the MS/DOS FDISK program to remove the existing partitions on the hard disc drive or drives. In doing so the contents of the disc or discs is removed, so backup any important files first. Having removed the existing partitions you have what is effectively a new and totally blank disc, and everything is reinstalled onto the disc using the same procedures that are adopted for a new disc. This means using FDISK to put the correct partitions back again, formatting the disc using the FORMAT program, and then installing the applications software and you data files. If an unusual problem reoccurs despite wiping the hard drive and starting from scratch, either there is an obscure hardware fault causing the problem, or you have a disc that is infected with a virus. It makes sense to thoroughly check for a virus first, rather than replacing the hard disc drive. If the problem is a virus, replacing the hard drive will not get rid of it. When you use the infected disc the problem will be spread to the new drive. The only solution is to use anti-virus software to locate the virus, and then remove it from any infected discs.

What is a virus?

There are actually various types of program that can attack a computer system and damage files on any accessible disc drive. These tend to be lumped together under the term "virus", but strictly speaking a virus is a parasitic program that can reproduce itself and spread across a system, or from one system to another. A virus attaches itself to other programs, but it is not immediately apparent to the user that anything has happened. A virus can be benign, but usually it starts to do serious damage at some stage, and will often infect the boot sector of the hard disc, rendering the system unbootable. It can also affect the FAT (file allocation table) of a disc so that the computer can not find files or the partition table so that the reported size of a disc does not match up with its true capacity. The less subtle viruses take more direct action such as attempting to erase or overwrite everything on the hard disc.

A virus can be spread from one computer to another via an infected file, which can enter the second computer via a disc, a modem, or over a network. In fact any means of transferring a file from one computer to another is a potential route for spreading viruses. A program is really only a virus if it attaches itself to other programs and replicates itself. A program is not a virus if it is put forward as a useful applications program but it actually starts damaging the system when it is run. This type of program is more correctly called a "Trojan Horse" or just a "Trojan".

Virus protection

This is a case where the old adage of "prevention is better than cure" certainly applies. There is probably a cure for every computer virus, but getting rid of viruses can take a great deal of time. Also, having removed the virus there is no guarantee that your files will all be intact. In fact there is a good chance that some damage will have been done. The best way to avoid viruses is to avoid doing anything that could introduce them into the system, but for most users this is not a practical proposition. These days computing is increasingly about communications between PCs and any swapping of data between PCs provides a route for the spread of viruses.

It used to be said that PC viruses could only be spread via discs that contained programs, and that data discs posed no major threat. It is in fact possible for a virus to infect a PC from a data disc, but only if the disc is left in the drive and the computer tries to boot from it at switch-on. These days there is another method for viruses to spread from data discs, and this is via macros contained within the data files. Obviously not all applications software supports macros, but it is as well to regard data discs as potential virus carriers.

Given that it is not practical for most users to avoid any possible contact with computer viruses, the alternative is to rely on anti-virus software to deal with any viruses that do come along. Ideally one of the "big name" anti-virus programs should be installed on the system and it should then be kept up to date. This should ensure that any infected disc is soon spotted and dealt with. Software of this type is designed for use before any problems occur, and it normally runs in the background, checking any potential sources of infection as they appear.

There is usually a direct mode as well, which enables discs, memory, etc., to be checked for viruses. Figure 2.19 shows the start-up screen for the Quarterdeck ViruSweep program, and selecting the "Scan For

Viruses" option takes the user into further screens that permit various options to be selected. The first screen (Figure 2.20) permits the user to select the parts of the system that will be checked. Viruses can exist in memory as well as in disc files, so checking the memory is normally an option.

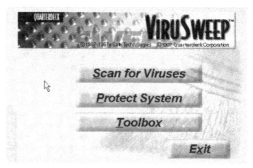

Fig.2.19 The ViruSweep start up screen

Further screens enable the type of scan to be selected (Figure 2.21), and the action to be taken if a virus is detected (Figure 2.22). Most anti-

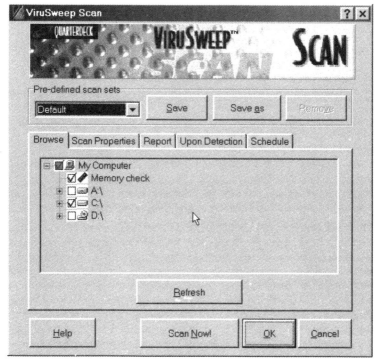

Fig.2.20 Selecting the parts of the system to be checked for viruses

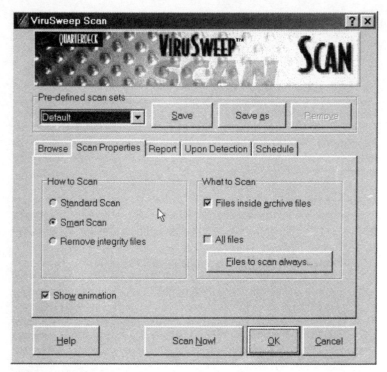

Fig.2.21 This screen enables various types of scan to be selected

virus software has the option of removing a virus rather than simply indicating that it has been detected. Note though, that in some cases it might not be possible to automatically remove a virus. The program will then usually give details of how to manually remove the virus.

Things are likely to be very difficult if you do not use anti-virus software and your PC becomes infected. On the face of it, you can simply load an anti-virus program onto the hard disc and then use it to remove the virus. In practice most software of this type will not load onto the hard disc if it detects that a virus is present. This may seem to greatly reduce the usefulness of the software, but there is a good reason for not loading any software onto an infected system. This is the risk of further spreading the virus by loading new software onto the computer. With a lot of new files loaded onto the hard disc there is plenty of opportunity for the virus to infect more files.

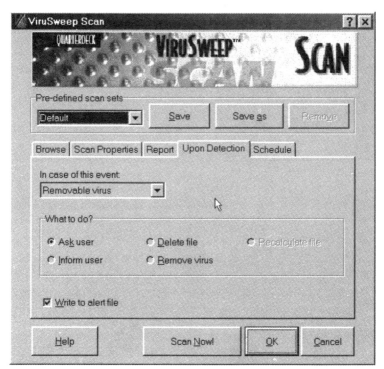

Fig.2.22 Various courses of action are available if a problem is detected

Most viruses can actually be removed once they have infected a system, but not usually by loading a major piece of anti-virus software onto the hard disc and using it to remove the virus. The method offered by many anti-virus suites is to boot from a special floppy disc that contains anti-virus software. With this method there is no need to load any software onto the hard disc, and consequently there is no risk of the anti-virus software causing the virus to be spread further over the system.

If attempts to remove a virus prove to be unsuccessful it becomes necessary to take drastic action in order to get the system running properly again. This means using the MS/DOS FDISK program to remove the existing partitions from the disc, which means losing the entire contents of the disc. Making backup copies of files first is decidedly risky since there is a good chance that the virus will be spread to the discs containing the backup copies. Restoring the files from these discs

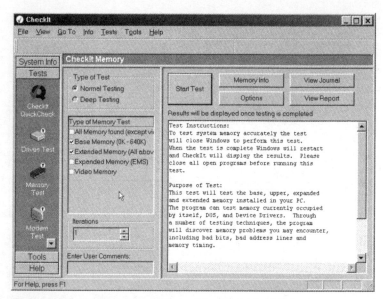

Fig.2.23 The memory test section of the Checkit program

could also restore the virus onto the hard disc. Once the partitions on the hard disc drive have been removed you have what is effectively a new hard drive, and everything is restored onto the disc utilizing the same methods that are used for a new hard drive.

Diagnostics software

Diagnostics software was mentioned in chapter 1, but it was only considered there as a quick means of obtaining information about the hardware present in a PC. If you have a PC that is largely working but seems to be a bit erratic or unreliable, software of this type may help to locate the source of the problem. Note though, that problems of this type are not necessarily due to hardware faults, and can be due to a software bug or software that is not installed properly. If a problem only occurs when a certain applications program is run, the problem probably has its origins in that piece of software. Of course, if it is the operating system that has the fault, problems can occur when running any applications software.

Where you have diagnostics software available and a PC seems to be generally unreliable, it is certainly worthwhile running the software to

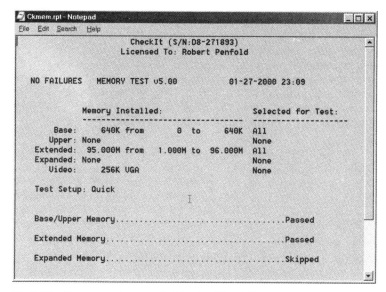

Fig.2.24 A test report generated by the Checkit program

see if it can find any problems. In my experience, if a PC has a tendency to simply grind to a halt with the display freezing, the problem is more likely to be in the hardware than the software. This is also the case where things come to a halt with the screen going blank. The fault is more likely to be in the software if the dreaded Windows error messages ("This program has performed an illegal operation and will shut down", etc.) keep appearing.

Diagnostics programs will run tests on many parts of the system, including hard and floppy disc drives, the main memory, video memory, the processor, and the ports. As pointed out in chapter 1, programs of this type sometimes operate under MS/DOS. This is primarily so that they can take control of the memory when making memory tests. Windows places restrictions on the way memory is allocated to programs, and would therefore place much of the memory beyond the reach of the diagnostics software. Even where diagnostics programs run under Windows, to make certain tests they will often reboot into MS/DOS to perform the tests, and then go back into Windows to display the results. Figure 2.23 shows the Checkit memory test screen, and Figure 2.24 shows an example set of test results after rebooting into MS/DOS and then back into Windows 98 again. This makes the testing rather longwinded, but it is perhaps a more convenient way of doing things than rebooting into MS/DOS and carrying out all the tests from there.

If a fault only occurs intermittently it might be necessary to repeat the test procedures a few times in order to coax the system into an error while the diagnostics software is running. Obviously you should try to concentrate on tests that are likely to bring results, and not bother too much about tests on parts of the system that are least likely to be causing the problem. Problems with the ports and the floppy disc drive are unlikely to be responsible for bringing the system to a halt at times when none of these are in use. On the other hand, you may as well give every part of the system a "quick once over" while you are using the diagnostics software, just in case the problem does actually lie in an unlikely part of the system. If the system has a tendency to hang up periodically, the memory, processor and video card are probably the most likely sources of the problem.

By far the most difficult type of problem to sort out is where a PC has a very intermittent fault. In other words, a fault that occurs every few days or weeks, rather than one that happens at intervals of a few minutes or hours. A fault of this type may conveniently crop up while you are running the right part of a diagnostics program, but your chances of winning the lottery are probably better. There is actually very little chance of locating the source of a very intermittent fault where the problem seems to occur randomly and simply results in the computer hanging up. A fault that only occurs when the hard disc is accessed gives a strong clue as to the source of the problem. A random fault gives you nothing to go on. Being realistic about matters there are really only three options when faced with a problem of this type;

1   put up with it

2   buy a new PC

3   start replacing parts of the computer in the hope that this clears the fault

None of these are very satisfactory, and most users simply learn to live with the problem, replacing the PC as soon as it starts to become "a bit long in the tooth".

Windows problems

Sorting out problems with PC operating systems is a complete subject in itself, and it is not possible to provide complete coverage of the subject here. However, it is certainly worthwhile taking a look at some of the more common problems and the solutions to them. A relatively simple operating system such as MS/DOS does not usually fail to boot unless there is damage to one of the boot files. It will throw up a few error messages during the boot process, and it may not operate exactly as you would like once the system has booted, but the system will usually boot.

The situation is different with a complex operating system such as Windows 98 which is dependent on numerous disc files being present and correct. If any one of these files is damaged or absent, or a configuration file erroneously specifies a file that is not present, the boot process will often stop about half way through the process. In fact quite minor problems seem to bring the boot process to a halt, such as the system running out of "environmental space", which seems to mean a lack of memory set aside for use as buffers, for use by the PATH command, etc. Windows 95/98 does not operate under the "boot anyway" philosophy of MS/DOS.

When repeated attempts to boot the system result in the boot process coming to a premature end, Windows can be set into a sort of "boot at all costs" mode, or "Safe mode" as it is called. In order to boot into this mode the F8 function key must be pressed as soon as the boot process begins. There is only a very brief gap between the BIOS finishing its start up routine and the system starting to boot, so you must press F8 as soon as the BIOS has finished its routine. In fact with some systems the only reliable way of entering Safe mode is to repeatedly press F8 as the end of the start up routine approaches. Pressing F8 does not take the system straight into Safe mode, but instead brings up the simple menu system shown here:

```
Microsoft Windows 98 Startup Menu

1.    Normal
2.    Logged (\BOOTLOG.TXT)
3.    Safe mode
4.    Step-by-step confirmation
5.    Command prompt only
6.    Safe mode command prompt only
```

Select option three to boot the system in Safe mode. Booting the system in this mode will get it into Windows, and the computer will be "up and running" to some extent. As pointed out by a warning message towards the end of the boot process, Safe mode provides a simplified version of the operating system. It is only intended to permit problems with the system to be traced and fixed, and it is not designed to permit the system to be used normally. One major difference between Safe mode and normal operation is the lack of hardware support. The video card will of course function, but only in a basic VGA mode. Exotic pieces of hardware will not function because their drivers will not have been loaded, and even some basic pieces of hardware such as the CD-ROM drive and the soundcard will not function for the same reason. Provided the mouse is a reasonably standard type is should still function in Safe mode. Some of the facilities provided by the operating system will also be lacking, which is a pity because this can make life more difficult when trying to sort out a problem.

If the problem with Windows is a minor one, it might actually be possible to boot into the normal version or something close to it, by taking a slightly circuitous route. Option number five on the mode menu permits the system to be started in MS/DOS mode. In other words, the system boots up into the Windows 95/98 version of MS/DOS, and you are then faced with a command prompt instead of a GUI (graphical user interface). Option number six does much the same, but it ignores the AUTOEXEC.BAT and CONFIG.SYS files and boots into a non-configured version of MS/DOS. This guarantees that the system will boot into MS/DOS, but there will be minor problems such as the pound sign key on an UK keyboard not producing the right character. Once into MS/DOS, try typing "win" and pressing the Return key. This may just produce an error message or cause the system to hang, but it will sometimes boot into the normal mode of Windows 95/98.

Once into Safe mode you can go into the Windows Device Manager and check for problems with the hardware. This is a process that is dealt with in subsequent chapters, but note that the facilities offered by Device Manager are reduced somewhat in Safe mode. This is to some extent inevitable, because a few items of hardware will not have their device drivers loaded. Consequently they will be non-operational in Safe mode even if the hardware and drivers are perfectly all right. It is worth running the Windows ScanDisk program, which can be run by operating the Start button and then selecting Programs, Accessories, System Tools, and ScanDisk.

This program offers two levels of operation, which are Standard and Thorough (Figure 2.25). In the Standard mode the disc is checked for errors in the files and folders, and even with a large hard drive the checking process is usually quite quick. The Thorough mode additionally

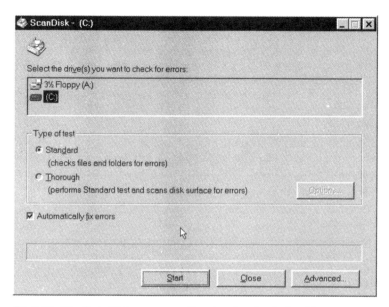

Fig.2.25 The ScanDisk program offers two levels of checking

scans the disc for weak spots, and with even moderate sized discs it takes a substantial amount of time to complete the task. Initially you might prefer to use the Standard mode to see if this unearths any problems. ScanDisk can automatically fix minor problems, but no hard disc utility can resurrect files that have been seriously damaged. If important system files have been overwritten or otherwise seriously damaged it will probably be necessary to reinstall the operating system.

Logging

Newly installed software that makes a mess of a configuration file is probably the most common cause of Windows start up problems. If the system refuses to boot just after some new software has been installed it is odds-on that the installation program has done something it should not. There are two options in the Windows 95/98 start up menu that help you to discover the root cause of the fault when the system refuses to boot. The first of these is option two, which provides a logged start up. Depending on the way your PC is configured, it may provide a long string of messages detailing what is happening during the boot process, or it may suppress these messages. Even if these messages are displayed, on a modern PC you often find that many of them scroll off the screen so fast that there is little chance of reading them. The basic function of the logged boot up is to write these messages to a file called BOOTLOG.TXT that is placed in the root directory of the boot disc. This file can be read using any text editor or word processor. Incidentally, the previous version of the file, if there is one, will be saved as BOOTLOG.PRV.

The list of messages is comprehensive and provides a full list of every action during boot up. The file also shows whether or not each action was successful. This is just a small sample from a long BOOTLOG file:

```
[00109EE9] Loading Device =
C:\WINDOWS\SETVER.EXE
[00109EE9] LoadSuccess     =
C:\WINDOWS\SETVER.EXE
[00109EE9] Loading Device =
C:\WINDOWS\COMMAND\ANSI.SYS
[00109EE9] LoadSuccess     =
C:\WINDOWS\COMMAND\ANSI.SYS
[00109EE9] Loading Device = C:\MTM\MTMCDAI.SYS
[00109F0B] LoadSuccess     = C:\MTM\MTMCDAI.SYS
[00109F0B] Loading Device =
C:\WAVRIDER\DRIVERS\SGIDECD.SYS
[00109F26] LoadFailed      =
C:\WAVRIDER\DRIVERS\SGIDECD.SYS
[00109F26] Loading Device =
C:\WINDOWS\COMMAND\DISPLAY.SYS
[00109F32] LoadSuccess     =
C:\WINDOWS\COMMAND\DISPLAY.SYS
[00109F32] Loading Device =
C:\WINDOWS\HIMEM.SYS
[00109F32] LoadSuccess     =
C:\WINDOWS\HIMEM.SYS
```

As with all faultfinding, resist the temptation to jump to conclusions. In this list there is one line that failed, but it is obvious that this did not bring things to an immediate halt because the boot process continued on for dozens more lines and processes. The system file (SGIDECD.SYS) that failed to load is a driver for a soundcard no longer fitted to the system.

The required file was no longer on the system, and was no longer needed. Its failure to load was ignored by the system, which continued to boot. It is conceivable that an error early in the proceedings could result in failure later in the boot process, but it is towards the end of the BOOTLOG file that the cause of the problem is more likely to be found.

Step-by-step

Option four in the Windows start up menu provides an alternative method of locating the problem, and is the one I would recommend using. Step-by-step confirmation, as one would expect from its name, means that the system will go through the boot process step-by-step, and that it will only include those steps that the user authorises. This enables the user to see exactly where things grind to a halt, and with further attempts it is possible to bypass certain stages of the boot process to see if this enables the system to boot. It is often helpful to try booting the computer without the CONFIG.SYS file being processed, or if that does not get the system to boot try again without the AUTOEXEC.BAT file being processed. If blocking one of these enables the system to boot, examine the relevant file (which will be in the root directory of the boot drive) using a word processor or text editor.

When editing any configuration file it is necessary to take great care not to make inadvertent changes to the file. If you are not very careful you could easily end up doing more harm than good. Always save an unchanged version of the file to provide a backup if you make a mess of things and need to return to the origin version of the file. I recommend making a backup on the hard drive called something like CONFIG.BAK or AUTOEXEC.BAK, and also making a backup copy on a floppy disc which should be write protected so that it can not be accidentally overwritten.

If you wish to get rid of a line in the file that seems to be causing the problem, a useful ploy is to add "Rem" followed by a space at the beginning of that line. This tells the operating system to ignore the line because it contains a remark that is merely there as an aid to anyone examining the file. The advantage of this method over deleting the line is that it is so easy to put things back the way they were. If you need to reinstate the line you simply delete the four characters you added. There is little chance of accidentally altering the line, because you never make any changes to the original text. It is worth looking for repetition in these configuration files.

Some installation programs make automatic changes to configuration files, and things do not always work quite as they should. For example, you will often find two or three almost identical PATH commands in the AUTOEXEC.BAT file. What seems to happen is that an installation program adds a new PATH command that is the same as the original except that it has one or two additions at the end. Presumably the original PATH command is supposed to be erased, but a flaw in the installation program leaves it intact. The same sort of thing can happen with other commands. The additional commands may seem to be of no consequence, but they will take up memory, and the memory set aside for this purpose may be used up. This usually produce error messages along the lines "not enough environment space". Lines in the configuration files that run drivers that are no longer necessary or undertake any unnecessary operations can waste memory and prevent the system from booting properly.

If the problem lies in the Windows registry or one of the Windows configuration files the problem could be difficult and time consuming to fix, even for those who are familiar with this type of problem. Some advocate reinstalling Windows sooner rather than later if a major problem occurs. I suppose there is good reasoning behind this view, since reinstalling Windows could actually be quicker than finding and rectifying the problem. There is no guarantee that you will actually be able to find and fix the problem, and ultimately it might be necessary to reinstall Windows anyway. Unfortunately, having reinstalled Windows the problem may persist, with the problem having been copied from the old installation to the new one. It is possible to get around this by totally removing Windows from the hard drive and then reinstalling it from scratch. This will probably require all the applications software to be reinstalled as well, and is therefore likely to be very time consuming.

Insurance

There are utility programs that monitor the system, make backup copies of important system files, and which should enable the user to repair the system if boot or stability problems should arise. If you are not particularly expert with Windows problems it would probably be worthwhile investing some time and money in using one of these programs.

Although many Windows problems are due to rogue software, plenty of them are due to the user confusing the system my moving or deleting files. Moving or deleting your data files should be safe enough, but it is certainly not a good idea with program and support files. It is certainly

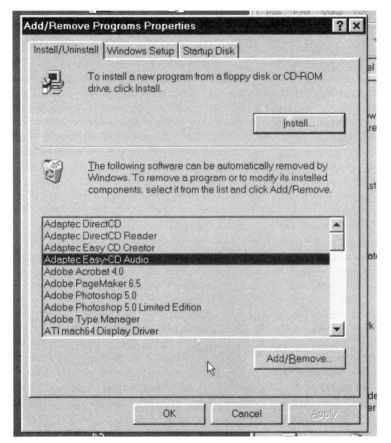

Fig.2.26 Windows 95 and 98 have a built-in uninstaller

asking for trouble with Windows system files. Simply erasing programs that are not needed any more is usually safe enough with MS/DOS software, but it should definitely not be done with more modern operating systems.

If a program must be removed from the system it should be removed using either its own uninstaller program, or the built in uninstall facilities of Windows 95/98. To run the built-in uninstaller, operate the Start button and then select Settings, Control Panel, and Add/Remove Programs. This will produce a window something like Figure 2.26, with a list of programs that can be uninstalled. In order to remove a program first left click on its entry in the list to highlight it, and then operate the Add/ Remove button. You will then be asked to confirm that you wish to uninstall this software, and it will be removed if you do so.

The uninstaller may not remove all files associated with the program from the system. Anything that may be needed by another program will be left, possibly together with any data files you have generated using the program. Obviously the folders containing any of these files will also have to be left on the hard disc. Provided you no longer need them, erasing your data files should not cause any problems, but removing any other files left by an uninstaller has to be regarded as a little risky. The uninstaller sometimes states that it has detected a shared file that is no longer needed by another program and it will then ask if you would like to erase it. It should be safe to do so, but the totally safe option is to leave any file of this type intact.

It is quite normal for some of the installed programs to be absent from the list in the uninstaller. In theory there should be proper uninstaller support for any Windows 95 or 98 program. In practice some of the smaller utilities do not seem to conform to this requirement. Programs that are written for Windows 3.1 will usually run under Windows 95 or 98 without any major problems, but they do not usually have any uninstaller support. Programs that can not be uninstalled by other means can be removed using one of the numerous uninstaller programs that are currently available. It is only fair to point out that using any form of uninstaller program, whether it is built into Windows or a third party add-on, does not totally guarantee trouble-free results. However, it does greatly reduce the risk of problems, and if anything does go wrong at least it was not your fault!

Charts

The charts from Figure 2.27 onwards summarise some of the faultfinding techniques described in this chapter, and they should be useful for quick reference purposes.

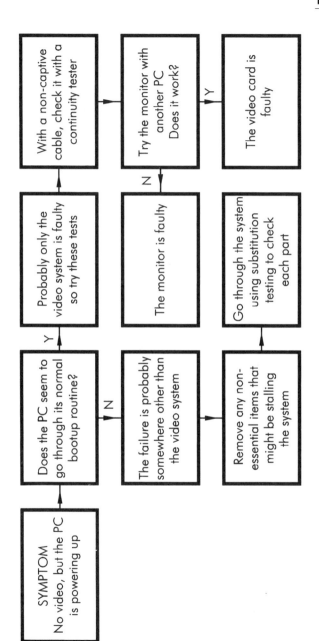

Fig.2.27 Test chart for a lack of video at switch-on

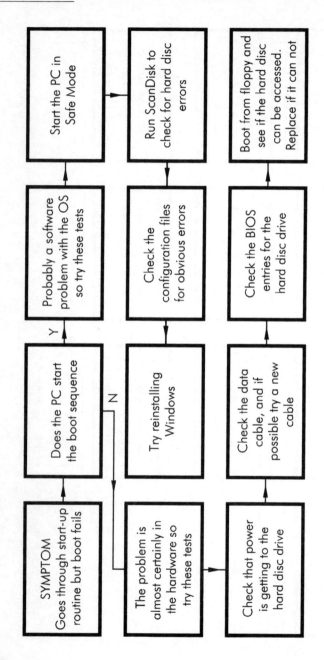

Fig.2.28 Test chart for boot failure problems

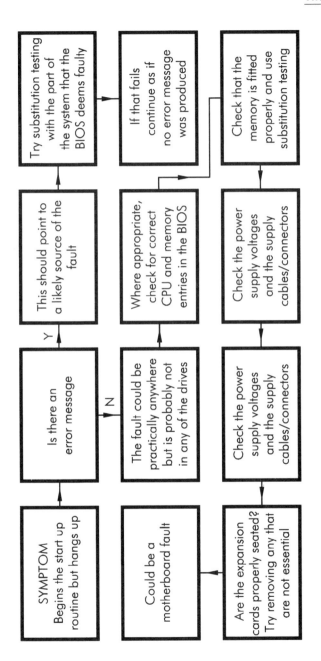

Fig.2.29 Troubleshooting chart for problems during the start-up routine

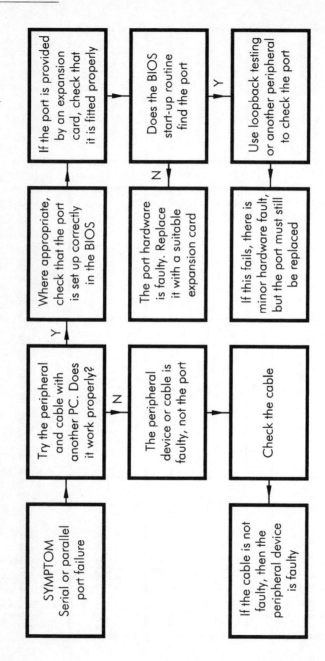

Fig.2.30 Test chart for problems with the serial and parallel ports

Disc drives

Floppy problems

For a stand-alone PC at least one disc drive is an essential feature, because the operating system is loaded from a disc drive and is not built-in. While in theory a single floppy drive will suffice, these days the minimum requirement is a fairly large hard disc, one floppy drive, and a CD-ROM drive. Most software will actually run quite happily without a CD-ROM drive, but software is mainly distributed on CD-ROMs, and without a suitable drive there is no way of installing it onto the hard disc drive. It is probably easier to get by without a floppy disc drive rather than a CD-ROM drive, particularly if the PC has some form of interchangeable mass storage device. However, most PC users still use a floppy drive for backing up small files such as word processor documents, and there are few "floppyless" PCs in use.

Floppy drives

There are five types of floppy disc drive used with PCs, and these are listed below. All five types use both sides of the disc incidentally.

3.5 inch, 80 track, 720K capacity

3.5 inch, 80 track, 1.44M capacity

3.5 inch 2.88M capacity

5.25 inch, 40 track, 360K capacity

5.25 inch, 80 track, 1.2M capacity

The data on a floppy disc drive is stored magnetically on the metal oxide coating. This is much the same as the way in which an audio signal is recorded onto the tape in an ordinary compact cassette. In the case of a floppy disc though, the data is recorded onto a number of concentric tracks, or "cylinders" as they are sometimes termed. Each track is divided into a number of sectors, and there are nine sectors per track for a 5.25 inch 360K disc for example.

Compatibility

Compatibility between the various formats is less of an issue than it once was, because many users now have only one size of disc and drive. However, you can still run into difficulty if you start dealing with old discs and (or) old PCs, so the following should be borne in mind if you have to deal with more than one disc format. It is easy to become convinced that a floppy drive is faulty when there is actually a compatibility problem. Of course, 3.5-inch discs and the 5.25-inch varieties are totally incompatible, and you can only read a disc using a drive of the right size.

There is quite good compatibility between the two 5.25 inch disc formats. It is something less than perfect though. A 1.2M disc can not be read by a 360K drive, and it would be unreasonable to expect it to do so. Apart from the higher data density used by 1.2M drives, they also use twice as many tracks. With its wider record/playback head and only 40 head positions, a 360K drive will read two tracks at once when fed with a 1.2M format disc. A 1.2M drive can read 360K discs, and in my experience there are not usually any reliability problems when doing this. A 1.2M drive can produce 360K discs, but there is a potential problem if this is done. What the drive actually does is to miss out every other track, so that it only uses 40 tracks per side of the disc. This is not quite the same as a genuine 40-track disc, in that the 80-track drive is effectively using only about half the width of each of the 40 tracks. When read using a real 40-track drive this can, and often does, produce problems.

If you start with an unused disc, the half-tracks on which nothing is recorded will produce noise, but the disc drive may well be able to read the data through this increased noise. On the other hand, it might not! If the disc has ever been used in a real 40-track drive and there has been data recorded across the full track width at some time, the chances of being able to read the data off the disc is negligible. The problem is that the original data on the disc is recorded across the full track width, but the 1.2M disc drive will only overwrite about half of each track. A 360K drive will therefore read back both sets of data simultaneously, giving a totally scrambled output. Paradoxically, another 1.2M drive will only read the half of the track which contains the wanted data, and will probably read a 360K disc of this type successfully, whereas a 360K drive will be unable to do so.

Compatibility between the two types of 3.5-inch disc is much better. The 720K drives can not read 1.44M discs, since they can not handle the higher data density. However, as both types of disc use 80 tracks, there are no problems if a 1.44M drive is used to produce 720K discs. They should be perfectly readable on both 1.44M and 720K drives.

I do not have much first-hand experience of the 2.88-megabyte drives, but they are supposed to have good compatibility with the earlier 3.5-inch disc formats.

Testing

Any general PC testing software should have a section that deals with the floppy disc drive or drives. In some cases this software will try to examine the disc controller to see if this is at fault. The BIOS often does something similar during the initial checking prior to boot up, and if there is a problem with the controller the BIOS will almost certainly report this, or simply that it can not detect the floppy drive. With any reasonably modern PC a floppy controller failure is a serious problem. In days gone by it required the controller card to be changed, which was not exactly cheap but was relatively inexpensive and easy.

With a modern PC the floppy disc controller is incorporated in the motherboard, and therefore requires the motherboard to be replaced. In theory, if the motherboard's floppy controller can be switched off, a floppy controller card could be added. In practice there is little chance of obtaining a card of this type, although a multi-function card that includes this facility might be available. The multi-function option is fine provided any facilities that duplicate those already present in the PC can be disabled. However, it is not a good idea to use a motherboard that contains faulty hardware. Faulty parts can overheat, and there is a risk of other items of hardware being damaged if the faulty components cause a catastrophic failure. The risk of using a motherboard that contains a minor fault is probably minimal, but it is one I would not take.

If a testing program or the BIOS reports a floppy controller failure, I would be inclined to check a little further before resorting to a replacement motherboard. Diagnostics software is generally very reliable, but it is possible that the problem lies somewhere other than the controller. You should certainly go into the BIOS Setup program and check that the entries for the floppy drive or drives are correct. If the BIOS has an option that enables the floppy disc interface to be switched off, also make sure that this interface is actually enabled. Last, and by no means least, check that the data cable is fully serviceable. Floppy data cables are amongst the least reliable because they have one or two connectors near the middle of the cable. These are to accommodate drive B, and

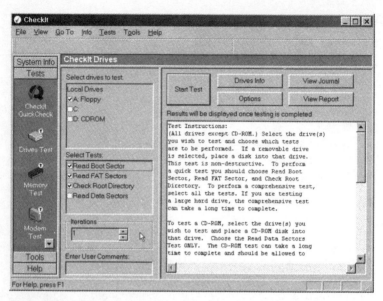

Fig.3.1 The disc testing section of the Checkit diagnostics program

will usually be present even in a PC that does not actually have a drive B. They are presumably included to make it easier to add a second drive if you should wish to do so. The problem with adding connectors into the middle of a cable is that they tend to weaken it, and if not fitted absolutely perfectly these connectors can tend to cut through the wires.

It is probably worthwhile trying another floppy drive, even if this means borrowing one from another PC. There is no need to remove the old drive from the PC. Simply disconnect the data and power cables from the drive and connect them to the replacement drive. This drive should be positioned in the PC where there is no danger of anything fouling and moving parts, and where it is not in danger of falling onto other parts and causing either physical damage or short circuits. In most cases it can be rested on the drive bays, but it is advisable to place it on a piece of paper or card to ensure that there is no risk of any connections on the drive short-circuiting to the metal chassis. If the replacement drive works properly, then the original was obviously faulty, and the problem was not in the controller. If, on the other hand, the new drive fails to work, it would seem that the controller is the cause of the problem.

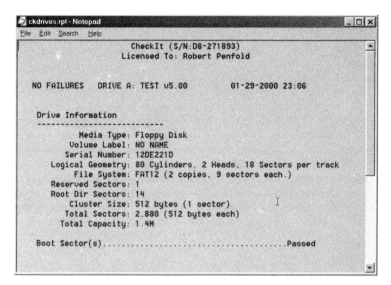

Fig.3.2 A report generated by the Checkit program

Unreliable discs

Probably the most common problem with floppy disc drives is poor reliability. This should not unquestioningly be put down to the floppy drive itself being worn out. There are large numbers of poor quality floppy discs in circulation, and experience would suggest that many discs that are otherwise of high quality start to become unreliable after a number of years, even if they have received little use. A floppy diagnostics program will usually test a floppy drive by repeatedly writing data to a disc and reading it back again. Figure 3.1 shows the disc testing section of the Checkit program. Each test is quite quick, but you can set the program to repeat the test procedure numerous times if desired (up to 100 times). Figure 3.2 shows a test report generated by this program.

When undertaking this type of test it is essential to use a modern disc of good quality. If the drive fails the test it is as well to repeat it with another disc to make absolutely certain that it is the drive and not the disc that is at fault. If you do not have suitable diagnostics software you can test a floppy drive by writing something like large graphic files to some floppy discs, and then reading them back into a graphics program to ensure that the data can be read properly.

A fair percentage of reliability problems with floppy disc drives are simply due to a build-up of oxide and other dirt on the record/playback heads. Floppy disc drive cleaning devices are readily available, and these should be used every month or so to ensure that the heads remain reasonably clean. If a floppy drive is proving unreliable it is certainly a good idea to clean the heads two or three times and then test it again. With some drives it is possible to see the heads if you remove the drive from the PC and examine it closely. It might then be possible to clean them using a proprietary cleaning fluid on a cotton bud. This sort of thing is not normally to be recommended, but if a drive has become unreliable to the point where it is unusable you do not have a lot to lose. If it is only possible to get at the heads by partially dismantling the drive, do not bother. Anything much more than the removal of a cover plate is unlikely to be reversible and the chances of getting the cleaned drive back into working order would be remote.

Replacement

Unless the problem drive can be restored to full reliability it should certainly be replaced. Replacement should not pose any major problems unless the faulty drive is an old type. The main problem will then be finding a suitable replacement. To remove the old drive take off the outer cover of the PC, and then disconnect the data and power cables from the drive. With any modern PC and many older types the drives are mounted directly into the drive bays. In order to remove the drive it is merely necessary to remove the four screws that go through the drive bays and into the sides of the drive. There can be a slight problem here in that one side of the drive bay may be inaccessible. With some cases a panel can be removed to provide better access, but with most the 3.5-inch drive bays can be removed. This usually involves undoing one or two screws and then sliding the drive bay backwards and free of the case. The bays are often reluctant to part company with the case, and it can take a certain amount of manipulation to get the bay assembly free. Once the old drive has been removed it is just a matter of reversing the process to fit the new drive.

Note that with very old PCs the drives are often mounted on guide-rails, and the guide rails are bolted to the drive bays. Figure 3.3 shows a pair of guide-rails, but the exact design varies somewhat from one case to another. Replacing floppy drives on old PCs of this type is not much different to the equivalent operation on a modern PC. When the drive is unbolted from the drive bay it will slide out complete with the guide-

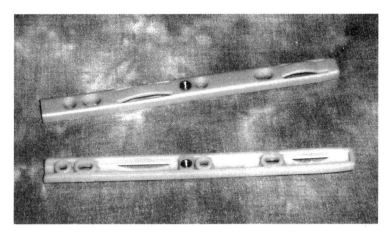

Fig.3.3 Some older PCs have the drives mounted via plastic rails

rails. These are then unbolted from the old drive and mounted on the new one. This assembly should then slide back into the drive bay without difficulty. The only minor problem is that there will probably be numerous mounting holes in the guide-rails, and possibly in the drive as well. If the wrong sets of holes are used the drive will be seated too far forward or backwards in the bay, but if necessary a certain amount of trial and error can be used to get the drive installed properly in the bay.

Cable

The data cables for floppy drives can be a bit confusing for the uninitiated and due care needs to be taken when refitting this cable. The standard PC floppy disc drive cable consists of a length of 34-way ribbon cable, which is fitted with 34-way edge connectors and IDC connectors at the floppy drive end. 3.5-inch floppy drives require the IDC connectors, and 5.25-inch types connect to the edge connectors (Figures 3.4 and 3.5 respectively). The connector at the controller end is not totally standardised, but any reasonably modern controller will require a 34-way IDC

Fig.3.4 An IDC connector for 3.5-inch drives

Fig.3.5 An edge connector for 5.25-inch drives

connector. As pointed out previously, most cables are for twin drives, and therefore have two sets of drive connectors. This makes like easier when adding a second drive, because you can normally use the existing cable.

In a standard floppy drive set-up, the two connectors would be wired in exactly the same way. Pin 1 at the controller would connect to pin 1 of both drives, pin 2 would connect to both of the pin 2s, and so on. The two drives do not operate in unison, with both trying to operate as drive A, because there are jumper leads on the drives which are set to make one operate as drive A, and the other as drive B. These jumper blocks are normally a set of four pairs of terminals marked something like "DS0", "DS1", "DS2", and "DS3" (or possibly something like "DS1" to "DS4"). The instruction manual for the disc drive (in the unlikely event of you being able to obtain it) will make it clear which of the many jumper blocks are the ones for drive selection. Drive A has the jumper lead on "DS0", while drive B has it on "DS1".

Things could actually be set up in this fashion in a PC, but it is not the standard way of doing things. Instead, both drives are set as drive B by having the jumper lead placed on "DS1". The so-called "twist" in the cable between the two drive connectors then reverses some of the connections to one drive, making it operate as drive A. This may seem to be an unusual way of doing things, but there is apparently a good reason for it. If you obtain a replacement PC disc drive, whether for use as a replacement for a worn out drive A or B, or a newly added drive B, the same drive configured in exactly the same way will do the job. This avoids the need for dealers to stock two different types of drive, which in reality is exactly the same type of drive with a slightly different configuration.

For the DIY PC repairer it makes life easier in that any drive sold for use in a PC should work perfectly without the need to alter any of the configuration jumpers. In fact many 3.5-inch drives are manufactured specifically for use in PCs, and do not actually have any configuration jumpers. Of course, if you buy a drive that is not specifically for use in a PC, it might not be set up correctly for operation in a PC. In fact a drive

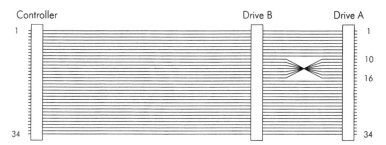

Fig.3.6 Connection details for a floppy drive data cable. There may be two different types of connector for each drive

not specifically designed for operation in a PC might not be fully PC compatible, so it is best to obtain the "real thing". If you use a drive that does have configuration jumpers or switches it is likely that it will be supplied ready for use in a PC, but the elusive instruction booklet for the disc drive is then more than a little useful.

The computer will still work if you get the connections to two floppy drives swapped over, but the one you required as drive A will be drive B, and vice versa. The connector at the end of the cable couples to drive A, while the other one connects to drive B. Figure 3.6 shows this general scheme of things. When doing a continuity check on a floppy drive data cable remember to allow for the "twist" in the cable, and the fact that some pins of one connector do not connect to the same pins on the other connector. It is leads 10 to 16 that have the twist, giving this method of interconnection on these terminals of the connector:

Motherboard/drive B	Drive A
10	16
11	15
12	14
13	13
14	12
15	11
16	10

Getting the floppy drive cables connected to the new drive should be straightforward, because the connectors should be polarised, so that they can not be fitted the wrong way round. The necessary "key" is just a small metal rod on the edge connector, which fits into a slot in the

Fig.3.7 5.25-inch power connectors will only fit the right way round

connector on the drive. A lump and a slot on IDC connectors serve the same function. Unfortunately, the polarising "keys" are sometimes missing. You should find that the connector numbers, or some of them, are marked onto the connector on the disc drive and on or around the motherboard connectors at the other end of the cable. As always with ribbon style data cables, the red lead should carry the pin 1 connection. If the data cable is accidentally disconnected from the motherboard make sure the right end of the cable is reconnected to the floppy disc drive.

With most data cables it does not matter which way round it is connected in this respect, but the twist in the cable makes it essential to get a floppy data cable the right way round. The fact that there is one connector on one side of the "twist" and two connectors on the other side (see Figure 3.6) makes it easy to get things right first time. If the PC has a cable that only supports a single floppy disc, the connector nearest the "twist" is normally the one that connects to the floppy disc drive.

The shape of a 5.25-inch power plug means that there is no risk of connecting it the wrong way round (Figure 3.7). If you look at the connectors on the cable and the drive itself it is obvious which way round the power plug should be fitted. The 3.5-inch power connectors are perhaps slightly less foolproof, and you can fit one upside-down if you are determined to. The concave side of the connector faces downward towards the connector on the drive and the other side faces upward (Figure 3.8). There is probably a greater risk of getting the power connector one pin out of alignment, so be careful to get the plug properly aligned with the connector on the drive before pushing it into place. If the plug does not fit easily and fully into place it is probably not aligned properly and powering-up the PC could result in damage to the drive.

Fig.3.8 A 3.5-inch power connector fits the drive this way up

Termination resistors

In the past every disc drive had a set of eight termination resistors. These connected to certain inputs of the drive, and tied them to the +5 volt supply rail. They are termed "pull-up" resistors. However many disc drives are used, only one set of termination resistors should be present. It is only the drive at the end of the cable that should have these resistors. Therefore, if you fit a new B drive it will fit mid-cable and it will not require its termination resistors. If you fit a new A drive it will fit at the end of the data cable and will require its termination resistors. These resistors are normally in the form of a single component, rather than eight individual resistors. They will be mounted in a socket of some kind, and this will often be of the standard 16-pin d.i.l. Integrated circuit type. A socket of this type has two rows of eight terminals 0.3 inches apart. The resistor pack itself will probably be in the form of a black plastic component having two rows of eight pins. The resistors have a value of 220 ohms, and so the component will be marked something like "220R", plus some other characters in most cases.

Some drives have a s.i.l. (single in-line) resistor pack. These have nine pins in a single row, usually with 0.1-inch pin spacing. Like the d.i.l. resistor packs, they are mounted in a socket so that they can be easily removed. In fact the s.i.l. variety are generally more easily removed than the d.i.l. type. With any d.i.l. component it is a good idea to use a screwdriver to carefully prise it free from the socket. Keep the termination resistor pack safe somewhere in case it should be needed at some later time. In fact you should always keep anything removed from the computer when performing upgrades. You never know when these odds and ends will be needed again. Another variation is for the termination resistors to be switched in and out via either a configuration jumper or a DIP-switch. With either of these methods the instruction manual for the drive is needed in order to configure things correctly, although the markings on the drive might give some clue as to the correct settings.

It is only fair to point out that many modern floppy drives do not have removable termination resistors. With drives of this type you simply connect them up and hope they work (which they invariably seem to). You are unlikely to encounter termination resistors on 3.5-inch floppy drives, but they will almost certainly be present on 5.25-inch drives. These days most 5.25-inch drives are used as drive B, and should therefore have the termination resistors removed or switched out of circuit. However, satisfactory results might still be obtained if they are left in circuit.

Hard discs

A hard disc is very much like an ordinary floppy type, but in a highly refined form. The disc itself is a permanent part of the drive, and is not interchangeable like floppy discs (hence the alternative name of "fixed" disc). The disc is made of metal and is rigid (hence the "hard" disc name). The disc spins at a much higher rate that is about ten or more times faster than the rotation speed of a floppy disc. With the faster modern discs the rotation speed is over 7000 r.p.m., but a speed of about 5400 r.p.m. is more common. The disc rotates continuously and not just when data must be accessed. This is an important factor, since one of the main advantages of a hard disc is the speed with which data can be accessed. Having to wait for the disc to build up speed and settle down at the right speed would slow down disc accesses by an unacceptable degree. In fact the high rotation speed would result in accesses to a hard disc actually being slower than those to a floppy disc.

A slight drawback of this continuous rotation is that computers equipped with hard discs are notoriously noisy! The high rotation speed of the disc aids rapid data transfers. Data can typically be read from a hard disc in less than a tenth of the time that a floppy disc would take to handle the same amount of data. In fact modern hard drives are more than100 times faster than standard floppy drives.

Although the disc of a hard disc drive is not changeable, it has a very high capacity so that it can accommodate large amounts of data and several large applications programs if necessary. This is achieved by having what is typically many hundreds of cylinders (tracks) with numerous sectors per cylinder. Early hard discs had capacities of about 10 to 20 megabytes, but the lowest capacity currently offered by most suppliers is well in excess of one gigabyte (1000 megabytes). Drives having capacities of 10 to 30 gigabytes are now commonplace. In most cases the "disc" is actually two, three, or four discs mounted one above the other on a common spindle. This enables around three to eight record/playback heads and sides of the disc to be used, giving higher capacities than could be handled using a single disc.

An important point that has to be made right from the start is that hard discs are highly intricate and quite delicate pieces of equipment. Modern hard drives are somewhat tougher than the early units, most of which had warning notices stating that the mildest of jolts could damage the drive. Even so, they must be treated with due respect, and protected from excessive jolts and vibration if they are to provide long and trouble-free service. You are unlikely to damage a modern hard disc drive simply by picking up the computer in which it is fitted, and carrying it across to the other side of the room. On the other hand, dropping a hard drive or the computer in which it is fitted could well result in serious damage to the drive.

Hard disc units are hermetically sealed so that dust can not enter. This is crucial, due to the high rotation speed of the disc. Apparently, the heads are aerodynamic types, which glide just above the surface of the disc, never actually coming into contact with it. If the two should come into contact, even via an intervening speck of dust, the result could easily be severe damage to the surface of the disc, and possibly to the head as well. Never open up a hard disc drive if you ever intend to use it again!

Testing

A hard disc problem could be caused by the drive itself, the controller, or the data cable. In a situation of this sort it is always a good idea to check the cable sooner rather than later, especially if any recent work has been done inside the computer. Make certain that both ends of the cable have their connectors fully pushed into place. These cables are non-locking types that can gradually work loose over a period of time. Some combinations of IDE connectors simply do not fit together as well as they should, causing the cable to fall out of position with the slightest provocation. If you have a spare IDE data cable try using this instead of the existing cable. Do not forget to check that the power cable is fitted reliably. A useful ploy is to swap the power cable with that of the CD-ROM drive, or if there is a spare 5.25-inch power connector use that instead of the one currently in use. If you try the swapping method and the CD-ROM drive fails to work, the problem clearly lies with the power lead and connector. Some of the power connectors are quite crude. If a visual inspection shows that it is coming apart, it is usually possible to fit the connector back together again without too much difficulty.

Often when a hard disc fails it is fairly obvious that the disc itself has failed, because there will be a considerable amount of noise from within the case of the drive, and it will probably be causing itself a great deal of internal damage. A fault in the controller could send the hard disc into convulsions and cause a fair amount of noise, but if there are sounds of metal grating against metal you know that the hard disc's "days are numbered", and the PC should be switched off immediately.

Often things will not be as clear cut as this and some investigation will be needed in order to ascertain whether it is the disc drive or the controller that has failed. An IDE hard disc has most of the control electronics built into the drive itself, and the drive is very complex mechanically. Consequently, the chances of the IDE interface on the motherboard being faulty are quite small, and it is likely that the drive itself is faulty. If there is a CD-ROM drive on the same IDE interface as the hard disc drive, and the CD-ROM is working fine, it is very unlikely that the IDE interface is faulty. On the other hand, if there is a CD-ROM on the same IDE interface as the hard disc drive and neither drive is working properly, it is odds on that the interface is the cause of the problem.

Practically all motherboards have two IDE interfaces, and you can therefore try moving the hard drive to the other IDE interface. There are one or two potential problems here, and you have to avoid these by ensuring that the drives are suitably configured. An IDE drive is set as

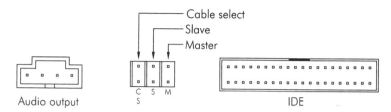

Fig.3.9 The configuration jumpers for an IDE CD-ROM drive

the main or slave device via a configuration jumper. On most CD-ROM drives and many hard disc drives there are three positions for this jumper (Figure 3.9). You simply place the jumper on the appropriate pair of terminals to select master, slave, or cable select operation, but the latter is not normally used with PCs. Some hard disc drives have a slightly more complex arrangement, with a fourth option. This is where the drive will be used as the main drive on that IDE channel, but there will be a slave device as well. The instruction manual for the hard disc drive should give concise information on setting the configuration jumpers to suit any normal arrangement. If you do not have the instruction manual for the disc drive it will almost certainly be available as a free download at the manufacturer's web site.

Probably the easiest way to test the hard disc drive on the secondary IDE interface is to disconnect any drives that are already connected on that channel, and have the hard disc as the primary drive on that channel. This will not require any changes to the configuration jumpers unless the hard drive was previously used on the same channel as another drive, and it is a type that requires different settings depending on whether it is the master device or the only device on that channel. You can either reconfigure the drive or transfer both drives to the secondary IDE interface. It is conceivable that the problem could be due to the slave device interfering with the hard disc drive, so reconfiguring the hard drive is the better option. If the BIOS is set to the auto-detection mode it will automatically adjust to the new configuration. Otherwise it will be necessary to go into the BIOS Setup program and reconfigure the BIOS to suit the new drive arrangement.

Some PCs will boot up from a hard disc on either IDE channel, but others will only boot from the primary channel or from the secondary channel if the BIOS is suitably configured. Where appropriate you must consult the relevant section of the motherboard's instruction manual and make any necessary adjustments to the BIOS settings. Alternatively, simply boot from drive A, and then check to see if the hard disc drive is fully operational.

It is sometimes worth trying a problematic hard disc drive as a non-boot drive anyway. If the drive works fine in this role, but it is not possible to boot from it reliably, the most likely cause of the fault is corruption of the data in the boot sector of the disc. Check that the hard drive parameters in the BIOS are correct, since errors here can also produce boot-up problems. If the boot data on the disc has become corrupted there is probably only one way of correcting matters. This is to reformat the disc and reinstall the operating system, all the applications software, and all your data. As the disc is still readable it should be possible to back up all the data it contains so that the data can be restored after the disc has been reformatted.

It is always a good idea to keep old IDE hard disc drives for testing purposes, and an easy way of checking that the IDE interface is working properly is to disconnect the existing drive and replace it with an old one. Once again, unless the BIOS is set to the auto-detection mode it will be necessary to reconfigure it to suit the old drive. If things work fine with the old drive, then the existing drive is almost certainly faulty. It is worthwhile trying the existing drive again just in case the problem was simply due to a bad connection or something of this type.

Bear in mind that the old drive will not probably not have the operating system configured to suit the hardware in the PC you are trying it in. If it has an old operating system such as MS/DOS this does not really apply, and it should boot up with a minimum or error messages. With something like Windows 98 things will probably falter during the boot-up procedure, with the operating system trying to reconfigure itself to suit the current hardware. Unless you wish to use the old hard disc drive temporarily there is no point in continuing with this. If the old drive is recognised correctly by the BIOS and the boot-up process gets underway correctly it is very unlikely that there is a problem with the IDE interface.

Utilities

If the problem is one of poor reliability rather than complete failure, there are hard disc testing utilities that can check each sector of the disc to locate the "soft spots" in the disc. The idea is to locate the bad sectors and mark them as such so that they are not used for data storage. The Windows 98 Scandisk program when used with the "Thorough" option

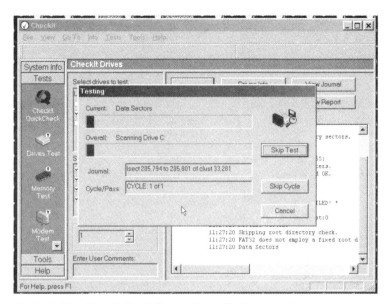

Fig.3.10 The Checkit hard disc testing utility in operation

will do this. I suppose that this type of thing is worth a try, and might provide many years of trouble-free service from the hard disc drive. However, practical experience would suggest that once a hard disc drive starts to experience problems it usually continues to go "down hill". If a hard disc becomes unreliable I would certainly recommend its replacement. Any PC diagnostics program will have a comprehensive set of hard disc test routines. Figure 3.10 shows the hard disc section of Checkit program in operation. This type of thing can be useful where there is some doubt as to whether an unreliability problem is due to the hard disc or a software problem. There is almost certainly a software problem if thorough testing of the disc fails to show up any hardware faults.

In days gone by there was a simple ploy that many used in order to bring an unreliable hard disc drive back into full working order. This was to back up all the data on the disc, do a low level reformat, a high level reformat, repartition the disc, and then restore all the programs and data. In other words, the disc was treated as if it was a new disc being installed from scratch. This sometimes worked due to the relatively simple mechanisms of the hard discs of that period. Some types of disc could gradually slip out of alignment so that the heads were no longer reading the tracks accurately. The low level reformatting put in new tracks to match the slippage of the heads. This type of thing does not really get you anywhere with modern hard disc drives. The low level formatting is part of the manufacturing process and normal low level formatting programs will not work with modern discs. Due to improvements in the design and construction of hard drives it is unlikely that this slippage problem will occur anyway. If a hard disc drive becomes unreliable it is likely to be due to some other form of mechanical failure or inadequacies in the magnetic media.

Backing up

A hard disc failure is potentially a major disaster for those who use the PC, but if you use PCs for some years it is a failure you are almost certain to experience. A complete failure of the disc means that all the data it contains is lost. There are companies that offer a data recovery service, but there is no guarantee that the contents of the disc will be recoverable, and the cost of a recovery service is too high for many users anyway. As a minimum, any important data files should be backed up onto floppy discs, CDRs, or any suitable media, so that they can be restored onto a new hard disc if the old unit fails.

Ideally the entire contents of the hard disc drive should be backed up using a program that enables it to be properly restored onto a new hard disc. This is very much quicker and easier than having to reinstall and configure the operating system, and then reinstall all the applications programs and data. Also, any customisation of the operating system or other software will be automatically restored. If you have heavily customised software, after reinstallation it can take a great deal time to get it set up to your satisfaction.

The problem with the full back up method is that it takes a fair amount of time to maintain an up to date copy of the hard disc. Also, it is only feasible if your PC is equipped with some form of mass storage device that can be used for backup purposes, such as a CDR writer or a Zip drive. Otherwise it could well require in excess of a thousand floppy discs to do a full backup of the hard drive! Looking on the bright side, if everything does have to be restored from scratch you will have a "clean" copy of the operating system. Over a period of time most modern operating systems seem to become slightly "gummed up" with numerous files that no longer serve any purpose, and things can generally slow down. By returning to a fresh copy of the operating system you will probably free up some hard disc space and things might run slightly faster.

Replacement

Replacing a hard disc drive is very similar to the equivalent operation with a floppy drive. One difference is that a floppy disc can usually be removed by sliding it forwards out of the drive bay, which is generally easier than taking it in the opposite direction. With a hard disc drive there will often be no opening in the case in front of the drive, and the only way of removing it will be to slide it backwards into the case. If there is only a plastic blanking plate in front of the drive, this can be carefully prised out using a flat bladed screwdriver, and the drive can then be slid out through the front of the case.

If the drive has to be removed from the rear of the drive bay be careful when pulling it back into the case. The interior of a modern PC is fairly crowded and a lack of care and attention could result in damage to other components. It will probably take some delicate manoeuvring to get the drive free, and it may be necessary to temporarily remove some other components such as expansion cards or memory modules.

The cabling for a hard disc is easier to deal with than that for a floppy disc drive. There are no cross couplings, so it does not matter which end connects to the hard disc, or to the motherboard. If the cable supports two drives it does not matter which drive connects to which connector. The jumpers on the drives handle the master and slave assignments. The replacement drive must be configured correctly, and it should be supplied with a manual that gives the jumper settings for the available options. The jumpers are often difficult to get at once the drive has been installed in the PC, so make any necessary adjustments to the jumpers prior to installing the drive. Hard disc drives, even the 3.5-inch variety, have the larger power connectors normally used for 5.25-inch drives. Getting the power cable connected properly is therefore almost foolproof, but make sure that the connector is fully pushed into place. Power connectors in general, and the 5.25-inch drive connectors in particular, need a fair amount of force to get them connected properly, or unconnected again.

Having physically installed the hard disc it will probably be necessary to go into the BIOS Setup program and set the appropriate parameters for the new disc. If the new disc is exactly the same as the old one, this will not be necessary, as the drive parameters will be exactly the same as before. Things move on quite rapidly in the world of hard disc drives, and it is more than likely that the new drive will have to be bigger and better than the original. Obviously no changes should be needed if the BIOS is set to the auto detection mode, since the BIOS should be able to detect the new drive properly. There may be problems if a new PC is used with a very large hard drive, and the potential problems with large drives are covered later in this chapter.

Operating system

If you have a backup utility and an image of the defunct hard disc that it can transfer to the new disc, then this is the easiest way of getting the replacement disc "up and running". These utilities generally work by having a special boot-up floppy disc that is used initially, and the restoration program is then run from a CD-ROM or a floppy disc. However, the exact way in which the process is handled varies from one program to another, and might also be different depending on the medium that contains the backup files. The instruction manual for the backup program should give concise information on the way that the image is transferred to the new disc. It might be necessary to partition the disc or even format it before the image is transferred, or the backup program might take this care of this. Again, the instruction manual for the backup software should give details of any preparation that is needed prior to transferring the image.

Being realistic about things, most people who find themselves installing a replacement hard disc will lack an image of the defunct disc drive. They will have the installation discs for the operating system and applications programs, plus some discs containing the user's data files. The first task is to do any necessary preparation of the hard disc drive, such as partitioning and high level formatting. Then the operating system is installed, followed by the applications software. Any customisation is then undertaken, and the user's data files are restored to the appropriate directories on the disc.

Methods of installing operating systems vary considerably from one system to another, and even from one version of an operating system to the next. Any fairly recent PC should be able to boot from the CD-ROM drive, but it will only do so if the CD-ROM drive is set as a boot device in the relevant section of the BIOS Setup program. This will usually be found in something like the "BIOS Features" section (see Figure 2.14 in chapter two), and there will either be various preset boot device options, or a facility to select the first, second, and third boot devices. It is probably best to choose an option that has the CD-ROM drive as the primary boot device, or to select this as the first boot device where appropriate. Once the operating system has been installed you can go back to the BIOS Setup program and set the hard disc as the primary boot device.

Most versions of Linux can be installed from CD-ROM, as can Windows NT and BEOS. The exact procedure varies enormously from one operating system to another, but the process is normally automated to a large degree. The user has to do little more than provide the correct responses to questions asked by the installation routine. Things are less straightforward with Windows 98, which is normally installed from CD-ROM, but the CD-ROM is not bootable. As Windows 98 (together with its predecessor Windows 95) is the most popular operating system, we will take a detailed look at reinstalling this system.

Partitioning

With MS/DOS, Windows 3.1, Windows 95, and Windows 98 the hard disc drive must be partitioned and formatted before the operating system can be installed. Start by rebooting the computer from floppy disc. The BIOS will probably be set to boot from the floppy drive already, but if necessary you must use the BIOS Setup program to set the floppy drive as a boot device. With the computer booted-up and running MS-DOS or the Windows 95/98 equivalent of MS-DOS, the hard drive will not be accessible. Modern hard disc drives are supplied with the low level formatting already done, but they still require high-level formatted using the MS-DOS "FORMAT" program. However, you must first prepare the disc using the "FDISK " partitioning program.

The system disc used to boot the computer should contain copies of both FDISK (and FORMAT, and it is also helpful if this disc contains a simple text editor program such as the MS-DOS EDIT program). With a Windows 98 set-up disc both of these programs will be placed on the disc for you when it is created. A set-up disc should have been created when Windows 98 was first installed, but it is easy to make one using any PC running Windows 98. To create the disc from the Windows 98 desktop select Start, Settings, Control Panel, Add/Remove Programs, Startup Disc, and finally Create Disc (Figure 3.11). Note that you will be asked for the Windows 98 CD-ROM, because some of the files required are not normally stored on the hard disc.

If you will be installing MS/DOS and Windows 3.1 you should use a boot disc containing the system files for the appropriate version of MS/DOS. With an MS/DOS boot disc you must copy the programs onto the disc yourself, from an MS/DOS installation on a hard disc drive. When booting from the Windows 98 set-up disc you are presented with a menu that offers three options. Select CD-ROM support, since this will be needed to install Windows 98 from the CD-ROM. Windows 3.1 is normally

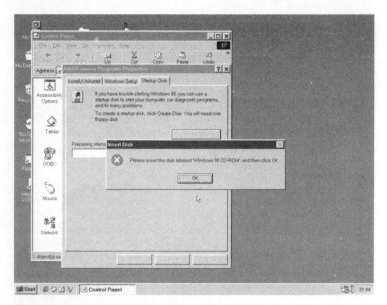

Fig.3.11 A recovery disc is easily made using Windows 95 or 98

installed from floppy discs, so there is no need to add CD-ROM to the
boot disc if you are installing MS/DOS and Windows 3.1.

FDISK

FDISK is used to create one or more DOS partitions, and with discs of
2.1 gigabytes or less you may wish to have the whole of the disc as a
single partition. The hard disc drive then becomes drive C. By creating
further partitions it can also operate as drive D, drive E, etc. The primary
partition is the boot disc, and this is where the operating system must
be installed. The MS/DOS and Windows 95 file systems set the 2.1-
gigabyte partition limit. There is also an 8.4-gigabyte limit on the physical
size of the drive. With Windows 98 and any reasonably modern BIOS
these limits do not apply, but you must use the FAT32 file system. To do
this simply answer yes when FDISK is first run, and you are asked if you
require support for large hard disc drives. Even if you do not wish to
have a large disc organised as one large partition, it is still best to opt for
large hard disc support. FAT32 utilizes the available disc space more
efficiently and reduces wastage. Note that if you only require a single

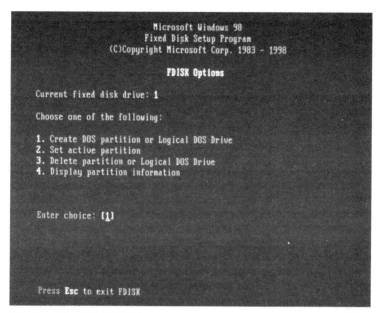

```
                    Microsoft Windows 98
                  Fixed Disk Setup Program
           (C)Copyright Microsoft Corp. 1983 - 1998

                        FDISK Options

   Current fixed disk drive: 1

   Choose one of the following:

   1. Create DOS partition or Logical DOS Drive
   2. Set active partition
   3. Delete partition or Logical DOS Drive
   4. Display partition information


   Enter choice: [1]




   Press Esc to exit FDISK
```

Fig.3.12 The initial FDISK menu

partition you must still use the FDISK program to set up this single partition, and that the FORMAT program will not work on the hard drive until FDISK has created a DOS partition.

Some hard discs are supplied complete with partitioning software that will also format the disc and add the system files, which will be copied from the boot disc. Where a utility program of this type is available it is probably better to use it instead of the FDISK and FORMAT programs. These MS-DOS programs are fairly straightforward in use, but using the software supplied with the drive will almost certainly be even easier. If you use the FDISK and FORMAT programs, make sure that you are not using ancient versions of them. Versions of MS/DOS earlier than version 3.3 are not able to provide two partitions, and are not really suitable for use with a modern PC.

Using FDISK

Once you are in FDISK there is a menu offering these four choices (see also Figure 3.12):

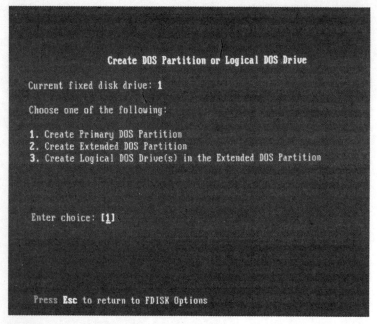

Fig.3.13 *The FDISK partition creation menu*

1. Create DOS partition or logical DOS drive

2. Set the active partition

3. Delete partition or logical DOS drive

4. Display partition information

The first thing we need to do is create a DOS partition, so select option one, which will be the default. This takes you into a further menu offering these three options (Figure 3.13):

1. Create primary DOS partition

2. Create extended DOS partition

3. Create logical DOS drive(s) in the extended DOS partition

It is a primary DOS partition that is required, so select option one, which should again be the default. You will then be asked if you wish to use the maximum space for the partition and make it the active partition. If you answer yes, the whole disc, or as much of it as FDISK can handle,

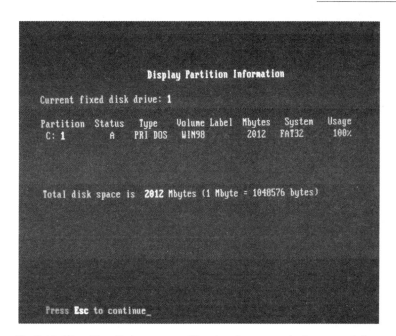

Display Partition Information

Current fixed disk drive: 1

Partition	Status	Type	Volume Label	Mbytes	System	Usage
C: 1	A	PRI DOS	WIN98	2012	FAT32	100%

Total disk space is **2012** Mbytes (1 Mbyte = 1048576 bytes)

Press **Esc** to continue_

Fig.3.14 Checking that a new partition has been created successfully

will be used for the partition. It will also be made active, which simply means that this is the partition that the computer will try to boot from. This is the partition to which the operating system should be installed. If you answer no, you will then have to specify the size of the primary partition in megabytes. This creates the partition, but does not make it active. Having created the partition you the press the Escape key to return to the original menu. It is a good idea to select option four to check that the partition has been created successfully (Figure 3.14).

If you did not use the maximum space for the partition it will not have been made active. To do this select option two from the main menu and then enter the number of the partition you wish to make active. As there is only one partition this will obviously be partition number one. Press return to implement this command, and then press the Escape key to return to the main menu again. It is then a good idea to use option four once again to ensure that everything has gone smoothly. In the Status column there should be an "A" to indicate that partition one is active (as in Figure 3.14).

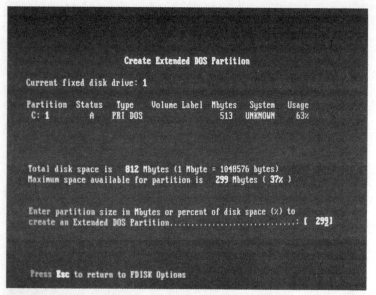

Fig.3.15 The screen for creating an extended partition

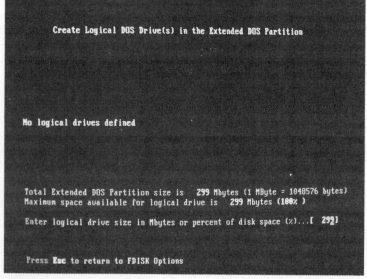

Fig.3.16 A logical drive must be created to use an extended partition

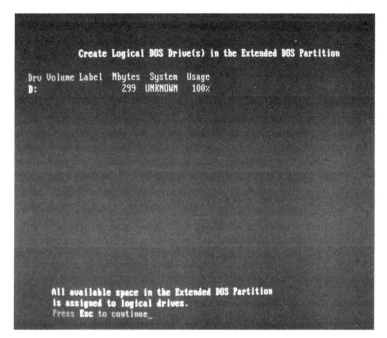

Fig.3.17 Confirming that a logical drive has been created

If a further partition is required select option one, and then option two, which is "Create extended DOS partition" (Figure 3.15). Enter the size of the partition you require and press the Return key to create the partition. Then press the Escape key, which will bring up a message saying "No logical drives defined" (Figure 3.16). In other words, you have created a partition, but as yet it does not have a drive letter. Assuming you require all the space in the partition to be one logical drive, simply press the Return key. This will make the partition drive D, and a screen giving this information will appear (Figure 3.17). Press the Escape key to return to the main menu, and use option four to check that the partition has been created successfully.

Formatting

Having created the partitions you require, the "FORMAT" command can then be run. First you will have to press the Escape key twice to exit FDISK, and then the computer must be rebooted so that the new partition information takes effect. To format drive C and place the system files onto it use this command:

format C: /s

This will bring up a warning to the effect that all data in drive C will be lost if you proceed with the format. As yet there is no data to lose, so answer yes to proceed with the formatting. It might take several minutes to complete the task, since there are a large number of tracks to be processed and checked. If the hard disc has more than one partition and is operating as drive C, drive D, etc., each partition must be formatted using a separate "FORMAT" command. Of course, the system should only be placed on disc C, so for the other logical drives do not use the "/s" addition to the command. This would not actually prevent drive D from working, but it would waste disc space on system files that would never be used. To format drive D this command would be used:

format D:

Windows

If you are still using MS-DOS, the PC is more or less ready to use once the hard drive is bootable. Suitable AUTOEXEC.BAT and CONFIG.SYS files will be needed in the root directory of the boot drive to initialise MS/DOS in the required manner. You will have to install all your applications software or course, and it is a good idea to copy the MS-DOS support files to a directory call "DOS", or something similar. The later versions of MS/DOS have an installation program that will do all this for you. Windows 3.1 can be installed onto the hard disc in much the same way as applications programs. For most users, putting the MS-DOS operating system onto the hard disc is simply a stepping-stone to installing Windows 95/98. In the unlikely event that you have the floppy disc version of Windows 95/98 there should be no difficulty in loading it onto the hard disc once the hard disc is bootable. You may find that you need to install the mouse in MS-DOS first, but otherwise it can be installed onto the bare drive. The situation is similar with the CD-ROM version provided you remember to opt for CD-ROM support during the boot-up process.

Windows Setup

To run the Setup program on the Windows 95/98 installation disc simply type "setup" and press the Return key. The Scandisk utility will run first and will check for errors on the hard disc drives and logical drives. Assuming all is well, press the "x" key to exit Scandisk and go into the

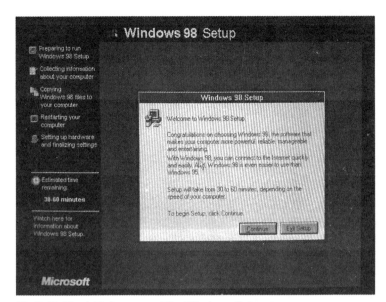

Fig.3.18 The initial screen of the Windows Setup program

first screen of the Windows Setup program (Figure 3.18). It is then just a matter of following the on-screen prompts to complete the Windows installation. Note that you can install the upgrade version of Windows 95 or 98 onto a "clean" hard disc, and that it is not essential to load your old version of Windows first so that you have something to upgrade. However, during the installation process you will probably be asked to prove that you have a qualifying upgrade product by putting the Setup disc into the floppy drive or CD-ROM drive, as appropriate. Do not throw away or recycle your old Windows discs, as this could leave you unable to reinstall the Windows upgrade.

You will be asked to select the directory into which Windows will be installed, but unless there is good reason to do otherwise, simply accept the default (C:\Windows). You will be offered several installation options (Figure 3.19), but for most users the default option of a "Typical" installation will suffice. Remember that you can add and delete Windows components once the operating system is installed, so you are not tied to the typical installation forever. The "Custom" options enables the user to select precisely the required components, but this can be time consuming and you need to know what you are doing. The "Compact" option is useful if hard disc space is limited.

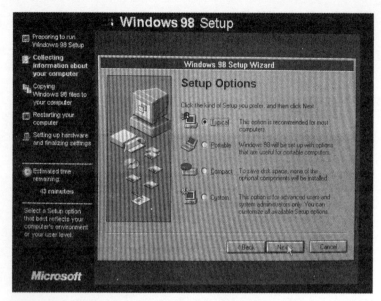

Fig.3.19 The Setup program offers four installation options

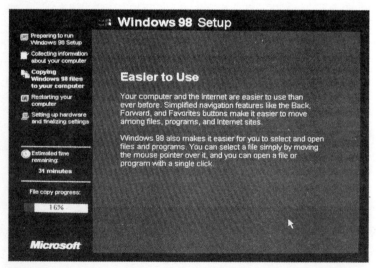

Fig.3.20 Once you reach this stage installation is largely automatic

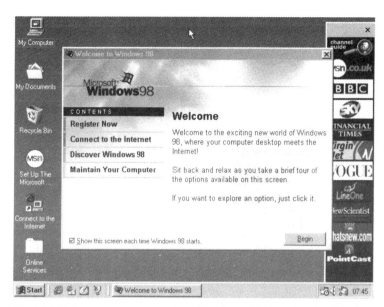

Fig.3.21 This screen appears when Windows 98 is run for the first time

After providing language information, etc., the program will progress to the main installation screen (Figure 3.20), and from thereon installation is largely automatic. The computer will reboot itself two or three times during the installation process, so if you opted to produce a Windows 98 start-up disc during the initial set-up procedure remember to remove this from the floppy drive. Otherwise the computer might reboot from the floppy rather than the hard disc, which would interfere with the installation process. Eventually you should end up with a basic Windows 98 installation, and the familiar initial screen (Figure 3.21).

Finishing

There will probably still be a certain amount of work to be done in order to get all the hardware fully installed, the required screen resolution set, and so on. To alter the screen resolution and colour depth, go to the control panel and double-click on the Display icon. Then left-click on the Settings tab to bring up a screen of the type shown in Figure 3.22. It is then just a matter of using the on-screen controls to set the required screen resolution and colour depth. To use the new settings left-click

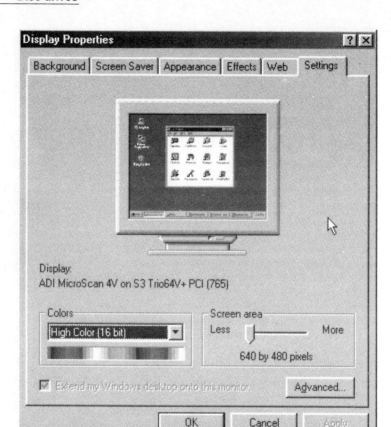

Fig.3.22 The Control Panel is used to adjust the display settings

the Apply button. It may be necessary to let the computer reboot in order to use the new settings, but in most cases they can be applied without doing this. Instead Windows will apply the new settings for a few seconds so that you can see that all is well. Simply left-click on the Yes button to start using the new settings.

If there is a problem with the picture stability, do nothing, and things should return to the original settings after a few seconds. This should not really happen if the monitor is installed correctly, because Windows will not try to use scan rates that are beyond the capabilities of the installed monitor. If a problem of this type should occur, check that the monitor is

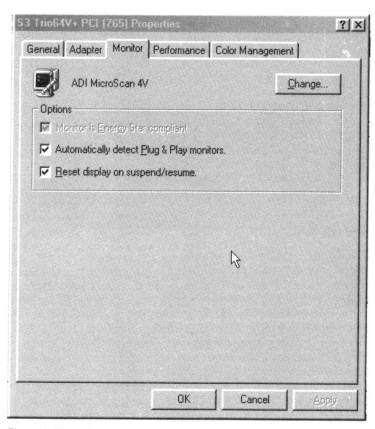

*Fig.3.23 The advanced display settings window enables the monitor
and video adapter to be changed*

installed properly. In the Display window of Control Panel select Settings,
Advanced, and then monitor. This will bring up a screen like Figure 3.23
which shows the type of monitor that is installed, if it is not right left-click
the Change button and select the correct one. If the picture is stable
with the new settings but the size and position are completely wrong,
there is probably no problem. It should be possible to position and size
the picture correctly using the monitor's controls. Many graphics cards
are supplied with utility software that helps to get the best possible display
from the system, and it is worth trying any software of this type to see if
it gives better results.

Windows 95/98 might have built-in support for all the hardware in your PC such as the sound and video cards, but this is unlikely. In order to get everything installed correctly you will probably require the installation discs provided with the various items of hardware used in the PC. These discs may be required during the installation of Windows 95/98, or they may have to be used after the basic installation has been completed. The instruction manuals provided with the hardware should explain the options available and provide precise installation instructions. These days even the motherboards seem to come complete with driver software for things such as special chipset features and the hard disc interface. It is once again a matter of reading the instruction manual to determine which drivers have to be installed, and how to go about it. Get all the hardware properly installed before you install the applications software.

Large Discs

When replacing a hard disc drive most users move up to a bigger and better drive. Sometimes this is by choice, but it is often due to a lack of a suitable replacement. Things move on rapidly in the world of hard disc drives, and a hard disc drive that was the latest thing a couple of years earlier is unlikely to be available any more. It is not just that the exact model used originally is likely to be unobtainable, it is unlikely that any drive of a similar specification will be available new. Second-hand hard disc drives are sometimes available from companies that deal in surplus and used computer equipment, and they are often available at computer fairs as well. Buying a second-hand drive that has a similar specification to the faulty drive is the easy option, because the replacement drive should be a trouble-free replacement. Having swapped the old drive for the new one it might be necessary to make some changes to the BIOS settings, and the "Auto" option can be used if you can not find the correct parameters for the drive. The replacement drive should then operate much like the original.

You may find that a modern high capacity drive can be used as a replacement without any difficulty, and this depends on the age of the PC. Older PCs were not designed to handle very high capacity disc drives, and in some cases they were not even designed to handle what would be considered quite small drives by current standards. In fact the limit for many older PCs is just 528 megabytes, and this limit is imposed by the BIOS. This does not necessarily mean that you can not use a larger drive in a PC that has an old BIOS, but either some compromises have to be made or the BIOS has to be upgraded.

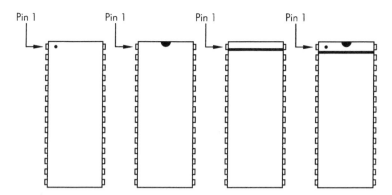

Fig.3.24 Methods of showing the orientation of integrated circuits

The best solution is undoubtedly to fit a new BIOS to the motherboard, but this may not be a practical proposition. With many older PCs fitting a new BIOS means removing the old BIOS chip or chips from the motherboard and replacing them with new ones. Removing the old chips should not be difficult since they will almost certainly be fitted in holders. If they are not, forget about fitting new BIOS chips. Your chances of removing the old ones without damaging the motherboard are slim. Removing a chip from its socket should be quite easy, even with the physically larger devices that are normally used for the BIOS in older PCs. Simply use a small screwdriver to prise one end upwards, and then do the same at the other end. This should leave the chip so loose in the socket that it easily lifts free, but if necessary repeat the procedure with the screwdriver before removing the chip.

However, before removing the BIOS chip or chips, make a note of which way round they are fitted. Older BIOS chips are invariable d.i.l. (dual in line) types having 24 or 28 pins, and there are various ways of indicating the pin-1 end of the chip. The usual ones are a notch or a dimple moulded into the case, or a line drawn across that end of the case (Figure 3.24). In fact there can be any combination of these, including all three on some chips. Make sure that the new chip or chips are fitted with the same orientation as the old ones. Fitting the new BIOS should not be difficult, but it is a peculiarity of all d.i.l. chips that the pins are splayed outwards slightly. They must be bent fractionally inwards before they will readily fit into a holder, and the easiest way of doing this is to press each set of pins against the workbench to squeeze them inwards slightly (Figure 3.25). Make sure that the BIOS chip or chips are fitted with the

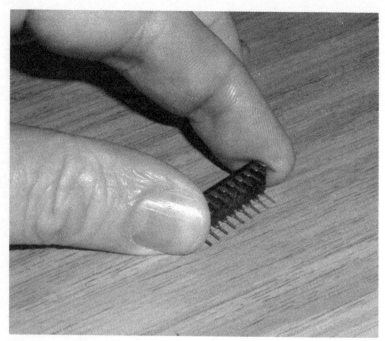

Fig.3.25 Bending the pins of an integrated circuit so that it will fit into its holder easily

correct orientation. If there are two chips you must fit them in the right holders. Normally one chip will be marked "H", and the other will be marked "L". These respectively contain the high and low bytes of a 16-bit BIOS.

The main problem with this kind of replacement BIOS is that suitable chips are unlikely to be obtainable. They are not the sort of thing that a normal computer store keeps in stock, and there is no guarantee that a suitable updated BIOS will have ever been made. You can enquire to the supplier or manufacturer of the PC to see if they can supply a new BIOS, but they are unlikely to have much in the way of spare parts and upgrades for an old PC. Modern PCs and some older types have a Flash BIOS, which refers to the type of RAM chip or chips used. The RAM chips used in older PCs are often re-programmable, but only by erasing them in a special eraser that uses ultra-violet "light", and then programming them in a suitable programmer unit. This is not really a practical way of changing the BIOS, even for most PC professionals.

Flash RAM is the type of memory used in the memory cards for digital cameras and notebook PCs. It can be erased and reprogrammed electronically much like ordinary RAM, but unlike ordinary RAM it does not "forget" when the power is switched off. This makes it possible to download a new version of the BIOS from the Internet, and load it into the existing BIOS chip with a suitable loader program. The latter is usually supplied with PCs and new motherboards, but it should also be available from the manufacturer's web site. When you download the upgrade the loader program will often be included.

The instruction manual for the PC or its motherboard should have a detailed explanation of how to go about the upgrade, and there will probably be a "read.me" file with the upgrade software that also gives this information. As pointed out previously, the upgrade is usually in the form of two main files, one of which is the program that actually performs the upgrade for you. The other file contains the new data for the ROM. If there is only one file it will be the new data for the ROM. It is only fair to point out that a BIOS upgrade of this type is a bit risky. You need to be absolutely certain that the data file you are using is the correct one for your motherboard. Using the wrong BIOS data file could easily render the computer unusable, and if it will not boot-up correctly it is impossible to restore the original BIOS.

Warning

Some PC users seem to be under the impression that any more recent BIOS can be used in place of an existing BIOS. I have to emphasise that this is definitely not the case, and apart from some early examples, each BIOS is customised to suit a particular motherboard, and the features of that board. If you use the wrong BIOS the Setup program will allow you to change all manner of things, but the data stored in memory might actually mean something completely different to the motherboard. Using the wrong BIOS might not stop the computer from working at all, but this is certainly a strong possibility. The computer is unlikely to be fully usable. Only use a BIOS upgrade that is designed specifically for the right make and model of computer, or for the exact version of the motherboard used in the PC.

The motherboard manufacturer's web site generally offers by far the best chance of obtaining an upgrade. Make sure that you accurately identify the motherboard, since there are often several versions of each one. Most PCs are supplied with the instruction manual for the motherboard, but this sometimes covers more than one board. The

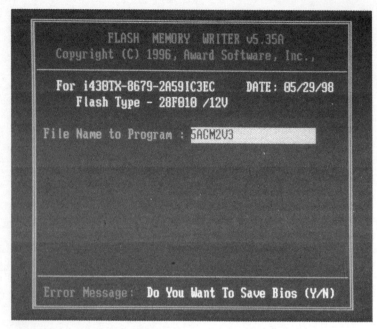

Fig.3.26 A typical flash BIOS upgrade program in action

board itself should be marked with the manufacturer's name and the make of the board. If the PC is fitted with a generic "no name" board it could be difficult to locate a suitable BIOS upgrade. In fact there is little chance of doing so unless the PC manufacturer's web site has BIOS upgrades.

Another slight worry when upgrading a BIOS is that of a power failure during the upgrade. This could leave the PC with a BI (half a BIOS)! With an incomplete or corrupted BIOS it is unlikely that the PC could be rebooted to restore the original or complete the upgrade. It only takes a few seconds to carry out the upgrade, so you would be very unlucky indeed if a power failure interrupted the process, but it is a slight risk. Obviously you must take due care not to do anything during the upgrade that could cause a brief power loss. No plugging in or unplugging the power lead of the printer for example.

The upgrade program usually has to be run from MS/DOS, and is normally very simple to operate (Figure 3.26). After you have supplied the name of the data file for the new BIOS (including any extension to the filename) the program should give the option of saving the existing BIOS onto disc. It is as well to do this so that you can revert to the original BIOS if the new version proves to be troublesome. After you have confirmed that you wish to continue with the upgrade the new data will be written to the BIOS ROM chip. Do not touch the computer during the flash upgrade, just stand back and let the upgrade program get on with it. The computer is then ready for rebooting and checking to see if the new BIOS has the desired effect.

Software fix

Most hard disc drive manufacturers supply some support software with their drives. This may include a software utility that provides a way around the 528 megabyte BIOS limit. However, do not expect a quick fix of this type to give ideal results. A software fix has to work around the BIOS limitations rather than eliminating them, and there will almost certainly be a compromise somewhere. This will often be in the form of the large hard disc "pretending" to be two or more smaller discs, probably with a maximum size of 528-megabytes per disc. While not exactly ideal, this arrangement will free all or some of the additional disc space, depending on the size of the drive and the number of notional drives you are prepared to have.

With some of these hard disc utilities there is no need to use the FDISK and FORMAT commands to partition and format the disc, since the utility itself partitions and formats the disc. Indeed, it is essential not to use the FDISK and FORMAT commands as to do so would prevent the utility from bypassing the 528-megabyte limit of the BIOS. This type of utility is not compatible with all operating systems, and it is clearly essential to read the installation instructions very carefully before using any program of this type. You should also read carefully through the "fine print" to see if there are any important limitations that you should know about.

There is actually another way of using a large hard drive in a PC that has the 528-megabyte limit imposed by the BIOS. This is simply to use no more than 528-megabytes of the hard disc's capacity. As pointed out previously, IDE hard drives can operate with practically any drive table size parameters that do not try to exceed the actual capacity of the drive. If you use (say) a 6.4-gigabyte drive as a 528-megabyte type, in theory at any rate, there should be no problems. In practice there can sometimes be odd difficulties with something like unreliable booting, but a little experimentation with the drive table parameters will usual iron out any problems of this type. It is clearly wasteful to use what could well be less than 10 percent of the hard drive's capacity. However, the new drive will probably cost a lot less than the original, and if a capacity of 528-megabytes is enough it does not really matter that most of the disc is not being used. 528 megabytes is inadequate for most Windows 95, 98, and NT4 systems, but most people still using MS/DOS will find this capacity perfectly adequate.

Other limitations

Assuming that that the BIOS in your PC does support hard discs having a capacity in excess of 528 megabytes, there are still one or two potential problems in adding a larger drive. These are limits imposed by certain operating systems, or to be more precise, by the disc filing systems used by those operating systems. There is a 2.1-gigabyte limit for MS/DOS or other operating systems that use the FAT16 file system. This does not mean that any capacity above 2.1 gigabytes can not be used, but the disc must be partitioned so that each partition is within this limit. In order to fully exploit a modern hard disc drive it could be necessary to have several partitions. This problem does not arise with Windows 95 or 98 using the FAT32 file system, where the maximum partition size is around 2 terabytes (2000 gigabytes).

The FAT16 file system also imposes an 8.4-gigabyte physical limit on each hard disc drive. In other words, you can have an 8.4-gigabyte drive set as four 2.1-gigabyte partitions, but a 10.5-gigabyte drive in the form of five 2.1-gigabyte partitions would not be acceptable because the total capacity would be greater than 8.4 gigabytes. At the time of writing this it is still possible to obtain drives of less than 8.4 gigabytes, but in the future it could be necessary to "lie" to the BIOS, and set a capacity of 8.4 gigabytes or less for what is actually a higher capacity drive.

Some versions of Windows 95 and all versions of Windows 98 can get around the 8.4-gigabyte limit, but only if the BIOS supports larger drives. In practice it is better to use the FAT32 file system wherever possible. The FAT16 system accommodates large partitions by using large sectors, and with large drives this means sectors as large as 32K. This may not seem to be of great importance, but each sector can only be assigned to a single file. Even if most of a sector is unused, the file system does not have the ability to allocate the any of the unused space to another file. This means that there is an average wastage of 16 kilobytes per file, or somewhat more than this if there are numerous small files. In practical computing there are normally numerous small support and data files, giving what is typically around 20 to 25 percent wasted disc space. In other words, about 400 to 500 megabytes is wasted per 2.1-gigabyte partition.

FAT32 provides much more efficient use of large partitions by using a smaller sector size of typically about 4 kilobytes. This gives greatly reduced wastage. Windows 98 is often installed with the FAT32 disc filing system already in place. This is achieved by opting for large hard disc support when first running the FDISK program. Once Windows 98 has been installed with the FAT16 file system it is possible to convert the disc to FAT32 operation using the built-in conversion utility. This is obtained by selecting Start, Programs, Accessories, System Tools, and Drive Converter. Any converter of this type can not be guaranteed to operate flawlessly, so it is as well to heed the warnings given by the program and back up the hard disc before using this utility. The few times that I have used this program it has never given any problems. Note that Windows 95 can use the FAT32 file system, but does not have any built-in facility to set up the disc for this system.

Compatibility

The IDE interface has gone through several changes over the years, and this is a brief description of the various versions:

IDE

IDE stands for Integrated Drive Electronics, which simply means that the controller electronics are integrated with the drive mechanism. The maximum transfer rate for data is about two or three megabytes per second and the maximum drive capacity is 528 megabytes. The limit is two devices per IDE controller.

EIDE

This is the enhanced version of the IDE interface, and it brings a number of benefits. One of these is an increase in the maximum disc size to 8.4 gigabytes, and it also permits the use of up to four drives per controller. Faster data transfers are also possible, up to a maximum of around 16.7 megabytes per second. However, the transfer rate depends on the mode used, the speed of the PC, and the capabilities of the hard disc drive. A brief explanation of hard disc modes is provided later in this chapter. The EIDE specification includes the ATA Packet Interface (ATAPI), which enables it to be used for other types of drive, such as CD-ROM drives, tape drive, Zip drives, etc.

Ultra DMA33

The "DMA" part of the name is an acronym for Direct Memory Access, and this is where something other than the processor takes over accesses to the system memory. The main difference between EIDE and Ultra DMA33 interfaces is the higher maximum operating speed of the latter. It is around twice as fast, offering a maximum transfer rate of around 33 megabytes per second.

Ultra DMA66

This is the newest form of IDE interface, and it offers a maximum transfer rate of 66 megabytes per second. This assumes that the hard disc drive can handle this rate, which is not necessarily the case with all drives that sport this interface. Ultra DMA66 operation requires a special data cable.

Compatibility between the various versions is very good, and there should be no problem in using an old IDE drive with the latest Ultra DMA66 motherboard, or the latest super-fast disc drive with an old motherboard having an original IDE interface. However, bear in mind that the simplest device in the system will be the limiting factor in any IDE set up. You can use the latest thing in hard disc drives in an old PC, but the interface and speed of the PC will not permit super-fast data transfers. As pointed out already, it might be difficult or impossible to use the full capacity of the drive in a set-up of this type. It would probably not be necessary to do so other than for testing purposes, but an old drive should work perfectly well with an otherwise up to the minute PC. The low speed and limited capacity of the drive would clearly hold back the overall performance and scope of the system.

Drive modes

When dealing with IDE interfaces and hard drives, etc., you will inevitably come across references to the various EIDE operating modes that were mentioned previously. In most instances you do not have to bother too much about these modes, and you can simply let the system "do its own thing". The BIOS program should correctly determine and use the right mode for any device connected to it. However, it is worth taking a quick look at the various modes and the ways in which they differ.

PIO mode

A PIO (programmed input/output) mode is where the processor has direct control of the hard disc via one of the support chips on the motherboard. In order to place data on the disc, or read it from the disc, the processor must issue the appropriate commands to transfer the data between the disc and the computer's memory.

Master mode

In a master mode the microprocessor is not in direct control of the hard disc, but instead this task is handed over to one of the support chips. Obviously the processor still has to issue commands to the chipset so that it knows which data to access and where to place it, but the processor has little involvement beyond that. A Master mode is not inherently any quicker at transferring data than a PIO mode. However, it places less of a burden on the processor and can therefore provide a boost in performance in other respects.

DMA

This is direct memory access, and any mode where the chipset moves data between the disc and memory independently of the processor makes use of DMA.

There are five PIO modes numbered from 0 to 4 and the higher the number, the greater the maximum data transfer rate possible. There are three DMA modes numbered from 0 to 2, and again, the higher the mode number the faster the maximum transfer rate. These are the maximum rates for the four PIO modes and three DMA modes, but not all hard discs and PCs are necessarily capable of providing these rates. Also, not all drives can use the faster modes.

PIO Mode 0	3.3MB per second
PIO Mode 1	5.2 MB per second
PIO Mode 2	8.3MB per second
PIO Mode 3	11.1MB per second
PIO Mode 4	16.6MB per second
DMA Mode 0	4.16MB per second
DMA Mode 1	13.3MB per second
DMA Mode 2	16.6MB per second

Any reasonably modern hard disc drive should be able to support the faster transfer modes, but other IDE devices such as CD-ROM drives and other interchangeable disc systems may not. Bear in mind that there is no point in using a fast transfer mode with a device that can only accept or supply data at relatively low rates.

SCSI drives

SCSI (small computer systems interface) is not an interface designed specifically for hard disc drives, and it is actually a general purpose parallel computer interface that can handle high speed data transfers with up to 15 devices. Incidentally, those in the computer business usually pronounce SCSI something like "scuzzy". This interface is often used for external peripherals such as scanners and external drives, but it is also used for internal devices such as hard discs and high performance CD-ROM units. Some motherboards are equipped with a SCSI interface, but this is a luxury feature rather than a standard one. In the past SCSI was popular for high-end workstations and network servers, where it permitted the use of fast data transfers and large disc capacities that were not supported by the IDE interface at that time. With improvements in the IDE standard over the years the advantage of SCSI has been eroded, although it still seems to remain the first choice for those who require the ultimate in hard disc performance.

The basic testing methods used with IDE drives can be applied to SCSI types, so that the exact nature of the fault can be located. Replacing the faulty component is also broadly similar to an equivalent operation with an IDE drive system, but SCSI drives are slightly less straightforward to deal with. In fact SCSI is a potentially confusing subject because it actually encompasses a number of standards. Like the IDE interface, SCSI has evolved over the years, but it does not have the same degree of compatibility as the IDE standard. Some manufacturers producing SCSI equipment that does not strictly adhere to the agreed standards have tended to further complicate matters. This has resulted in some equipment that works fine with its matching SCSI interface card, but other SCSI equipment can not be used with the card due to non-standard cabling or other problems. With SCSI equipment it is essential to carefully read through the manuals to determine exactly what you have, and to check the "fine print" to see if there are any little gems of information there that you need to know about.

Versions

SCSI exists in various versions, starting with the original specification, and then versions two and three. Version two exists in standard, fast, and wide versions. The SCSI-3 variations are wide, Ultra, and Ultra2. Devices that are designed for use with a SCSI-2 or SCSI-3 interface may not work properly with an original SCSI interface. Things are better in the opposite direction, and a standard SCSI device should work with a modern SCSI interface. However, as already pointed out, you need to be wary of non-standard interface cards that are generally incompatible with other SCSI devices. The practical implication of all this is that replacing a SCSI hard disc drive might also require the interface card to be changed. Before buying a SCSI adapter for an old PC, check that it will work properly with your PC. Modern high-speed adapters and some older AT class PCs are not compatible.

SCSI devices are connected together using the "chain" method. In other words, each SCSI device has an input port and an output port, and if there is only one device in the system its input connects to the output of the controller. If there is a second device, this has its input connected to the output port of the first device. A third SCSI unit would have its input connected to the output of the second device, and so on. A SCSI cable for internal devices is usually a fairly substantial 50-way type, but a 68-way cable is used for Wide versions of this interface. In either case the cable uses "straight" connection, with no crossed-over wires. In a hard disc context there will usually just be the controller card and the hard disc itself, with no other SCSI devices to contend with. It is then just a matter of connecting the output of the controller to the input of the hard disc drive. Pin one on the cable and connectors might be identified, but it is essential to check with the instruction manuals and make quite sure that everything is connected the right way round.

The SCSI interface makes use of termination resistors, and there should only be termination resistors at each end of the system. By default these resistors are normally in-circuit, and with only a controller and a hard disc drive they should be left in-circuit. They are only removed or switched out on a unit that is not at one end of the "chain". When fitting a new SCSI controller card or hard disc drive you should obviously consult the instruction manual and check the hardware to ensure that the termination resistors are properly switched into circuit.

Like IDE drives, the SCSI variety has the low level formatting done at the factory. Do not attempt to undertake low level formatting on a drive of this type. Also like an IDE hard drive, it is necessary to partition the drive using the FDISK program, even if only one partition is needed. The disc must then be high level formatted, after which the operating system and applications programs are installed.

CD-ROM drives

Audio CD players seem to go on working forever, but in my experience computer CD-ROM drives do not offer the same degree of long term reliability. In defence of CD-ROM drives it has to be pointed out that they have a generally tougher time than their audio counterparts. They read computer data at many times the speed audio data is extracted, there is a great deal of stopping and starting, and there is also a fair amount of jumping around each disc to find the data you require. Anyway, I seem to replace far more CD-ROM drives than any other type of drive. The drive will often fail gradually, with the odd disc giving difficulty, and then most discs being partially or totally unreadable. It is possible to obtain cleaners that will attempt to polish the optics and restore normal operation to a failing drive. However, it is not necessarily the optics that are at fault, and simple cleaning may not do the job anyway. If there is a sudden failure it pays to be cautious.

Rather than jumping in and immediately replacing the drive, first make sure that the problem is not due to a faulty cable or bad connection. It could also be due to a problem with the IDE interface. This is a matter of substituting another CD-ROM drive to see if the problem persists. If it does, the interface or the cable is at fault, not the drive. It is not essential to use another CD-ROM drive in the substitution test, and something like an old IDE hard disc drive will do. Where appropriate, check that the BIOS settings are correct for the substitute drive. If no substitute drive is available you can try swapping the hard drive and the CD-ROM drive. Depending on the set-up of the PC, this will require some swapping over of the data cables, and (or) changes to the jumper settings. For example, if the hard drive and CD-ROM drive are the master devices on the primary and secondary IDE channels, no changes to the jumper settings will be required. It is just a matter of connecting the cable for the primary IDE interface to the CD-ROM drive and fitting the secondary IDE cable to the hard drive.

Any necessary changes to the BIOS settings should then be made, and the easy option is to use automatic detection for both drives. There is potentially a problem with the BIOS not permitting the system to boot from the secondary IDE interface. Most will, but a few will not. One way around this is to boot into MS/DOS from the floppy drive, and to install

CD-ROM support, or simply use a Windows 98 start-up disc and opt for CD-ROM support when asked. Once the system has booted you can then check to see if the hard drive and CD-ROM drives are both accessible.

Speed ratings

Fortunately, new CD-ROM drives are relatively cheap these days, and the new drive is likely to have far faster reading rates than the original unit. The speed ratings of modern CD-ROM drives have to be taken with the proverbial "pinch of salt", and in practical tests they often fall short of their rated speeds. It also has to be borne in mind that data can be read at faster rates from the longer tracks towards the outer edge of the disc than from the shorter tracks near the middle. Thus a drive that is rated at 48x can only achieve this rate on the outermost tracks, and may not achieve even 20x on the inner tracks. The speed rating is relative to an ordinary audio disc player incidentally, which is equivalent to a read rate of just over 150 kilobytes per second. In theory at any rate, a 40x drive can therefore read data from some tracks at over 6 megabytes per second. Even though modern drives may struggle to achieve their theoretical transfer rates, a substantial improvement in performance should be noticed after changing from something like a 2x or 4x drive to a modern 40x or higher drive. Unfortunately, the higher rotation speed of a modern disc results in a longer wait for the disc to get up to speed and the drive to start reading data. Modern drives also tend to be far more noisy than old 2x and 4x units.

Replacing an old and slow CD-ROM drive with a modern unit should not give any compatibility problems. Like modern hard disc drives, up to the minute CD-ROM units are fully compatible with older versions of the IDE interface. Replacing a CD-ROM drive is very much like replacing a hard disc drive, as described previously. However, there should be no difficulty in removing the drive by moving it forward out of the drive bay. The new drive can be inserted into the drive bay from the front, making replacement much easier.

Things could be slightly fraught if the faulty CD-ROM drive does not use an IDE interface. In the early days these units used several different types of interface, and a drive was only usable if the PC had a suitable interface card. Many drives were actually sold in multimedia upgrade kits that included an audio card, and the CD-ROM interface was included on this expansion card. Even if the CD-ROM is operated via an interface on an audio card or dedicated expansion card, it could still be an IDE

Fig.3.27 Do not forget the configuartion jumpers of IDE drives

type. If a standard 40-wire IDE data cable is used, then the interface is almost certainly an IDE type. However, it would still be advisable to check this point in the PC's instruction manual. If the drive uses some other interface, such as a Panasonic type, there is little chance of obtaining a suitable spare part. The only realistic option is to abandon the original interface and use an IDE drive. There may be a suitable interface on the audio card or on the CD-ROM interface card, or the motherboard might have a suitable interface and a spare IDE channel available. Adding an IDE interface card could be another option. It is a matter of reading through the instruction manuals and weighing up the options.

Configuration

Do not forget to check that any IDE devices, including CD-ROM drives, have the configuration jumpers set to the correct mode. Most CD-ROMs are supplied with the jumper set for slave operation, which is fine if it is

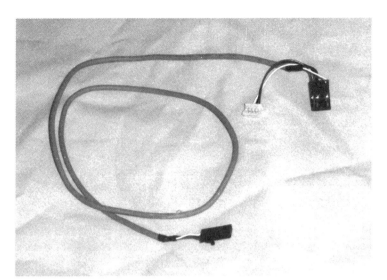

Fig.3.28 Some CD-ROM audio leads have two connectors so that they can be used with a wider range of soundcards

operating on the primary IDE port as a slave to the hard disc drive. If the CD-ROM drive operates on its own on the secondary IDE port, the BIOS will probably be looking for it as the master device. When I am asked for assistance with a replacement CD-ROM drive that fails to work it is almost always because no one has bothered to set it to the correct operating mode. The jumper terminals are hidden away in the connectors and are easily overlooked (Figure 3.27) Configuring IDE drives was covered in the section of this chapter that deals with hard disc drives. Configuring an IDE device is much the same whether it is a hard disc, CD-ROM drive, or some other mass storage device such as a ZIP drive, so the notes on configuring IDE hard drives apply equally well to CD-ROM drives.

IDE conflicts

There can occasionally be problems with IDE devices that seem unable to operate reliably together. This should not really occur, and thankfully it is something that is rare these days. Problems seem to arise due to the various equipment manufacturers interpreting the IDE specification in slightly different ways. The problem is not usually insurmountable, and if two devices will not operate properly on the same IDE interface, try using them on separate IDE ports. Conversely, if they will not operate properly on different IDE ports, try using them on the same port. Before swapping things around make quite sure that both drives are configured properly, because an incorrect jumper setting is far more likely to be the cause of the problem.

Audio cable

With CD-ROM drives you often find that there is an extra cable that runs from the rear of the drive to a connector on the sound card. This cable is usually quite thin (Figure 3.28), and its purpose is to couple the audio output signal from the CD-ROM drive to the audio card. It is then possible to hear audio tracks via the loudspeakers connected to the audio card. This coupling is not really necessary if you will not play audio tracks on the CD-ROM drive, or if audio tracks will be monitored via the headphone socket on the CD-ROM drive. However, if this cable is present it makes sense to connect it up just in case you need to play audio tracks via the soundcard. There is a potential snag, which is simply that more than one type of connector has been used at both the CD-ROM and the soundcard ends of these cables. If you change either the CD-ROM unit or the soundcard you might find that the audio cable has to be replaced as well.

The rest

There are now numerous types of drive that can be fitted to a PC, and it is not feasible to give detailed coverage of them here. With IDE devices the same general testing principles apply regardless of whether the drive is a hard disc, CD-ROM unit, ZIP drive, or anything else. First do some cable testing and substitution testing to ensure that the problem is due to a faulty drive, and not something else such as a broken cable or faulty interface on the motherboard. If possible, try the drive in another PC to double-check that it is indeed faulty. Having established which component is broken it is then replaced.

Video and sound

In common with most other aspects of PCs, the video and sound capabilities have undergone a number of changes over the years. The internal loudspeaker is still included in modern PCs, but a soundcard and external loudspeakers that can produce excellent synthesised music and sound effects almost invariably augment it. In fact modern soundcards go beyond this, and can record high quality stereo sound. They also feature a port that acts as both a MIDI interface and a games port. The situation is similar with the video side of things. The original PC display was a text-only type, which included some basic graphics characters. This screen mode is still supported by modern video cards, as are many of the other early PC screen modes. However, they are little used these days, and high-resolution graphics modes are required for a graphical user interface (GUI) such as Windows.

Sound diagnosis

If a soundcard appears to have failed it is essential to look at other possibilities before trying a replacement. Apart from the soundcard itself, the audio system includes active loudspeakers that contain a stereo amplifier, a couple of connecting cables, and a set of software drivers. A fault in any of these can cause a complete loss of the audio signal or other problems.

For a soundcard to function properly it must have the software drivers installed correctly, and there are usually three or four of these drivers. It may seem a bit "over the top" to have several drivers for one piece of hardware, but you have to bear in mind that a PC soundcard actually fulfils several functions. It handles the recording and playback of sound samples, at least one and often two or three forms of sound synthesis, plus it provides games and MIDI ports. If you go into the Windows 98 Device Manager and look at the entries for the soundcard there will be

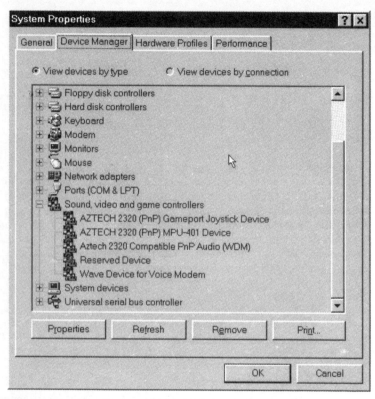

Fig.4.1 Checking the soundcard entries in Device Manager

about three or four of them (Figure 4.1). Possibly because there are several drivers, some of which are quite complex, problems with these drivers are far from rare. Things are not as bad as they were some years ago when getting the soundcard to work with each MS/DOS program was a series of puzzles. Once a soundcard is correctly installed in Windows it should work properly with all Windows programs. Unfortunately, some soundcards seem to uninstall themselves quite regularly, and have to be periodically reinstalled.

If there is a problem with the sound system, unless it is obviously a hardware problem I would certainly recommend investigating the drivers first. Sometimes driver problems do not produce any error messages from applications software or the operating system. In most cases though, there will be error messages along the lines of "can not find X", where "X" is a hardware or software resource associated with the soundcard.   Do not assume that the hardware is at fault because an error message indicates that a hardware resource can not be used.   A problem with a driver can make the operating system "blind" to a piece of hardware.

Yellow peril

In theory at any rate, if there is a problem with a driver there will be a yellow exclamation mark or question mark against the device's entry in the Device Manager's list of drivers.   Double clicking on the entry will bring up another window (Figure 4.2) that may shed some light on the problem. It is only fair to point out that many computers operate perfectly well with what Device Manager considers to be one or two problem devices.   It is as well to check the list of drivers before anything goes wrong, so that you can look for new problems.   In the example of Figure 4.2 the "Reserved Device" is actually an IDE port on the soundcard, and it is not operating because there is no spare interrupt line for it to use. This does not matter because the soundcard's IDE port is not required in this PC, and it can be left in an inoperative state.   It is sometimes possible to delete a rogue device of this type from Device Manager, but due to the Plug and Play feature it might simply reinstall itself.   The "Disable in this hardware profile" option is a usually better way of making sure a device of this type does not give any problems.

If a driver has become damaged, the only solution is to reinstall it.   With a Plug and Play device one way of doing this is to remove it in Device Manager.   To do so simply left-click on the entry for the device and then left-click on the "Remove" button.   This brings up a warning message, and you then either select "OK" to go ahead or "Cancel" to leave the driver intact.   Having removed the driver or drivers the computer must be restarted.   The Plug and Play system should then reinstall the driver correctly.   In practice this method does not always seem to work properly, and the damaged driver can be reinstated.   If a damaged driver seems reluctant to go away, it can usually be banished by removing it from Device Manager, shutting down Windows, and then switching off the computer.   Remove the soundcard and then start up the PC so that Windows loads and runs without the card.   Then shut down Windows again, reinstall the soundcard, restart the computer, and let the Plug and Play feature reinstall the drivers for the card.   This is clearly a bit of a rigmarole, but normal operation should then be restored.

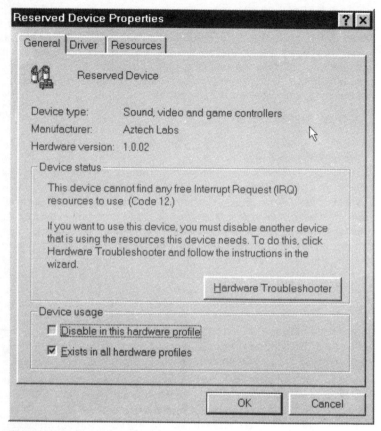

Fig.4.2 Investigating a troublesome device using Device Manager

An alternative method of reinstalling a driver is to double click on its entry in Device Manager, select the "Update driver" option, and then follow the instructions that appear on the screen. Of course, if a device continually runs into driver problems it needs genuinely updated drivers. Provided the soundcard is produced by one of the main manufacturers it should not be difficult to find their web site so you search for a newer driver for your card. With inexpensive generic cards this might not be possible, but it is worth looking through the card's instruction manual to see if there is a web address. If not, the manufacturer of the PC may well have a suitable driver available at their web site. Updated drivers often come complete with a text file that gives some installation instructions, and these should be studied carefully. The instructions might suggest that the "Update driver" option in Device Manager is used, but these improved drivers are often in the form of a program that is launched from the "Run" option in the Start menu. The program then checks that the correct hardware and drivers are present, and makes any necessary changes to the driver software.

In order to check the card it is necessary to install it in another computer to see if it then works. Unfortunately, this means removing any existing soundcard in the other PC, and then installing the drivers for the troublesome card. After the check, everything then has to be put back the way it was in the other PC. If the soundcard is a very inexpensive type, or is simply a bit old and out of date, you may prefer to simply opt for trying a replacement. Before replacing the card it is advisable to try physically reinstalling it, preferably in a different expansion slot. This often removes problems with expansion cards.

If the card does appear to be faulty and a replacement is needed, as with most PC spare parts, you are unlikely to find the original part still available. There will probably be no option but to move onto something newer and better. Looking on the plus side, this means that the computer's sound system should be significantly improved, and the replacement card should not cost a great deal of money unless you require the latest "state of the art" audio card. On down side, there are one or two potential problems in changing to a different soundcard. Most of the current soundcards are for PCI expansion slots, but an old PC might only have ISA slots. You choice may be a bit limited, but at the time of writing this there are still some ISA audio cards available.

There could be problems if the audio card provides the interface for the CD-ROM drive. Any form of CD-ROM interface on a soundcard is now something of a rarity, and there is little chance of finding a suitable card if the CD-ROM drive uses anything other than an IDE interface. Using a separate card to provide the CD-ROM interface is one way around the problem, but there is again little chance of finding a suitable card if the CD-ROM drive uses something other than an ordinary IDE interface. Consequently, changing the audio card might necessitate switching to a new CD-ROM drive as well. This will clearly increase the cost of the repair quite substantially, although the repaired PC should have much better multimedia capability than the original.

Speakers

Checking the loudspeakers and connecting cables should not give any problems. PC audio leads normally use 3.5-millimetre stereo jack plugs, and there are only three wires connecting the audio card to the speaker that contains the amplifier (left-hand channel, right-hand channel, and earth). The lead that connects the main speaker to the secondary speaker is a simple two-way type that uses 3.5-millimetre monophonic jack plugs, or the stereo variety with one terminal of each plug left unused. Continuity testing will soon determine whether or not each terminal of one plug connects to the equivalent terminal of the other plug.

Before testing the leads you can do a simple check to see if there is anything wrong with this part of the audio system. Disconnect the loudspeaker lead from the audio card and try touching the non-earth terminals of the plug with the blade of a small screwdriver. Figure 4.3 identifies the three terminals of the jack plug. Make sure that you are touching the blade of the screwdriver and not just the insulated handle, because this test relies on "hum" and other electrical noise being picked up by your body. This signal should produce mains "hum" and other general noise from the loudspeakers provided the volume control is well advanced.

If you have an item of audio equipment that has a 3.5-millimetre stereo output socket, such as a personal stereo unit, use this as the audio source. Either way, a lack of sound from one or both of the loudspeakers indicates a fault in a cable or the loudspeaker units. If the cables pass the continuity test it is presumably the loudspeakers that are at fault. If the loudspeakers are mains powered, as most are, check the fuse in the mains plug and ensure that everything is connected together properly.

A common problem with soundcards is that they function perfectly for some time, but fail when you try to record sound via a microphone. This is not usually due to a fault in either the soundcard or the microphone. The problem is more usually due to incompatibility between the microphone and the audio card. There would seem to be a lack of true standardisation with this aspect of audio cards, and a microphone that works perfectly well with one card might give no signal at all when used with another. The substitution method of testing is therefore unreliable in this instance.

The microphone problem stems from the fact that the microphone inputs of early SoundBlaster cards, and many of the compatible cards of a similar age, are intended for use with a carbon microphone. This is a

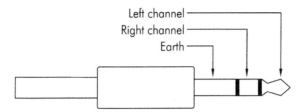

Left channel
Right channel
Earth

Fig.4.3 The standard connector for computer audio is a 3.5mm jack

rather crude form of microphone, as used in early telephone handsets. The audio quality of a carbon microphone is usually quite low, but the output signal is very high. Hence the microphone inputs of most early soundcards, and some recent ones come to that, are very insensitive. Although the microphone connector on the card is a stereo 3.5-millimetre jack socket, this is normally a monophonic input. The third terminal is used to provide power to the carbon microphone, and not to provide a second stereo channel. By no means all soundcards have this type of microphone input. Some have a monophonic input with one terminal of the input socket left unused, while others do actually have a stereo microphone input.

Carbon microphones are little used with soundcards these days, and probably never were used very much with them. The normal choices at present are electret and dynamic microphones. Electret microphones require a power supply to operate, and this is often in the form of a built-in battery. However, some electret microphones are designed for use with a SoundBlaster style microphone input, and use the soundcard as the power source. Dynamic microphones do not require a power source, but often have very low output levels. There is clearly plenty of scope for incompatibility problems when using the microphone input of an audio card. If you use a low output microphone with an insensitive input there will probably be too little audio signal to be of any practical use. If you use a microphone that requires power from the soundcard, it will only work if the card actually provides a suitable power source. Using a stereo microphone will clearly not give the desired result if the card only has a monophonic microphone input.

Sorting out microphone problems tends to be difficult. In theory it should be possible to obtain information about suitable types of microphone from the soundcard's instruction manual or the manufacturer's web site. In practice the information available on this subject is often sketchy to the point of being virtually non-existent. You often end up trying any microphone you can lay your hands on in the hope that it will work. In general, the safest option is a dynamic microphone that has a fairly high output level. This type of microphone will work properly regardless of whether or not the soundcard provides a power supply output, and it will give usable results with an insensitive input.

If a microphone fails to give a satisfactory signal level, or no signal at all, investigate the software side of things before giving up on it. A little loudspeaker icon usually appears on the Windows 98 taskbar when the soundcard drivers are installed. Double clicking on this may produce nothing more than a simple volume control, but it often produces a screen that provides various audio controls. A facility of this type might be available from the Control Panel, either via the multimedia icon, or by way of an icon for the audio card.

Where it is possible to select the recording source, make sure that the microphone input is enabled. By default the system might only record from the "line" input socket. If there is a slider control for the microphone, make sure that this is well advanced and not fully backed off. There is sometimes a switch that can be used to boost or reduce the recording level by 20 decibels. In other words, it boosts or reduces the signal by a factor of 10. If there is a lack of microphone signal, make sure any switch of this type is set to give the higher level of sensitivity. On the other hand, where there are problems with distortion due to overloading when the microphone is used, set the switch for lower sensitivity.

Monitors

One point that has to be made right at the outset is that ordinary monitors, which use a cathode ray tube (CRT), operate with very high voltages and are potentially lethal. Some of these high voltages can remain present for some time after the monitor has been switched off. Only suitably trained engineers should remove the outer casing of a monitor and attempt to repair it or make adjustments. With some monitors, and mainly the older units, there are one or two controls tucked around the back that can be twiddled if there are problems with picture stability, and most modern monitors have external controls for adjusting picture size, position, brightness, etc. The services of trained engineers at a service centre are required if these standard controls can not produce a satisfactory picture.

Before deciding that a monitor is faulty do check that the problem is not simply due to the controls going out of adjustment. On more than one occasion I have been asked for help with an apparently blank monitor screen, only to discover that the brightness or contrast control had been knocked back to zero. This usually happens when a monitor is moved, but the non-digital brightness and contrast controls of many monitors are easily knocked out of adjustment.

When most parts of a computer become faulty there is no option but to replace them. The situation is different with a monitor, and it is often worthwhile getting a faulty unit repaired. Obviously each case has to be taken on its own merits, and something like a 14-inch monitor that is ten years old is unlikely to be worthwhile repairing. It might not be possible to get spare parts for an old monitor anyway, and the cost of repair is likely to be substantially more than the value of the monitor. At the other extreme, with a high quality 17 or 19-inch monitor that is just out of guarantee it would almost certainly be worthwhile getting it repaired.

If you suspect that a monitor is faulty, and adjustment of the controls does not produce a usable picture, the substitution method of testing can be used. You need to be careful when testing the iffy monitor with another PC since some monitors have greater scanning capability than others do. In general, monitors that can scan at high rates can also scan over a range of lower frequencies. However, some older monitors in particular can only scan at high rates when used at high and medium resolutions. There is a real risk that the monitor will seem to be inoperative simply because it is receiving a video signal that is too high or low in frequency.

With a Plug and Play operating system you may find that the change in monitor is detected, and that the operating system then proceeds to install the "new" monitor. If the monitor had previously been completely blank or otherwise unusable, even during the initial testing and boot-up process when low scan rates are used, but it produces a proper picture with another PC, the monitor is almost certainly all right. Installing it into the operating system of the test PC would seem to be pointless. Do not forget that having installed the iffy monitor it will then be necessary to reinstall the original monitor when the test PC is returned to its original configuration. When the monitor works during the initial boot process, but seems to fail when the system switches to a higher resolution mode, there is little option but to go ahead with installation on the test system.

Where no Plug and Play system comes into operation the new monitor must be installed manually. This might not actually be necessary if the monitor works properly once the new PC has booted and gone into a higher resolution screen mode. This would seem to suggest that the monitor is working properly, although there is the possibility that it is working in a different resolution or scan rate on the test PC. Ideally the

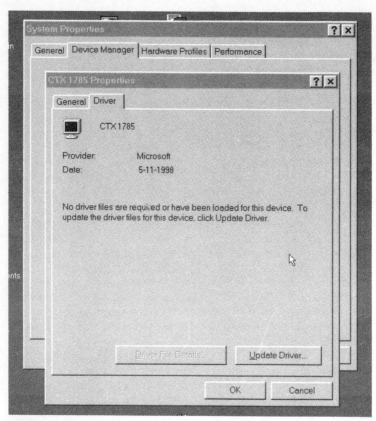

Fig.4.4 Installing a different monitor in Device Manager

test system should run the monitor in exactly the same screen mode that it normally uses. Whether or not this is possible depends on the capabilities of the test system. If the monitor fails when the test system goes into high resolution mode, the system must be reset and restarted in "Safe Mode", or an equivalent for operating systems other than Windows 95 and 98.

Manual installation of a monitor can be tricky, because many facilities are disabled in Safe Mode. On the other hand, there is no point in booting in normal mode if the monitor will fail to produce a picture. You will probably find that the monitor type can not be changed via the obvious route of the "Display" icon in the Control Panel. Going into

Device Manager and double clicking on "Monitors" is a usually a more successful route. Double click on the entry for an installed monitor, left-click on the "Driver" tab, and then select the "Update Driver" option (Figure 4.4). It should then be possible to follow the process through and install the iffy monitor in place of the original. Of course, only do this if you are sure that you can restore the original settings when the original monitor is restored to the system.

NT4 monitor testing

A PC running Windows NT4 is ideal for testing monitors provided it is equipped with a reasonably good video card. Unlike Windows 95 and 98, NT4 does not make use of Plug and Play, but instead enables the user to select from a range of resolutions and scan frequencies supported by the video card. Furthermore, it provides a simple test facility that makes it easy to check a monitor with each set of scan frequency and resolution settings (Figure 4.5). Not only does this make it quick and easy to test a monitor with a wide range of settings to determine its capabilities, but it also makes it easy to reinstate the original set-up afterwards.

Warning

One final note of warning is in order here. It is not a good idea to leave any faulty equipment switched on for more than brief periods, and with complex mains powered equipment such as a monitor it is definitely a bad idea. One reason for this is that one thing can lead to another, causing one fault to produce further damage. What starts as a minor fault can become a major problem if faulty equipment is left running. There is also the safety aspect to consider. Faults can sometimes cause high current flows in parts of a circuit. A fuse or other protection circuit in the monitor might prevent any serious damage from occurring, but there is a real risk of something overheating with this type of fault.

If you think that a monitor might be faulty, do not leave it switched on for any longer than is really necessary. Needless to say, but I will say it anyway, if a monitor or any other piece of equipment shows any sign of overheating it should be switched off at once. By any sign I do not just mean smoke coming from the top of the unit! Hot electronic components have a characteristic smell that anyone dealing with electronic fault finding soon learns to recognise.

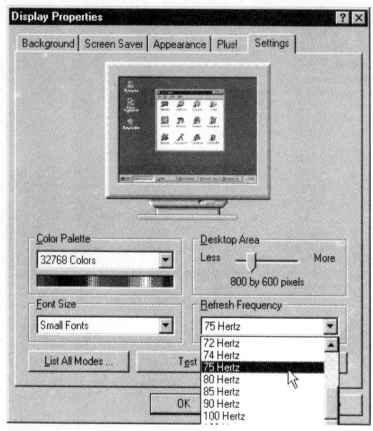

Fig.4.5 Windows NT4 has facilities that are good for testing monitors

Video card

If a PC produces no picture and the monitor is found to be fully operational it is easy to jump to the conclusion that the video card is at fault. However, there is a wide range of faults that can cause a loss of the video signal. These include power supply failures, problems with the motherboard, the processor, and even the memory circuits. If it is indeed the video card that is at fault there is usually a strong hint to this effect when the PC is switched on. If it seems to go through the normal boot-up process but with no picture, it is quite likely that the video card is the source of the problem. If the usual start-up "beep" or "beeps" from the BIOS are

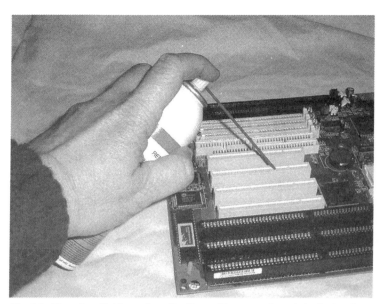

*Fig.4.6 Cleaning fluid can be effective with expansion slots, but only
use a proper contact cleaning spray*

absent and there is a lack of the usual hard disc activity as the system
boots from disc, the fault almost certainly lies elsewhere.

Assuming that the video card does appear to be faulty, it can be tested
in another computer and (or) another video card can be tried in the
faulty PC.   The usual expansion card routine should be tried before
resorting to substitution testing. Try removing and reinstalling the card
in case the problem is simply due to a bad connection or the card
becoming slightly displaced. Where possible, try the card in a vacant
expansion slot, or in the absence of a vacant slot try swapping it over
with another card. This type of thing is not possible with AGP video
cards, because motherboards are only equipped with one AGP slot. It
can usually be done with ISA and PCI cards though, as there will normally
be at least two slots of each type. If moving the video card to a vacant
slot cures the problem, I would simply leave it in the new location and
investigate no further. The problem is probably due to dirty contacts or
minor mechanical damage to the original expansion slot. If the
troublesome slot is required at some later date, the problem with it can
be sorted out then. In all probability it will not ever be needed.

The situation is very different if swapping the video card with another card restores the picture but results in the other card failing. The slot originally occupied by the video card is then clearly faulty. With no spare expansion slot it is necessary to get the faulty one working, or to replace the motherboard. If the problem with the slot is electronic in nature there is no realistic chance of mending it, and replacing the motherboard is the only option. It is more likely that the problem is simply due to a dirty contact and cleaning the slot with a contact cleaning fluid or spray should cure the fault (Figure 4.6).

Where the motherboard has integrated video circuits, a lack of video output is a very serious fault. With most integrated motherboards it is possible to disable the video circuits, so check that the problem is not simply due to the integral video generator somehow becoming switched off. The video generator can be controlled via the BIOS Setup program, jumpers, or DIP switches, and the manual for the PC (or its motherboard) should have full details. If the video circuits are enabled and no video signal at all is being produced, even during the BIOS start-up routine, the inevitable conclusion is that the on-board video circuits are unusable.

In cases where these circuits can not be switched off, a new motherboard is probably the only solution. A video card could be used in a vacant expansion slot, but there is usually no AGP slot on a motherboard that has integrated video circuits. A PCI video card could be used if there is a suitable slot available, but there is a risk of conflicts between the video card and the faulty video circuits. Also, having faulty circuits running is a bit dubious. If the onboard graphics generator can be switched off, it should then be possible to use a PCI video card in a spare PCI expansion slot with a minimum of risk. However, there may be some loss of performance compared to an onboard AGP video generator. Also, running a board that contains faulty circuits, even if those circuits are disabled, has to be considered a little risky.

Modems

The word modem is a contraction of modulator-demodulator, and the original modems operated using a simple system of tone decoding. Computers operate using ones and zeros, and as far as a computer is concerned, all programs and data consist of groups of ones and zeros. The original modems operated on the basis of using one audio tone to represent logic zero, and a different tone to represent logic one. Serial data from an RS232C computer port was fed into the modem, and the characteristic warbling sounds were generated as the modem converted a string of ones and zeros into an audio tone of alternating pitch. At the other end of the system the changing audio tone was converted back into logic ones and zeros that were fed into the serial input of a computer.

The problem with this basic method of encoding and decoding is that it allows only quite low data rates to be used. In fact this method does not intrinsically limit the rate at which data can be sent, but it does when applied to a system that has a very limited bandwidth. An ordinary telephone system certainly has a limited bandwidth, and the original modems only operated at around 300 to 1200 baud. In other words, they could handle transfers at around 300 to 1200 bits per second, or about 30 to 120 bytes per second. Modern modems have been refined to the point where they do not really use true tone encoding and decoding any more. You may still hear the familiar warbling sound when the modem is first establishing contact and is operating at a relatively low speed, but this soon changes to what sounds very much like random noise. These refined techniques enable baud rates of up to 33600 baud (33.6-kilobaud) to be used when sending data, and 56000 (56-kilobaud) when receiving it.

Speed considerations aside, there are three categories of modem these days. One of these is the external variety, which is the traditional modem that connects to the PC via a serial port and has its own mains power supply unit or battery supply. The other two types are internal modems that are in the form of a standard expansion card. For older modems the card is usually an ISA type, but modern internal modems are in the form of PCI expansion cards. The difference between the two types of internal modem is in the amount of hardware they contain. Older internal modems are basically the same as an external type, but the expansion card includes a serial port. Obviously an internal modem does not have a case or its own power supply, which generally makes it cheaper than an equivalent external type..

Some recent internal modems are of this type, but the majority seem to be so-called Windows modems, or "Winmodems". A modem of this type is relatively simple (Figure 4.7), and is really more of a soundcard than a modem. In order to operate as a modem it requires a complex driver program, and it is this program plus the PC's processor that does most of the hard work. Modems of this type usually require a reasonably powerful PC, with something like a 150MHz Pentium and 20 megabytes of RAM being a typical minimum requirement.

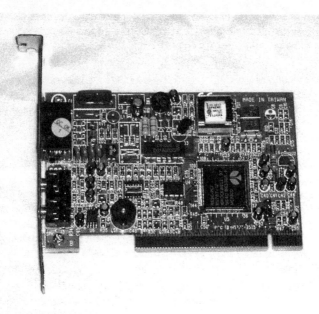

Fig.4.7 Most internal modems use relatively simple hardware and rely on the software to do most of the work

External modems

If an external modem ceases to operate it will probably have some indicator lights that give some clue as to the nature of the problem. In the event that the power indicator light does not come on, make the usual checks to ensure the fuse in the mains plug is all right, the mains lead is plugged into the modem reliably, and that the modem is actually switched on! Modems often have lights that show whether or not there is any signal being received on the serial port or the telephone port. When one or other of these lights fails to respond at the correct times you should check the appropriate connecting cable. Check the telephone line by plugging in an ordinary telephone instead of the modem. If you get the dialling tone when the handset if lifted it is unlikely that the telephone line is faulty, but you can always telephone a friend if you wish to make quite sure. With the fault apparently on the PC side of the modem, try the modem with another PC and (or) try another modem or serial device with the PC. Where the modem works with another PC, or another modem fails to work with the original PC, it is the PC's serial port and not the modem that is at fault.

Although it is uneconomic to have most PC peripherals repaired, it might be worthwhile with one of the more up-market external units. This obviously depends on the age of the modem and the cost of a comparable unit to replace it, as well as the likely cost of the repair. With one of the more expensive modems, especially if it is not very old, it would probably be worthwhile contacting the manufacturer's service department to get an estimate for repairing it.

Internal modems

With an internal modem, first check the cable and the telephone line, as described in the previous section. Also make the usual checks for an expansion card that is giving problems. Remove it from the PC and reinstall it, preferably in a different expansion slot. If it still does not work try it in another computer. This will require the modem to be installed in the new PC, which should be quite straightforward for older style modems. For a Windows modem it will require a large amount of driver software to be installed, although most of these installation procedures are largely automatic. The instruction manual for the modem should give concise installation instructions. If a large amount of driver software has to be installed it might be worthwhile reinstalling the driver software on the original PC before trying another PC. It is not unknown for complex driver software to become corrupted, and reinstalling the drivers should cure the problem if this occurs.

With some devices it can be difficult to get rid of the corrupted drivers, and they can tend to keep reappearing. The usual solution when this occurs is to delete the drivers in Windows Device Manager and then shutdown and switch off the PC so that the device can be physically removed. Then reboot the PC so that it runs without the problem device present. After shutting down and switching off the PC again, refit the card, switch on the PC, and finally reinstall the drivers "from scratch". This should result in a totally "clean" copy of the drivers being installed, and normal operation should then be resumed.

If the drivers refuse to install it is probably because the hardware is faulty, and when the drivers check that the correct hardware is present they fail to detect it. This could also be caused by a bad connection, so make quite sure that the card is properly installed in its expansion slot and that it is making good contact with the connector on the card. If the modem card fails to work in any slot in the original PC, and will not work in another PC, it is certainly faulty and a new card must be installed. If the new card is exactly the same as the old one it should just be a matter of installing the new card and then using the computer without the need for any software installation. In practice the operating system may have detected that there was a problem with the old card, and could go through a reinstallation routine. Things move on quickly in the PC world, and it is very likely that the new card will not be the same as the old one. It is then advisable to make sure that the old drivers are deleted in Windows Device Manager before the new modem card is installed. This ensures that the operating system is not fooled into thinking that there are conflicts between the old modem and the new one.

Motherboard, Memory, Processor

Memory problems

The processor and memory are separate entities, but could also be considered part of the motherboard. Hence we will consider these three parts of a PC together in this chapter. If a PC is failing to operate correctly and you have eliminated possibilities such as a faulty video card, power supply unit, or hard disc drive, you then have to turn your attention to the motherboard, processor and memory. Determining which of these is faulty can be difficult and time consuming. In some cases the computer will work perfectly well for much of the time, with only the occasional glitch. This could be due to a problem with any of the components under consideration here, but is most likely to be caused by an iffy memory chip or processor. We will consider memory problems first, since these are probably the most likely to occur.

Often a memory problem will become apparent during the initial BIOS start-up routine, either because an error message is produced or because the amount of memory reported is inaccurate. With the early PCs you could manually adjust the memory setting via the BIOS Setup program, but a modern BIOS automatically detects the memory and enters the appropriate figure on to the standard BIOS page. If the figure it reports is inaccurate it is possible that the BIOS is at fault, or that there is a problem with the motherboard, but it is far more likely that the problem lies in the memory itself. The BIOS might report that the problem is in a particular bank of memory, or even in a specific memory module, but often you will know nothing more than that there is a fault somewhere in the memory circuits.

If you are dealing with an old PC that has the memory in the form of numerous chips in sockets on the motherboard, life tends to become very difficult when a memory error occurs. Things are much easier with any reasonably modern PC that has memory modules. Rather than having to find which one of two or three dozen memory chips is at fault you only have between one and about six memory modules to deal with. On the downside, when you throw away a memory module you are likely to be disposing of one faulty chip and three or more perfectly good ones. This is rather wasteful and expensive, especially when replacing high capacity modules, but there is no practical alternative.

With no help from the BIOS in locating the faulty memory module there will probably be no alternative to using substitution testing. It is important to bear in mind that many types of memory module are used in pairs. If you have (say) four memory modules on the motherboard, the obvious way to locate the faulty module is to remove all four of them, and then tried them one by one on their own. With some types of memory module this approach is perfectly valid, and it is usually quite acceptable with modern DIMMs. It will not usually work with SIMMs, since with one or two exceptions no motherboards that use these modules can use them in the odd numbers. If you have a module of the correct type that can be used for substitution testing, things become much easier. However, bear in mind that each size of memory module exists in various types of RAM, speed rating, etc., and that you must be careful to ensure that any module used for test purposes is of exactly the right type. The test module can be tried in place of the existing modules, working through them one by one until the PC works normally. The module that is not installed when the PC works properly is clearly the faulty module.

It is probably worthwhile trying the faulty module back in the PC again just to double check that it is genuinely faulty. Memory modules tend to suffer from similar problems to expansion cards, and can appear to be faulty when the problem is simply a bad connection. Also, there can be problems in getting some memory modules fitted into their holders correctly. I have mainly found this problem with 72-pin SIMMs rather than the 30-pin variety or with DIMMs. When memory problems occur it is worthwhile removing and carefully reinstalling the modules, and it could be worth trying some contact cleaner as well.

Removing modules

Removing a SIMM is usually quite straightforward, and it is just a matter of pulling the metal clips at each end of the module outwards. The memory module should then drop forwards at an angle of around 45 degrees, and it can then be pulled clear of the holder. In practice things are not always quite this easy, and the close spacing of the modules can

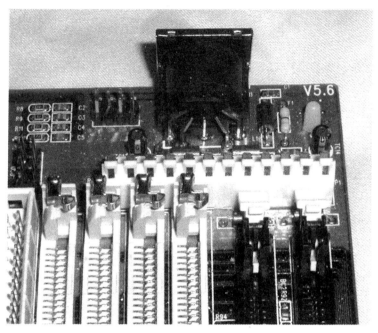

Fig.5.1 SIMM (left) and DIMM (right) retaining clips

give minor problems. One module may be prevented from falling forwards by a module in front of it. This means that you have to remove the front module first, and then work towards the back removing the modules one by one. They can be reluctant to drop forwards, but a little gentle persuasion should do the trick. However, never use force to get a module into or out of its holder. The modules themselves are actually quite tough, but the holders on the motherboard can be distorted and rendered useless if they are not treated with due care.

DIMMs are locked into their sockets using a different method. If you look at a DIMM in its holder you will notice that there is a simple plastic clip at each end which holds it in place. If both clips are pulled outwards the DIMM will be released, and should rise slightly out of its socket. It can then be easily pulled clear of the holder. Again, if a DIMM is reluctant to part company with its holder do not be tempted to use force. This could easily result in damage to the holder. If a DIMM will not pull free from its socket it is because one of the retaining clips has not been fully pulled out into the release position. Figure 5.1 shows the retaining clips on four SIMM holders (left) and two DIMM sockets (right).

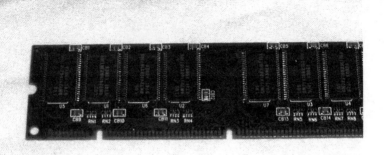

Fig,5.2 The two polarising keys in a DIMM

Fitting memories

As pointed out in chapter one, there are various types of memory available in each size of module, so make quite sure that you identify the faulty memory module correctly and obtain a suitable replacement. There is little chance of the PC working properly if you fit a memory module that contains the wrong type of RAM, lacks the parity bit when it should have it, or something of this nature.

Fitting DIMMs is very easy, and it is impossible to fit them the wrong way round because the DIMM's circuit board has a polarising "key". This is just an off-centre notch cut in the circuit board that matches a bar in the DIMM socket (Figure 5.2). In fact there are two of these keys, and they are apparently in slightly different positions depending on the supply voltage of the module and the type of RAM fitted. This should make it impossible to fit a DIMM of the wrong type. Because one notch and bar are well off-centre it is easy to determine in which way around the module should go. The module simply drops into place vertically and as it is pressed down into position the plastic lever at each end of the socket should start to close up. Pressing both levers into a fully vertical position should securely lock the module in place, if the levers do not snap into this position anyway. Make sure the levers are pulled fully outwards before you try to fit the DIMM. Figures 5.3 and 5.4 respectively show a DIMM that is ready to be pushed down into place and one that is locked in position.

Fig.5.3 A DIMM fitted in its holder but not locked in place

Fig.5.4 The DIMM with the retaing clips locked in place

In my opinion at any rate, SIMMs are slightly more awkward to fit. Although in theory it is impossible to fit a 72-pin SIMM the wrong way round, in practice it does happen occasionally. This seems to be due to the rather flimsy and slightly too basic SIMM holders used on some motherboards. There is the usual polarising notch in the module and matching bar in the socket, but they are small and only very slightly off-centre. Also, there is one corner of the circuit board missing. The old 30 pin SIMMs are somewhat easier to deal with.

When fitting SIMMs, orient the motherboard so that the sides of the sockets having the metal clips are facing towards you, and the plain sides are facing away from you. Take the first SIMM and fit it into the first socket, which is the one that is furthest away from you. The SIMM must be leaning toward you at about 45 degrees and not fully vertical. Figure 5.5 shows a properly positioned module, but viewed from the other side in order to give a clearer view of things. Once it is right down into the socket it should lock into place properly if it is raised to the vertical position (Figure 5.6). If it refuses to fit into position properly it is almost certainly the wrong way round. If you turn it through 180 degrees and try again it should fit into place correctly. You can then move on to the next socket, and fit the next SIMM in the same way. Because SIMMs

Fig.5.5 A SIMM fitted in its holder and ready to be locked in place

Fig.5.6 Raising the SIMM into a vertical position locks it in the holder

have to be inserted into their sockets at an angle, and the sockets are tightly grouped on the motherboard, you normally have to fit them in the right order. Otherwise you put in one SIMM which then blocks access to the socket for one of the others. You therefore have to work your way along the sockets in a methodical fashion. When replacing a SIMM it might be necessary to temporarily remove some of the others in order to gain access to the one you wish to replace.

Chip memory

You will only encounter memory in the form of individual chips on the motherboard if you are dealing with a pretty old PC. Provided the memory is fitted on the motherboard in sockets it should not be too difficult to remove and replace the memory chips. Special tools for removing integrated circuits are available, but in most cases they can be removed by prising one end free with the blade of a small screwdriver (Figure 5.7), and then repeating the process at the other end. If necessary repeat this process a couple of times to get each chip really loose so that it can be pulled free without difficulty. It is often difficult to see exactly what you are doing when removing chips, so be careful not to get the blade of the screwdriver between the board and the holder. Fortunately this is very difficult or impossible with most holders, but with some types you can seriously damage the holder and the board if you are not careful.

Fig.5.7 Prising an integrated circuit from its holder

Replacing a chip that has been removed should not be difficult, because the pins will probably be formed to accurately match up with the socket. Matters are usually less straightforward with new chips, where the pins are splayed out slightly and will not fit into the holders. In fact the pins of a chip can tend to spring outwards slightly when it is removed from its holder, so the same problem can arise when refitting a chip on the board. The easy solution is to press each row of pins against the worktop to bring them into the correct position (refer back to Figure 3.25 in chapter three). The chip should then fit into the holder without difficulty, but always proceed slowly and carefully when fitting chips. If you go about things a little too hastily or without paying due care and attention it is likely that one or more of the pins will buckle instead of fitting into the holder correctly.

Should a pin buckle outward it will be fairly easy to spot, but if it buckles underneath the body of the chip everything may look all right. Make sure all the pins are properly aligned with the holder and starting to slot into it correctly before pushing the chip fully into place. It should not take a lot of force to fit a chip into its socket, so look carefully to see what is wrong if a chip can not be pushed into place with moderate pressure.

The chips must be fitted the right way round, and will almost certainly be destroyed if they are fitted with the wrong orientation. The pin one end of the chip is indicated by a notch, "dimple", or line at that end of the chip, of any combination of these (refer back to Figure 3.24 in chapter three). The motherboard and (or) the integrated circuit holders are usually marked in some way to indicate the correct orientation of the chip. For example, pin one of each holder is often marked on the motherboard, and most integrated circuit holders have the notch to indicate the pin-1 end of the holder. However, as always, it does not do any harm to take notes and make some sketches so that you can easily reassemble everything correctly.

Processor

If you suspect that the processor is faulty, check that the motherboard is set up correctly for the processor in use. With many modern motherboards this means going into the BIOS Setup program to see if the processor settings are correct. The BIOS will probably refer to the processor as the CPU (central processing unit) incidentally. With most motherboards it is a matter of checking that the configuration jumpers or switches on the motherboard are set correctly, and that there are no bad contacts. Remove and replace the jumpers, or set the switches to the wrong setting and back to the right one a couple of times per switch. If there are any obvious signs of corrosion on any jumper terminals, clean them with contact cleaner.

Remember that the correct processor settings are often something less than obvious. The manual for the motherboard should give the correct settings for all the processors it supports, but it is a good idea to look on the processor itself to see if it is marked with the main parameters. Where there is conflicting information between the motherboard's manual and the processor itself, always set up the motherboard using the parameters given on the processor. Some processors exist in more than one version, and the only way of determining the correct settings for these is to look at the markings on the chip itself. The main parameters, and usually the only ones, are the processor's core voltage, the bus speed of the motherboard, and the multiplier value. The processor operates "x" times faster than the motherboard, and with a 450MHz Pentium III for example, the motherboard operates at 100MHz and processor operates with a multiplier value of 4.5.

If the motherboard is set up correctly and the BIOS is producing messages that suggest the processor is being identified correctly, any problem is presumably due to a fault in either the processor or motherboard. In order to get to the root of the problem some substitution testing is required, and it is easier to swap processors than motherboards. In fact substitution testing with motherboards is not very practical due to ɘ large amount of work involved in changing this component. It is a matter of eliminating all the other possibilities so that the only possible cause of the fault is the motherboard. The motherboard must then be replaced, even if it does require a large amount of time and effort.

Right processor

Each motherboard only accepts certain processors, and substitution testing is only feasible if you have two PCs that have some degree of processor compatibility. Ideally you would swap the two processors of the faulty PC and the test bed computer. However, if you can only try another processor in the faulty PC or the processor out the faulty PC in another PC, that should tell you all you need to know. If the processor from the faulty PC works in another computer it is reasonably certain that the motherboard in the faulty PC is the cause of the problem. If the processor fails to work when tried in another PC, it is certainly the processor that is at fault. Life is easier if the two computers use precisely the same processor, as this avoids having to reconfigure either of the motherboards. If the processors are of a different type, make sure that any necessary reconfiguring of the motherboards is undertaken before any swapping of the processors takes place. Also remember to do any reconfiguration that is required before any processors are returned to their original homes.

If you do not have a PC that can provide a processor for test purposes, a new processor must be purchased. This is slightly risky, since it is possible that the old processor is not the cause of the problem, and that the new processor will not ultimately be used. In this case it would simply eliminate the processor as a possible cause of the problem. Things move on in the PC world, and it is possible that for a modest price you will be able to obtain a better processor than the one currently in the PC. If the processor is not the cause of the problem, the new processor will at least give you a faster PC for your expenditure, and the money will not have been wasted. Before buying a newer and faster processor, make quite sure that the motherboard can accommodate it. The motherboard's manual should give a full list of the compatible processors and the correct settings for them. It is also worthwhile taking a look at the motherboard manufacturer's web site to see if there are any updates that apply to the board you are using. There might be settings for additional processors, and (or) a BIOS update that enables further processors to be accommodated.

With PCs that are a few years old it is increasingly common for the upgrade strategy to be taken a stage further. Do not bother to find whether the fault is in the processor, motherboard, or memory, but instead replace all three! This may seem a wasteful approach, which to some degree it is. Clearly it is also an expensive way of tackling the repair, since it involves replacing components that are in perfect working order. On the other hand, for your money you will get a repaired PC that will typically be around two to 10 times faster than the original, and it will probably have much more memory as well. When viewed as a simple repair the amount of money spent will be quite large, but with the increased capabilities of the computer taken into account it will probably still look like a real bargain. The "new" PC will be able to run your existing software much more quickly, and it will be capable of running new software that was beyond the capabilities of the original PC.

I suppose that one reason for the increase in major upgrades as a method of repairing older PCs is that suitable spares for older PCs can be difficult to obtain. If you require an AT format Socket 7 motherboard there should be plenty available, and they should all be able to accommodate a wide range of processors. However, if you have an early Pentium processor it may be incompatible with the many of these motherboards. Older microprocessors can be difficult to obtain, and are not stocked by many PC component suppliers. If you are lucky you might be able to find one that has been left unsold for some time, and it could well be on offer at a bargain price. It is more likely that you will end up paying a high "spare part" price. Older forms of memory are still available, albeit not as widely as was once the case, but price is again something of a problem. Older forms of memory seem to cost at least twice as much as an equivalent amount of modern RAM, and in some cases very much more than this. Upgrading your way out of trouble will almost certainly be more expensive than a straightforward repair, but it is in some ways a more simple option since there will be plenty of modern parts at low prices to choose from. Also, you are getting a major increase in performance for your money as well as getting the PC repaired.

Socket 7

When changing a Socket 7 processor it is necessary to proceed carefully as they have large numbers of pins that can easily become bent. If even one pin becomes slightly bent it will probably be impossible to fit the processor into its socket until the pin has been carefully straightened.

Socket Locked

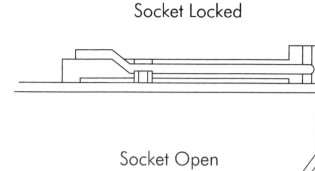

Socket Open

CPU

Fig.5.8 The ZIF socket is opened by raising the lever

This can be done with the aid of a small screwdriver blade, but is best avoided. It is more than a little tricky and can be very time consuming if several pins have to be straightened. Unless your eyesight is very good at short ranges you will probably need the aid of a magnifier.

Removing and installing a processor is much the same for Socket 7 and Socket 370 devices, which are conventional integrated circuits. Both types of socket are forms of ZIF (zero insertion force) holders. Conventional integrated circuit holders, even when used with integrated circuits that have only a few pins, are something less than easy to use. It is often quite difficult to squeeze the integrated circuits into them. The Socket 7 and Socket 370 chips have literally hundreds of pins. In fact the "370" in the Socket 370 name refers to the number of pins. Getting

Fig.5.9 A missing hole in
          the socket (bottom
          left corner) makes it
          impossible to fit the
          processor the wrong
          way around

Fig.5.10 A dot and a
           chamfered corner
           indicate the missing
           pin and the correct
           orientation for the
           chip

a chip of this size into a holder could be bordering on the impossible,
but the situation is greatly eased by the use of ZIF sockets. The holder
has a lever that is raised to the vertical position in order to open the
socket (Figure 5.8). The lever normally has to be pulled outwards slightly
in order to unlock it before it can be raised. With the socket open the
processor should simply pull free and the replacement should then drop
into place without any difficulty. Return the lever to its original position
to lock the processor in place.

The processor must be fitted with the correct orientation, and with modern
socket processors it impossible to fit a processor the wrong way round.
If you look at the socket you will find that there are three corners that
have provision for a pin on the processor, and one that does not (Figure

5.9). It is this missing hole in the socket that prevents the processor from fitting into it unless the processor has the correct orientation. If you look at the upper surface of the processor you will find a dot in one corner, and that corner of the casing will probably be chamfered as well (Figure 5.10). If you match that corner of the chip with the missing hole in the socket, the processor should drop easily into place.

If you are dealing with a pre Pentium board I would certainly recommend upgrading to a new motherboard, processor, and memory, rather than opting for a replacement processor. However, if you are determined to simply replace the old processor and a suitable replacement can be found, in the case of 80386 and 80486 chips it will not look much different to a Socket 7 or Socket 370 processor. It will be approximately square with large numbers of pins on the underside. The processor will almost certainly be fitted in a socket, but it might not be a ZIF type. If the processor is not fitted in a socket it is not practical to replace it, and a new motherboard and processor will be required. If the socket is a ZIF type it should be similar to a Socket 7 holder, but will probably differ in points of detail. Changing the processor is then just a matter of setting the socket to the open position, lifting the old processor clear, fitting the new one, and locking the socket again.

If the socket is a non-ZIF type the processor must be prised free. Use the blade of a small screwdriver to gradually lever it free, moving around the processor until all four edges have been lifted free of the socket. Start with a minimal amount of force at first, but be prepared to use more force if the processor is reluctant to leave its socket. Having been in the socket for many years it may well need a fair amount of force to remove it. It will probably require a fair amount of pressure to get the new chip into the socket. Note that with some of these older processors it might be possible to fit them into the socket the wrong way round, so make sure that you accurately identify pin one on the socket and the processor, and that you get the processor fitted with the correct orientation.

Processors prior to the 80386 series are rather like scaled-up memory chips, and are removed and fitted in much the same way. However, with 40 or more pins you have to be more careful about getting the chip properly aligned with the holder before fully inserting the chip. ZIF sockets were little used with these early processors incidentally, and a fair percentage were soldered direct to the motherboard.

Slot 1

Slot processors do not use conventional integrated circuit holders, but instead fit into a socket that is more like a holder for memory modules or an ordinary PCI expansion slot. The slot style processors are often referred to as "cartridges", and in appearance they are more like some

form of video cartridge than a conventional integrated circuit. In common with PCI slots and DIMM holders, there is an off-centre break in the rows of connections that makes way for a polarising key in the casing of the processor (Figure 5.11). This makes it easy to see which way round the processor should be inserted into the slot, and makes it impossible to fit it the wrong way round. A

Fig.5.11   The Slot 1 polarising key

cartridge holder is needed to keep the processor firmly in position, and this should be clearly visible at both ends of the processor. The Pentium II or III processor simply pushes down into the slot, and no more than moderate pressure should be needed to get it into place. As it moves down into position the clips on the cartridge holder will close and lock it in place. In order to remove the processor push the clips to the open position and pull the processor free.

Heatsink

Modern processors soon overheat without the aid of a cooling system, but in the pre-Pentium era it was rare for processors to be fitted with heatsinks. Some 80486 were in fact fitted with heatsinks, and these were usually glued to the top of the chip. If you replace a processor of this type it could be impossible to remove the heatsink from the old processor, and a new heatsink will be required.

With Socket 7 and 370 chips, removing and fitting the heatsink and fan can be rather fiddly and in some cases you may find that the heatsink does not clip in place really securely. The side-on view of Figure 5.12 shows the simple method of fixing that seems to be used for all Socket 7 and 370 heatsinks. Fitting the heatsink is just a matter of fitting one end of the spring clip on the heatsink under one of the plastic retaining clips on the socket. Without letting this end slip out of position, the other end of the clip is then secured on the other side of the socket. With some combinations of heatsink and processor it is a rather tight fit, but once the heatsink is actually in place it should stay there and work efficiently.

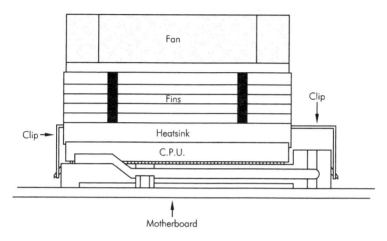

Fig.5.12 The heatsink and fan clip on to the ZIF socket

If the heatsink is a loose fit it may not work very well, and there is a real risk that before long it will become dislodged. If you look carefully at the clip that secures the heatsink to the motherboard you will probably find that part of the clip can be removed and repositioned further up the main section of the clip. Using this second position should result in the heatsink and fan being held in place much more securely.

With some processors, particularly the faster Socket 370 types, there may be a pad of a rather sticky rubber-like material on top of the processor. This is designed to ensure that there is a good thermal connection between the processor and the heatsink. Do not remove this pad and be careful not to damage it. Doing either of these could seriously reduce the efficiency of the heatsink, and could even result in the processor overheating.

Removing a heatsink is just a matter of pressing down on the appropriate side of the clip to free it from the holder, and moving it outwards to completely free it. With some heatsinks simply pressing down on the clip will result in it moving outwards and completely free of the holder. Others can be reluctant to properly unclip themselves, and a small screwdriver blade can then be inserted between the holder and the clip. With the clip pressed down it can then be gently levered free from the holder using the screwdriver.

Slot 1 heatsinks seem to vary somewhat in the way that they are mounted on the processor. Usually it is just a matter of slackening off four screws, fitting the heatsink assembly in position, and then tightening the screws to clamp it in place. Apparently another type simply clips in place, but I have no first hand experience of these. Either way it might be a bit tricky to fit everything together, but the way in which it all fits together and comes apart again should be fairly obvious.

Fig.5.13 A fan that takes its power from a 5.25-inch drive power lead

Fan

Apart from a few early examples, Pentium class processors have a cooling fan in addition to the heatsink. The cooling fan can usually be removed from the heatsink, but there is usually no point in doing so. Unless there is a good reason to remove it, leave the fan on the heatsink. The cooling fan will require a 12-volt supply, and there are two normal ways of obtaining this. In the past the most common method was to obtain power from one of the 5.25-in. disc drive supply outputs of the power supply unit. There will not always be a spare output of this type, but the fan will almost certainly be fitted with a lead that has two connectors (Figure 5.13). One of these connects to the output of the power supply and other connects to a 5.25-in. drive. This enables a single output of the power supply to provide power to both the cooling fan and one of the drives. The alternative method, and by far the most common one on recent PCs, is to power the fan from the motherboard. Virtually all modern motherboards have a small three-pin connector that can supply 12 volts to the cooling fan, and most processor cooling fans are now fitted with this type of connector (Figure 5.14). There is no need to worry about getting this connector fitted the right way round, because it will only fit with the correct orientation.

In most cases it will not be necessary to disconnect the cooling fan when changing the processor. However, once the processor has been changed it is essential to check that the supply to the fan has not been accidentally disconnected. Without the aid of the cooling fan it is likely that the processor would soon overheat. Some motherboards have temperature

Fig.5.14 A fan that takes power from the motherboard has a standard three-way power connector

sensors and automatic cutouts or warnings, but with most of the older boards there is no warning if the processor starts to get dangerously hot.

Motherboard

If the motherboard is faulty and has to be replaced, or you opt to repair the PC by implementing an upgrade of the motherboard, processor, and memory, a fair amount of work is involved. An experienced PC repairer can actually undertake a change of motherboard in an hour or two, but for those who are new to this type of thing it is important to take a more leisurely approach. The important thing is to complete the task successfully, and not to do it in world record time. The approach taken to changing the motherboard depends on whether the new board is the same as the old one. In most cases the original motherboard will be long out of production and no longer available. Buying a newer motherboard is then the only option. In the unlikely event that the original motherboard is still available, you can make notes and some quick drawings to show how the various leads connect to the motherboard. Even if you have the manual for the motherboard, I would still recommend making notes and drawings. Following these should ensure that everything is put back together to precisely match the original configuration.

Next everything is disconnected from the motherboard, and the board is removed from the case. The processor and memory are then transferred to the new board, and where appropriate the configuration jumpers or switches on the new board are set to match the settings used on the old board. This assembly is then mounted in the case, and everything is reconnected to the motherboard. Although one might reasonably expect the repaired PC to work exactly as before, it will almost certainly fail to do so.

It has to be remembered here that a change in motherboard is also a change of BIOS, and it will therefore be necessary to enter the BIOS Setup program and make any necessary changes to the settings. Also, some operating systems may detect that there has been a change to the hardware, and might undertake a certain amount of reinstallation when the new system is first booted. I do not know if this is really necessary, but there is probably no way of dissuading the operating system from going through its routine.

If there is a change of motherboard things proceed in a similar fashion, but there is probably nothing to be gained by making notes and drawing of the original cabling to the motherboard. You must rely on the instruction manual for the new motherboard when reconnecting everything. You can not simply copy configuration settings from the original motherboard either, since the new board will have its own way of doing things. Again, the motherboard's instruction manual should tell you everything you need to know. As before, the BIOS must be configured once the new motherboard has been installed.

With an operating system such as Windows 98 it is virtually certain that it will detect the change of motherboard and start to install any new hardware, and some of the existing hardware may be reinstalled. On the face of it this is unnecessary, but it has to be borne in mind that many operating systems install drivers to support hardware on the motherboard. The new motherboard will probably have different support chips to those fitted on the old motherboard, and it will therefore require different driver software. The operating system may have this software as part of its standard driver set, or you may have to use the drivers supplied with the motherboard. The motherboard's instruction manual should give details of the drivers supplied with it, and how they are installed.

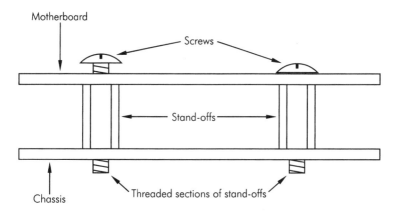

Fig.5.15 The most common form of stand-off for motherboards

Stand-offs

Before trying to remove the motherboard make sure that all leads, including the power supply lead or leads, have been disconnected from it. The motherboard is mounted on the metal base panel or side panel of the case, but it is essential that the connections on the underside of the board are held well clear of this panel so that short-circuits are avoided. The board is therefore mounted on some form of stand-off. Sometimes these are metal and are built into the chassis, but more usually they are metal and are screwed into the chassis (Figure 5.15). The motherboard is fitted to these types of stand-off by screws that fit into threaded holes in the stand-offs. There will usually be at least one stand-off of this type, since at least one of these is required to provide a low resistance connection from the motherboard to the chassis. It is possible that they will all be of this type, and then it should be very easy to remove the motherboard.

With all the mounting bolts removed, and there will usually be about five of them, it should be possible to lift the board clear of the case. With some types of case there can be obstructions that make it difficult to lift the board clear, and the 3.5-inch drive bays tend to get in the way with some of the smaller cases. If necessary, obstructions of this type must be temporarily removed, and reinstated when the new motherboard has been fitted.

Motherboard

Screw

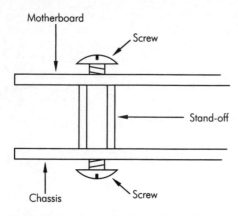

Stand-off

Chassis

Screw

Fig.5.16 An alternative form of stand-off

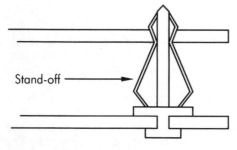

Stand-off

Fig.5.17 A plastic stand-off clips into place

A similar type of stand-off is fixed in place by a screw, as in Figure 5.16. There are also plastic types that clip into the motherboard and then slide into cutouts in the chassis, and this type is also depicted in Figure 5.17. These operate in conjunction with one or two metal stand-offs that enable the board to be bolted in place, and provide an electrical connection from the earth rail of the motherboard to the case. The slide-in approach can be a bit awkward in practice with some of the stand-offs tending to buckle under the board rather than sliding nicely into place. When fitting a board using this type of mounting always check that everything has fitted into place correctly. If there are any signs of problems slide the motherboard back out again and try again, and do not simply leave the board supported by buckled stand-offs. They may fall out of position and permit the board to short-circuit to the case. There are other types of stand-off in use, but they are mostly variations on the types described here. It should not be too difficult to work out how other types are used.

In order to remove the motherboard you must look carefully so as to see how it is held in place, remove any fixing screws, and then slide or pull it clear of the case. If you are unlucky the motherboard will to some extent be mounted on plastic stand-offs that are bolted to the chassis. If it is possible to gain access to the rear side of the chassis plate the stand-offs should be dismounted so that the motherboard can be pulled free, complete with the plastic stand-offs. It will still be necessary to remove the stand-offs from the motherboard so that they can be moved over to the new motherboard, but this operation is usually much easier once the board has been removed from the case. In order to remove the stand-offs the top section must be squeezed inwards slightly using pliers, and the board can then be slid upwards and clear of the mounting. You have to release the pliers at just the right moment so that the motherboard can be lifted clear of the mounting, but you should soon get the knack of this.

Size variations

It is virtually certain that the new motherboard will not be the same size and shape as the original. However, provided you use an AT board for an AT style case or an ATX board for an ATX case there should be no major problems. The board should still fit into the case properly, and sockets, etc., should align with the cutouts in the case. Note that it is possible to use most modern AT motherboards in an ATX case because they have both types of power connector, and ATX cases normally have provision for the off-board serial and parallel port connectors of an AT motherboard. On the other hand, there is a much better selection of ATX motherboards available, and there is probably no point in complicating matters by opting for an AT motherboard with an ATX case.

The new motherboard might have mounting holes that precisely match up with those of the original, but there will probably be one or two differences. These differences occur because modern motherboards do not usually have a full set of mounting holes, and typically have just five of these holes. Depending on the size of the board, there will be either six or nine mounting points for it on the case. It is important not to have a metal stand-off in the case at a point where there is no mounting hole in the board. This could result in connections on the underside of the board being short-circuited to the case.

If necessary, remove any metal stand-offs that are not required, and where appropriate relocate them to a position where they can be used. Having done any necessary juggling with the metal stand-offs, fit any plastic types that are required and then carefully fit the motherboard back into position. Replace the mounting screws, and the board is then ready for the cables and expansion cards to be fitted.

There should be no problems when fitting the data cables provided you remember that the red lead denotes lead one of each cable (Figure

Fig.5.18 The red lead (left) indicates pin-1 of the connector

5.18). Pin one of each connector on the motherboard is often marked on the motherboard itself, but there will be diagrams in the instruction manual that provide this information if you can not find it on the board. Motherboards are almost invariably supplied complete with a basic set of data leads. On the face of it there is no point in using these, and it is better to take the easy course and use the leads already in the PC. This may work properly in some cases, but in others there is no option but to use the leads supplied with the board. There are two issues here. Firstly, the data cables for the drives are well standardised, and the existing cables should provide the right connections. The potential problem is due to differences in the methods used to polarise these connectors. There are three methods:

1.   No polarising key at all

2.   The usual cutout in one connector and matching lump on the other

3.   As above plus one pin missing on one connector and the corresponding hole blanked off in the other

It is the third type of cable that is the main cause of problems. If the existing connectors have blanked holes for the missing pins on the motherboard connectors, but the connectors actually have this pin, it will not be possible to fit the existing cables to the new motherboard. It is not too difficult to drill out the pieces of plastic covering the holes in the connectors, but this requires a fine drill bit of around 0.7 to one millimetre in diameter. It is easier to use the data cables provided with the motherboard, which will presumably match the motherboard correctly.

The second problem only occurs with AT boards and the leads that carry the connections to the serial and parallel port connectors at the rear of the PC, and possibly other connectors such as those for mouse and USB ports. Although they may look very much the same, the serial and parallel port leads supplied with motherboards are quite definitely not all the same. You could certainly end up with a non-operating port

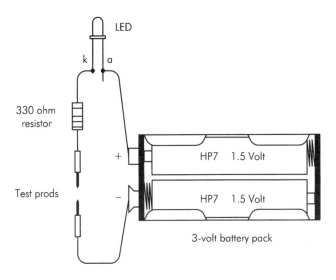

Fig.5.19 A simple low current continuity tester

by using the lead from one motherboard with a different motherboard. The safe option is to change to the leads that came with the new motherboard, but it is possible to do a quick check to determine if the existing leads are suitable. This involves connecting the leads to the motherboard and then making a simple check with a continuity tester. However, a torch bulb continuity tester of the type described earlier is not suitable for this type of testing. The test current used is too high, and could damage the port hardware.

Only use a proper test meter that is designed for this sort of testing. Alternatively, use a modernised version of the continuity tester that uses a LED rather than a torch bulb. Figure 5.19 shows a suitable arrangement. All the parts should be available from a shop or mail order company selling electronic components and equipment. Note that the LED will only work if it is connected the right way round. The cathode ("k") terminal is normally indicated by that lead being shorter than the anode ("a") lead and the cathode side of the body is usually (but not always) flattened slightly. Do not omit the resistor. Without this component a high current will flow, resulting in almost instant destruction of the LED.

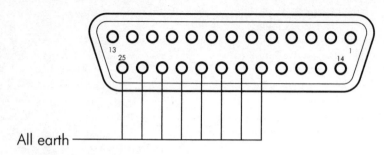

All earth

Fig.5.20 The earthed pins on a parallel port connector

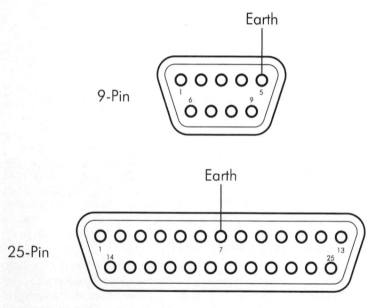

Fig.5.21 The earthed pins on serial port connectors

The quick and easy way of checking that the leads are connected properly is to check for continuity between the chassis of the computer and whichever terminal or terminals of the port connector should be earthed. For a parallel port it is pins 18 to 25 that should be earthed (Figure 5.20). For 25 and 9-pin serial ports it is respectively pins seven and five that should be earthed (Figure 5.21). If the right pins are not earthed and some of the other pins are earthed, either the cable is connected incorrectly at the motherboard or the cable is unsuitable. Only carry out continuity checks while the PC is switched off. There seems to be a great variety of USB leads in use, so I would only recommend using the USB lead supplied with the motherboard. Note that this lead may not be supplied as standard with the motherboard, and is often an optional extra.

The serial and parallel port connectors on motherboards are often simplified versions of IDE connectors, making it possible to connect the lead either way round. With a motherboard of this type you must refer to the manual to find pin one on each of the connectors, and then make quite sure that the red lead of the cable connects to this pin. It is also possible to fit many of these connectors one row of pins out of alignment. Fortunately, these cut-down connectors are now relatively rare, but due care needs to be taken if you should encounter a motherboard that uses them.

Power supply

The power supply of an ATX case connects to the motherboard by way of a single cable, which has a polarised connector (Figure 5.22). Consequently you can only fit it the right way round. This type of connector can be rather unyielding, and it is not a good idea to simply go on pushing harder until it fits into place or the board gives way! With a really stiff and awkward power connector the safest approach is to remove the motherboard again. Then fit the power connector while using one hand to support the board underneath the power connector, so

Fig.5.22 ATX power connectors

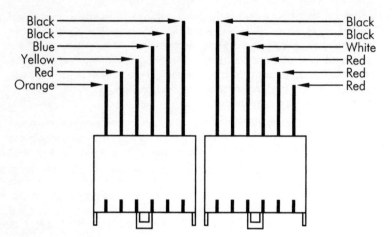

Fig.5.23 With AT power leads connected correctly the black leads are grouped together in the middle

that you can use really firm pressure without damaging anything. Having fitted the connector in place the board is then carefully manoeuvred back into the case and fixed in position.

An AT power supply has two power cables, and although the connectors on these are polarised, they are identical (or something close to it), and it is possible to get them swapped over. The motherboard's instruction manual should show which one connects to each terminal block on the motherboard, but all you have to remember is that the black leads should be grouped together in the middle (Figure 5.23). If the black leads are at each end of the line of leads, the power plugs are the wrong way round. In the event of a mistake the power supply should actually detect that the power leads are not connected correctly, and it will then fail to switch on. This should prevent any damage to the motherboard, but with anything like this it is as well not to put it to the "acid test" just in case things go awry.

The expansion cards may all fit perfectly into place, but it is quite common for some of them to give problems. This happens because the motherboard is not positioned perfectly in the case. The easy solution is to first slacken off the mounting bolts for the motherboard so that it is free to move around to a limited degree. Then fit the expansion cards, and once they are properly in place retighten the mounting bolts for the motherboard.

Connector block

The motherboard will have a connector block that accepts leads from various items on the case (Figure 5.24). This block is a common cause of confusion for newcomers to PC repair, because the facilities of the case never seem to perfectly match up with those of the motherboard. A typical set of connectors for an ATX case is shown in Figure 5.25.

Fig.5.24 A typical connector block

There may be some features of the case that are not supported by the motherboard, and there will almost certainly be several motherboard features that the case is unable to accommodate. This is something where you have to take a down to earth attitude, and provided a few basic features are implemented on both, which they will be, that is all that is needed to get your repaired PC operating successfully. These are the functions that you should be able to implement:

Power LED

This connects to what is usually a green LED on the front of the case that switches on whenever the computer is operating. Note that an LED, unlike an ordinary light bulb, will only work if it is connected with the right polarity. The instruction manual for the motherboard will have a diagram showing the functions of the various pins in the block, and this with have a "+" sign on one of the pins that connects to the power LED. The connectors on the leads that connect to the LEDs, etc., will be marked with their functions, and the connector for the power LED might have its polarity marked. If not, it is usually the white lead that

Fig.5.25 A set of ATX case connectors

is the "–" connection and the coloured lead that is the "+" one. There is little risk of an LED being damaged if it is connected with the wrong polarity, so you can use trial and error if necessary.

IDE activity LED

This is sometimes called the hard disc light, and in days gone by it would probably only switch on when the hard disc was active. However, this light actually switches on when any IDE device is active, and these days there will normally be other IDE devices such as CD-ROM drives and CD writers. This LED must be connected with the right polarity.

Reset switch

This is the switch on the front panel that can be used to reset the computer if it hangs up. Its lead can be connected either way round. Some users prefer not to connect this switch, so that it is not possible to accidentally reset the computer. However, without the reset switch the only means of providing a hardware reset is to switch the computer off, wait at least a couple of seconds, and then switch on again.

Loudspeaker

This is the lead for the computer's internal loudspeaker, which is little used in modern computing. This loudspeaker is normally used to produce one or two beeps at start-up to indicate that all is well or a different set of beeps if there is a fault. The leads on this connector will probably be red and black, but it can actually be connected either way round and it is not polarised.

Power switch

This facility is not used with an AT power supply, which is switched on and off by way of an ordinary mains power switch (Figure 5.26). With an ATX power supply the on/off switching is controlled via a signal from the motherboard. The on/off switch connects to the power supply via the motherboard and the supply's main power output lead. Pressing the power switch turns on the computer, pressing it again switches off the computer, and so on. This switch appears to operate like a normal power switch, but note that the computer will be in the off state if the mains supply is removed and then reinstated. This lead can be connected either way round.

These are some of the functions that might be implemented on the motherboard, but they are non-essential:

Keylock

It used to be standard practice for PCs to have a key that could be used to operate a special type of switch fitted on the front panel. This switch

Fig.5.26 An AT power supply unit has a conventional on/off switch

enabled the keyboard to be switched off, thus preventing anyone from tampering with the PC while you were not looking. This feature was never very popular, and when control of PCs was partially handed over to the mouse it failed to fulfil its intended task anyway. It is probably not worth implementing even if this feature is supported by the case.

Temperature warning

Because modern PCs contain a lot of components that get quite hot it is now very common for some sort of temperature monitoring and warning feature to be included on motherboards. Exactly what happens when something in the PC starts to get too hot varies from one motherboard to another, but the internal loudspeaker will probably start to "beep", a warning LED might start flashing, or the PC might even switch itself off. If there is an output for a temperature warning LED and the case has a spare LED indicator, I would recommend implementing this feature. Note that the LED will only work if it is connected the right way round, and that it is normally switched on under standby conditions.

Suspend switch

This switch can be used to enable and disable the power management function. This is probably something you can live without, which is just as well since few cases have the necessary switch. There is sometimes an output for an LED that operates in conjunction with this feature.

There may well be other functions available, and it is a matter of consulting the motherboard's instruction manual for details of any additional features. As time goes by, motherboards seem to gain more and more features. However, unless the case has some spare switches and (or) LEDs any "extras" will only be of academic interest. When fitting a new motherboard into an old PC it is unlikely that the case will be able to accommodate these additional features.

Configuration

If the replacement motherboard is the same as the original, the configuration settings will presumably have been copied from the original board, as described previously. If the new board is different, it may have jumpers or DIP-switches that need to be configured using information provided in its instruction manual. Some motherboards do not require any hardware configuration, but are instead configured using the BIOS Setup program. In fact most of these boards configure themselves using probing techniques to determine what processor is fitted, and manual configuration is only needed if you do not agree with the default settings for some reason.

Whichever method is used, it is essential for the motherboard to be configured correctly. There is a slight risk of damaging the processor if the motherboard is not set up correctly. We will therefore consider the configuration process in some depth here, particularly the type that requires jumpers or DIP-switches to be set, as this is often something less than straightforward. Note that it is best to do any hardware configuration prior to installing the motherboard if access to the board will be difficult once it is fitted in the case.

Manuals for pieces of electronic equipment and computer software tend to get ignored, and are only read as a last resort. This is not an option when dealing with motherboards, and it is essential to read through the manual and constantly refer to it for vital pieces of information. With a hardware configured board you will certainly need to study the instruction manual for details of how to set it up to suit the particular processor you are using. The parameters that are set via the jumpers or switches depends on the type of motherboard in use.

With a Socket 7 motherboard there are usually several things that need to be set up correctly. The processor and motherboard clock speeds must be set, and the two are linked. The correct clock rate for the motherboard is set, and then a multiplier is used to produce the required clock frequency. As a couple of examples, a Celeron processor operating at 500MHz with a 66MHz motherboard clock frequency would require a multiplier value of 7.5 (66 x 7.5 = 495). A Pentium III operating at 500MHz with a 100MHz bus frequency would require a multiplier value of five (100 x 5 = 500).

As will be apparent from the first of these examples, the mathematics is not always perfect. In the Celeron example, the actual processor clock frequency will be slightly lower than its nominal value, or the motherboard bus speed will be fractionally higher (66.66 MHz instead of 66 MHz). It does not really matter which, and there will be no noticeable difference in performance between clock rates of 495 and 500 MHz.

Cyrix clock rates

There is a slight complication with the processor frequency for the Cyrix chips in that their actual clock frequencies are lower than the name of the processor would suggest. Also, there can be more than one version of the chip, with each version requiring a different clock frequency. For example, the 300MHz Cyrix chip has been produced in versions that require 225 and 233MHz clock frequencies. The 300MHz figure is a sort of Intel equivalent rating, and takes into account the fact that the Cyrix processor needs fewer clock cycles to perform some instructions. The actual performance of PC processors depends on the software being run, so any equivalent of this type has to be taken with the proverbial "pinch of salt". Anyway, the actual clock frequency is either 225MHz (75MHz x 3) or 233MHz (66 MHz x 3.5). Although the 233MHz version might be expected to outperform the 225MHz processor, the higher system bus

Fig.5.27 A Cyrix processor marked with the system clock and multiplier values

frequency of the 225MHz chip compensates for the lower processor clock frequency. The two versions therefore have very similar levels of performance.

Obviously there is the potential for confusion with processors that are available in more than one version. How do you know which version of the chip you have? To avoid mistakes these processors have the bus frequency and multiplier marked on the top of the chip, and the correct core voltage is usually indicated as well (Figure 5.27). Always set up the motherboard to suit the clock frequency and multiplier indicated on the processor itself, even if the bus frequency and multiplier stated in the motherboard manual are different. It will always be the multiplier value and bus frequency on the chip itself that will be correct.

Core voltage

With a Socket 7 board it is also necessary to set the processor core voltage. Conventionally logic circuits operate from a 5-volt supply, but in order to get the highest possible performance it is common practice for other supply voltages to be used in parts of the computer. Memory circuits and some sections of the processor often operate at 3.3 volts, and the main processor circuits often work at a somewhat lower voltage. It is this second voltage, or core voltage that is set via the jumpers or DIP-switches. The instruction manual for the motherboard should give the correct settings for all the usable processors. It is common for the correct core voltage to be marked on the top surface of the processor, particularly with non-Intel devices. If the marked core voltage is different to the one indicated on the chip itself, set up the motherboard to provide the voltage indicated on the chip.

There may be other settings to make, but these additional parameters vary a lot from one motherboard to another. One virtually standard feature is a jumper that enables the CMOS memory to be disconnected from the backup battery. By default this should be set so the board functions normally, with the backup battery ensuring that the BIOS is free from amnesia, with the correct drive parameters, etc., being used each time the computer is switched on. Setting this jumper to the "off" position for a few minutes wipes the CMOS memory of all its contents. With the jumper restored to the "on" setting the computer is able to function again, but it is a matter of starting "from scratch" with the CMOS memory settings.

In effect, this jumper provides a means of resetting the CMOS memory. This would be probably only be necessary if someone started to use the password facility and then forgot his or her password. The only way of getting the computer to boot if this happens is to clear the current set-up from memory. The next time the computer is started it uses the default settings, which means that it starts up without implementing the password facility. Unless there is a good reason to do so, it is best not to use any BIOS password facility. Note that it is not necessary to clear the CMOS memory in this way if you manage to make a complete mess of the BIOS settings. From within the BIOS Setup program it is usually possible to revert to one or two sets of default settings, and then do any necessary "fine tuning".

There can be other jumpers or DIP-switches to set such things as the supply voltage for the memory modules, to disable the built-in audio system, and this type of thing. You really have to read the manual for the motherboard to determine what jumpers or DIP-switches have to be set up correctly, if any. The modern trend is towards as much as possible being set using auto-detection methods, or via the BIOS Setup program. Many motherboards only have one switch or jumper that can be used to power-down the CMOS memory.

Setting up

Actually setting any jumpers or switches should not give any major problems. There are two types of jumper, which are the straightforward on/off type and the two-way variety. The on/off type has two pins and you fit the jumper over the pins to connect them together ("on") or do not fit the jumper at all ("off"). This simple scheme of things is shown in Figure 5.28(a). It is common practice to fit the jumper on one of the pins to provide the "off" setting. If you should need to change the setting at a later time you then know exactly where to find the jumper. The jumpers are minute and are likely to get lost if you store them somewhere other than on the motherboard. The second type of jumper block has three pins, and the jumper is used to connect the middle pin to one of the outer pins (Figure 5.28(b)). The jumper is connecting together two pins, as before, and the jumpers are exactly the same whether they are used on a two-pin block or a three-pin type.

DIP-switches are normally in blocks of four or eight switches, but not all the switches in a block will necessarily be utilized. They are a form of slider switch, and are more or less a miniature version of the switches often used in small electronic gadgets such as cassette recorders and personal stereo units. The block of switches is marked with "on" and (or) "off" legends (Figure 5.29) to make it clear which setting is which.

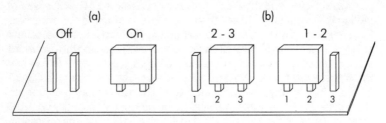

Fig.5.28 The two types of jumper normally used on motherboards

The motherboard's instruction manual normally includes a diagram showing the correct switch or jumper settings for a given processor. There is a slight problem here in that these diagrams are open to misinterpretation. In the two examples of Figure 5.30, which pins do the

Fig.5.29 A typical DIP-switch

jumpers connect and which switches are in the "on" position. My guess would be that the black blocks represent the jumpers and the control knobs on the switches, but there is no way of telling for sure without some further assistance. The manual should provide this assistance in the form of another diagram showing exactly how the switch or jumper setting diagrams

should be interpreted. These diagrams will be something like Figure 5.31 and 5.32. Never rely on guesswork when setting jumpers and DIP-switches. Mistakes are unlikely to result in any damage, but it is not worth taking the risk. Carefully study the instruction manual for the motherboard and get things right first time.

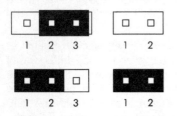
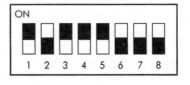

Fig.5.30 Some switch and jumper diagrams are clearer than others

Fig.5.31 An explanatory diagram for jumper settings

Fig.5.32 An explanatory diagram for DIP-switches

1 to 4 = ON

5 to 7 = OFF

CPU configuration

With a new motherboard fitted to a PC it is essential to configure the motherboard before the computer boots for the first time. Configuring the BIOS is covered in chapter two, and will not be covered again here. However, chapter two does not cover motherboards that have their CPU configuration handled via the BIOS, and we will briefly consider this aspect of things here. The parameters controlled by this section of the BIOS depends on the type of processor used, and will be the same as those controlled by jumpers or DIP-switches on a conventional motherboard. With a Socket 7 motherboard it should be possible to control the motherboard clock frequency, core voltage, and the processor clock multiplier. With a Celeron, Pentium II or Pentium III processor the core voltage will probably not be controllable. A CPU settings screen for a Socket 370 motherboard is shown in Figure 5.33.

The BIOS will try to identify the processor and automatically set the correct figures. It is advisable to check that the processor has been correctly identified and that the parameters used by the BIOS are correct. If they are, there is no need to do anything further. If you are sure that an error has been made, there should be a facility that enables the correct figures to be set manually. With Socket 7 motherboards identification errors do seem to occur from time to time, and are usually where the BIOS is a bit over-optimistic about the clock rating of the processor. Note that with Socket 370 Celeron processors the processor itself controls the clock multiplier, and this value can not be changed manually.

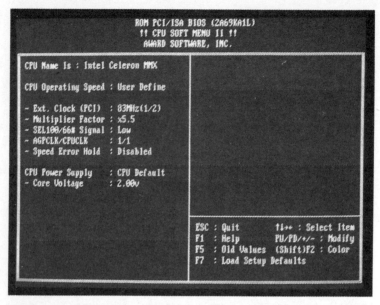

Fig.5.33 *An example of a separate screen for controlling CPU settings*

Finally

As explained previously, changing the motherboard will usually result in Windows 95 or 98 doing a certain amount of hardware installation and reinstallation. It is a good idea to have the Windows CD-ROM and the support discs for the hardware to hand when the PC boots for the first time, as some of them will almost certainly be needed. Follow the on-screen prompts and supply any discs that are requested. This can sometimes be a fairly protracted process, with several reboots being needed before the operating system finally boots properly. The motherboard will almost certainly be provided with a disc of drivers and utilities. Carefully read through the motherboard's instruction manual to see what, if any, additional software must be loaded once the operating system has finally booted. Once any additional software has been loaded it is as well to reboot the computer and then check that the soundcard, etc., are working properly. The rejuvenated PC is then ready for use.

Other
components

Keyboard

The keyboard is the part of a PC that requires most frequent replacement, and one reason for this is simply that it tends to receive a great deal of use. Another factor is undoubtedly that the keyboard tends to come in for a great deal of abuse, and tea or coffee being spilt on to a keyboard is not exactly a rare event. A further problem is that the keyboard is open to the air, and dust will inevitably find its way under the keys. If a keyboard is not cleaned reasonably regularly it is likely that before too long the amount of dust that will accumulate will prevent it from working properly. A lot of keyboard problems can certainly be avoided by working on the basis that prevention is better than cure. Keep liquid refreshment well away from keyboards, and you will not be faced with the task of trying to clean a keyboard that has been given a drenching.

Maintenance

A keyboard requires only some very simple and basic maintenance. The most important thing is to regularly clean off any dust, and ideally the keys should be given a quick clean with a small vacuum cleaner. This should help to remove any dust that gets down into the keys. Even with regular cleaning, after some years of use it is likely that a fair amount of dirt and dust will find its way down into the keyboard mechanism. With the current low cost of most keyboards you may simply take the view that it is not worthwhile spending time trying to resurrect a well-used keyboard. If the unit in question were a very cheap type I would certainly agree with this. The cheaper keyboards tend to wear out relatively quickly and have to be regarded as expendable. With one of the more up-market keyboards it is probably worthwhile giving the keyboard mechanism a thorough clean out. This will normally restore full operation but can be quite time-consuming.

All the PC keyboards I have ever encountered have been fitted with keys that can simply be prised off the switches on which they are mounted. A small screwdriver or any similar implement that can be used as a lever should do the job, but with anything like this you obviously have to proceed carefully. Otherwise there is a real risk of damaging either or one of the keys or the switches, and the keyboard will then be unusable.

In order to thoroughly clean the mechanism it will be necessary to remove all or most of the keys. Many spacebar mechanisms are easily damaged, and most are awkward to fit back together, so I would strongly recommend leaving the spacebar in place. You should be able to clean the keyboard quite well with the spacebar still in position. With the keys removed it should be quite easy to brush away or vacuum up the accumulated dust and fluff. The keys can then be pressed back into place, preferably in the right places!

When keys fail to operate reliably the problem is often due to dust under the keys preventing them from moving down far enough to operate the key-switches reliably. The method of cleaning the keyboard described previously will often cure this type of fault, but it will be ineffective if the problem is due to corrosion on the switch contacts. Lifting off the key top and then applying switch cleaner on and around the key-switch can often remove this corrosion. If the switch is a type that is comprehensively sealed it will not be possible for the contact cleaner to penetrate into the switch, and the keyboard then has to be regarded as non-repairable. If the switch cleaner is able to get into the switch it should remove any corrosion and restore normal operation. If the problem goes away for a while and then recurs it is likely that the problem is due to contact wear rather than corrosion. A new keyboard must then be obtained.

Many keyboards, particularly the cheaper types, do not have individual key-switches, but instead use what is called a "membrane switch". Looking at things in slightly oversimplified terms, this is just a thin membrane having one set of contacts that is held just above a rigid base that has a matching set of contacts. Pressing a key forces one of the contacts on the membrane downwards and onto the corresponding contact on the base. Cleaning the contacts with this type of keyboard is not usually feasible. When a membrane keyboard becomes unreliable and cleaning out the dust under the keys fails to provide an improvement, there is nothing to lose by trying some contact cleaner, but a new keyboard will probably be required. These keyboards are mostly of the "cheap and cheerful" variety, so a replacement should not cost very much.

Washout

Even if you undertake PC repairs on a very occasional basis it is a matter of if rather than when you will be asked for help with a keyboard that has had coffee, a soft drink, or some other sticky liquid spilt all over it. There are actually two problems when this type of spillage occurs. The keyboard mechanism itself is the main problem, and practically any liquid getting into the key-switches is likely to cause corrosion, and may dry to form a layer of insulation. If the liquid is sticky, it could obviously cause the switches to stick in the down position. A membrane keyboard is probably less vulnerable than a type that has individual switches, but a large amount of liquid poured into any type of keyboard is almost certain to find its way to some of the switch contacts.

The second problem is that of the liquid damaging the electronics. If a keyboard gets an unwanted shower you should always unplug it immediately. Liquid getting onto the circuit board is not too serious in itself, and provided it is washed off and the circuit board is dried it is unlikely that any major harm will occur. If the keyboard is left switched on, the voltages on the circuit board can produce electrolysis, which in turn results in thin wires and copper tracks being rapidly eaten away.

With an inexpensive keyboard, particularly if it has received a fair amount of use, you have to be realistic about the merits of trying to rescue it. A new one will only cost a few pounds and there is no guarantee that the cleaned keyboard will work properly. The quick way to attempt a rescue is to first unplug the keyboard from the PC and remove the batteries if it is fitted with any. The usual advice is to immerse the keyboard in a large bowl of distilled water, but this is probably not a practical proposition. Also, the distilled water will not remain distilled for long once the dirty keyboard is placed in it.

Having soaked the keyboard in water, pour away the dirty water, replace it with fresh water, and soak the keyboard again for a minute or two. Then drain as much water as possible from the unit, wipe it as dry as possible, and then leave it standing on one end for a day or two to thoroughly dry out. It is advisable to leave it standing on a cloth because a certain amount of liquid will probably drain out of it during the drying period. If you are lucky, the keyboard will then work properly, but there is probably only an evens chance of success at best.

You can take the longer approach of opening the keyboard case, drying the electronics with a cloth, and giving just the keyboard mechanism the dunking treatment, but this probably makes only a marginal improvement in your chances of success. Also, most keyboards come apart much more easily than they go back together, so you could end up with a sparkling clean keyboard that you can not reassemblecorrectly!

When buying a replacement keyboard bear in mind that there are two types of keyboard connector, both of which are in widespread use today. AT motherboards are equipped with the original 5-pin DIN socket, whereas ATX motherboards have the smaller PS/2 style connector (see

Figure 1.8 in chapter one). Some keyboards are supplied with a lead that has both types of connector, while others have a DIN plug plus a PS/2 adapter (Figure 6.1). In either case the keyboard should be usable with any standard PC. Many keyboards are supplied with only one connector and no adapter, so you have to be careful to obtain a keyboard that is compatible with your PC.

Fig.6.1 A DIN to PS/2 keyboard adapter

If you are using an operating system other than Windows 95 or Windows 98 you do not require the extra keys that are included on most of the current PC keyboards. You may find it difficult to find an ordinary 102-key type, but there should be no difficulties if you use a 105-key unit instead. The three extra keys will probably be ignored by the operating system, but it is highly unlikely that they will cause any problems. It is possible that with some older PCs these extra keys will have no effect even when using Windows 95 or 98. This is not a major problem, since they are something less than essential, but it might be possible to implement these keys properly by upgrading the BIOS.

Mouse

Most mice are supplied complete with one or two test utilities, and these should provide a definitive answer if you think a mouse is faulty, but do not overlook the possibility of a faulty port. If Windows or some other operating system ignores the mouse, it does not necessarily mean that it is faulty. Apart from the possibility of a faulty port, the problem could be due to a glitch in the software causing the mouse to be uninstalled. As a simple initial check, make sure that the mouse lead is connected reliably, and then shut down the computer. With luck, when the PC is rebooted the mouse will be picked up properly by the operating system, and will then be reinstalled. Try looking in the Windows Device Manager to see if any problems are reported with the mouse, and try reinstalling the drivers. If the drivers will not install properly it is possible that there is a software problem, but it is more likely that the hardware is faulty, and the drivers will not install simply because the system can not detect suitable matching hardware.

If the mouse is a serial type and there is a spare serial port on the PC, the obvious initial test is to try moving the mouse to the other serial port. If the mouse fails to work it is not certain that it is faulty, since a fault in the motherboard's input/output chip could result in both serial ports becoming faulty. However, if the mouse works when used on the other serial port, the mouse is clearly not at fault.

Where a change of serial port is not possible, or the mouse is not a serial type, the "acid test" is to try using another mouse, or to try using the suspect mouse on another system. Ideally two identical mice should be swapped, but in the real world if you have ten PCs they are quite likely to use eight or nine different types of mouse. Provided you swap two mice of the same general type (either serial mice or mouse-port mice) you should discover if it is the mouse that is at fault, or something else such as the port. Changing a mouse, like changing most items of hardware on a modern PC, is almost certain to involve installing the new device before the system will boot up properly.

Even if the new mouse is the same general type as the original, the operating system will probably detect that it is not quite the same. It is probably not worthwhile going through with the installation process if the mouse is found to give proper cursor and button control once the system has gone through the initial stages of booting up. The mouse and the port it is connect to are clearly fine if this happens. Keep selecting the "Cancel" option, shut down the system at the earliest opportunity, and then switch back to the original mouse.

In the event that the mouse works properly when used with another PC, but a different mouse does not work with the faulty computer, the port used with the mouse is almost certainly faulty. However, I would strongly recommend reconnecting the mouse and trying to reinstall it again, just to make quite sure that the problem is not due to corrupted drivers.

With this type of thing it is always a good idea to completely remove the original installation by deleting the driver in Device Manager, and then booting the computer without the device connected. Then shut down the PC, reattach the mouse, reboot the computer and reinstall the mouse "from scratch".

Remember to make some basic checks on the port used with the mouse. If it is a port that can be switched off in the BIOS Setup program, go into the Setup program and check that the port is switched on. With a PC that has an AT motherboard make sure that the lead from the motherboard to the mouse port connector is fitted properly.

Failure of a mouse port is a potentially serious matter. Whether the port is a PS/2 mouse type or a serial port, it is almost invariably provided by the motherboard. Ideally the motherboard would be replaced, but there are probably few people prepared to replace a motherboard if a way of working around the problem can be found. It is not a good idea to leave faulty hardware operating, so the first task is to enter the BIOS Setup program to see if the faulty port can be switched off. Unless the motherboard is pretty old it will certainly be possible to switch off any of the standard ports. The ports are usually controlled via a page in the Setup program called something like "Integrated Peripherals", but you may have to search through the pages to find the control for the port you wish to disable.

With the faulty port switched off you then have two basic ways of reinstating a mouse. The obvious one is to use another of the standard ports, assuming that these ports are not also affected by the problem with the motherboard's hardware. If the mouse is a serial type, and the other serial port is unused, the obvious ploy is to simply switch it to the other serial port.

If there is no spare serial port, does the PC have a mouse port? Some serial mice are supplied with an adapter that enables them to be used with a standard mouse port, and any odd accessories such as this should always be kept just in case they come in useful one day. In my experience these adapters do not always work, but it is worth a try if you have one and a PC with a suitable port. Even if you have to buy a mouse-port mouse, this is cheaper and easier than replacing the motherboard. As pointed out in the previous chapter, changing the motherboard in an older PC can necessitate other changes such as a new processor and memory. This makes it a relatively expensive and difficult repair that many users would prefer to avoid, despite the performance increase provided by what is also an upgrade.

If there is no spare serial port and no mouse port either, it is possible to use a serial port on an expansion card to replace the faulty port. Serial port cards are less widely available than they once were, but it should be possible to obtain one from one of the larger computer equipment retailers. A serial port card usually has jumpers to select the address range and the IRQ number, and there should be no problems if you use the same settings that were used for the disabled port. This should avoid the possibility of any hardware conflicts. These are the base addresses (in hexadecimal) and IRQs normally used for serial ports one and two:

Port	Base address	IRQ
1	3F8	4
2	2F8	3

If the problem is a faulty mouse-port mouse, it is unlikely that it will be possible to obtain a mouse port expansion card, although there is no harm in searching through a few catalogues to see if anything suitable is available. The more probable way around the problem is to change to a serial mouse. Again, it is worth looking through you box of computer bits and pieces to see if the mouse-port mouse came complete with an adapter (Figure 6,2). If not, a new serial mouse is quite inexpensive these days, and even if a mouse port expansion card is available, a new serial mouse could be the cheaper option.

Fig.6.2 A PS/2 mouse to serial port adapter

Mouse maintenance

Usually when there are problems with a mouse they are not in the form of a complete failure. If the mouse works intermittently, the most likely cause of the fault is a broken wire in the connecting cable. In most cases it is not too difficult to replace the cable and the connector. The connector for a serial mouse is a nine or 25-way female D connector, either of which should be available from one of the larger electronic component retailers. They should also be able to supply multi-way connecting cable. The connector for a mouse port mouse is less common, and could be difficult or impossible to obtain. Whether it is worth trying to fit a new lead and connector is another matter. The cost of the connector and cable could actually be higher than that of a cheap mouse, which renders the exercise rather pointless.

Probably the most common problem with mice is erratic movement of the on-screen pointer, with the pointer failing to follow all movements of the mouse. It is possible for this type of thing to be caused by problems with the drivers, or other software problems, but it is far more likely that fluff has found its way into the mouse. Virtually all modern mice have a ball covered in a rubber-like material, and as the mouse is moved around the ball rotates. The movement of the ball rotates two metal rods at right angles to each other. One rod rotates when the mouse is moved backwards and forwards, and the other rotates when it is moved from side to side. Either electromagnetic or opto-electronic components convert the rotation of the rods into signals that are fed to the PC.

If the ball and (or) the rods become dirty the mouse will not operate efficiently. There is usually a cover plate on the underside of a mouse

(Figure 6.3) that is easily removed to reveal the interior of the mouse (Figure 6.4). The ball can then be washed and dried, and any dirt or fluff on the rods can be removed. If any fluff has become wound around the rods it may be necessary to carefully cut it away using a modelling knife. Normal operation should be restored

Fig.6.3 The baseplate of most mice is easily removed

once the cleaned mouse has been reassembled. The mouse is simply worn out if it is still a bit erratic in operation, and it should be replaced.

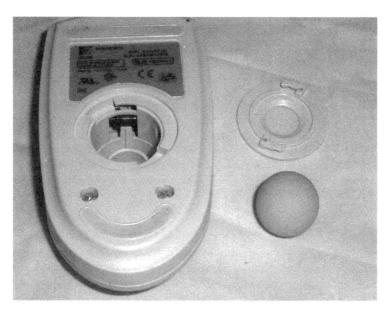

Fig.6.4 With the baseplate removed a mouse is easily cleaned

Mouseless operation

When a mouse fails to operate at all it can be difficult to operate the computer having a graphical user interface such as Windows 98. This can in turn make it difficult to investigate the problem and get things sorted out. It is not impossible though, and Windows can be controlled via the keyboard, as can practically every piece of Windows application software. The relevant Help system should give details of keyboard control, and what you need to know will usually be under the heading "keyboard shortcuts". Pressing the F1 function key is the standard method of bringing up a help screen for the current window. Pressing the Alt key and the text character that is underlined in the menu heading activates pop-down menus. The menu usually includes the key codes that select each item. The same basic methods of control are also used with dialogue boxes, etc.

Serial ports

Serial ports seem to cause more problems than the other standard computer types, and even computer experts can run into difficulties when using them. In fact some modern hardware is reasonably foolproof and comes complete with software and cables that handle everything for you, making it unnecessary to have any idea how a serial port operates. You just connect everything together as per the diagrams, load the software, and start using the digital camera or whatever. In an ideal world all hardware would be supplied in this easy to use form, but in real world computing things are not always that easy, and some knowledge of the way in which serial interfacing operates can often be a decided asset.

Bit-By-Bit

A serial interface sends all eight bits of data over a single line, and it must therefore send bits one at a time. Serial interfaces have a reputation for being slow at data transfers, and it is this bit-by-bit approach that causes the problem. A parallel interface transfers at least whole bytes (eight bits) at a time whereas a serial type literally transfers data on a bit-by-bit basis. A normal RS232C serial interface is asynchronous, which means that there are no additional connecting wires carrying a clock signal or some other form of synchronisation signal. The transmitting and receiving circuits must, of course, be kept correctly synchronised somehow. Synchronisation is achieved by using standard transmission rates and sending additional bits with each byte of data.

The two example waveforms of Figure 6.5 show how this system operates. The signal voltages are not at standard 5-volt logic levels, or any other common logic levels. Instead they are at nominal levels of plus and minus 12 volts. In fact the signal voltages can be as low as 3 volts when fully loaded, but would more usually be at around eight to 10 volts. Never connect serial outputs to any other type of computer port, as this could result in damage to the hardware of the other port.

The device at the heart of a serial interface does actually operate at normal logic levels, but it interfaces to the RS232C connector via special line drivers and receivers. These provide level shifting so that the interface operates at the correct voltage levels, and they also provide an inversion. Hence positive and negative voltages respectively represent logic 0 and logic 1, which is the opposite of the normal logic convention. These waveform diagrams may look completely wrong to anyone familiar with normal logic circuits, but they are in fact correct!

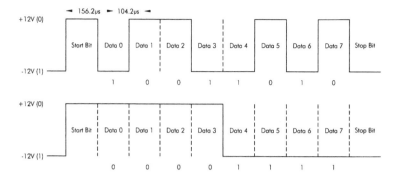

Fig.6.5 Two example serial waveforms

RS232C serial interfaces operate at a number of standard transmission rates, or baud rates as they are known. The baud rate is simply the number of bits sent per second if there is a continuous data stream. All the standard baud rates are listed here:

50	75
150	300
600	1200
2400	4800
9600	19200

The slowness of serial ports will be all too apparent from these rates. They provide data transfers at rates of around five to something under 2000 bytes per second. In an attempt to obtain more respectable transfer rates it is quite common for PC serial ports to be pushed beyond the normal maximum of 19200 baud, and any modern PC should quite happily operate at a maximum of about 115000 baud. Clearly, where a choice is available it is best to use the highest possible baud rate so that the fastest possible transfer rate is obtained. The only exception is where very long connecting cables are used, since the maximum usable cable length reduces as the baud rate is increased. In normal computing the cable lengths are not great enough for this to be a factor.

With only eight bits of data per byte, the transfer rates mentioned previously might seem to be slightly pessimistic. However, the transfer rate is significantly slowed down by the inclusion of synchronisation bits with each byte of data. Including the synchronisation signals there are typically ten bits transmitted per byte, which means that baud rates of 9600 and 19200 provide maximum data transfer rates of just 960 and 1920 bytes per second. Even at 115000 baud the transfer rate is only about 11500 bytes (11.5 kilobytes) per second.

The synchronisation signals are called stop and start bits, which are, as one would expect, sent immediately before and after the data bits. The start bit indicates to the receiving circuit that it must sample the signal line after a certain period of time, and this time is equal to the period of 1.5 bits. In the examples of Figure 6.5 the transmission rate is 9600 baud, which works out at approximately 104.2μs per bit (1000000μs divided by 9600 baud equals 104.2μs). Sampling the input line after 156.2μs (1.5 bits) therefore results in the logic level being tested in the middle of the first bit. This is always the least significant bit (D0). The input line is then tested every 104.2μs until bits D1 through to D7 have been read into the receiver register. The data line is then returned to its standby state for 104.2μs to produce the stop bit, which really just provides a guaranteed minimum gap from one byte of data to the next. This gives the receiving device time to deal with one byte of data before it starts to receive the next one.

Word formats

The serial signal in this example has one start bit, eight data bits, one stop bit, and no parity checking, which is probably the most common word format. However, there are many others in use, with anything from five to eight data bits, one, one and a half, or two stop bits, and odd or even parity checking. There is always a single start bit incidentally. In the present context you will normally require eight-bit data transfers. Some early printers could only handle seven-bit ASCII codes, but modern printers, etc., all require full eight-bit bytes. Parity checking is a simple method of error checking that relies on an extra bit being sent at the end of bytes, where necessary, so that there is always an even number or always an odd number of bits. This method of checking is not very reliable since a double glitch can result in data being corrupted but the parity being left intact. It is little used in practice and I would recommend avoiding word formats that involve either type of parity checking.

Serial interfaces have a reputation for being difficult to deal with, and this is at least partially due to the numerous baud rates and word formats in use. It is not simply enough to get the transmitting and receiving devices connected together correctly. Unless both ends of the system are set up to use the same word format and baud rate it is unlikely that

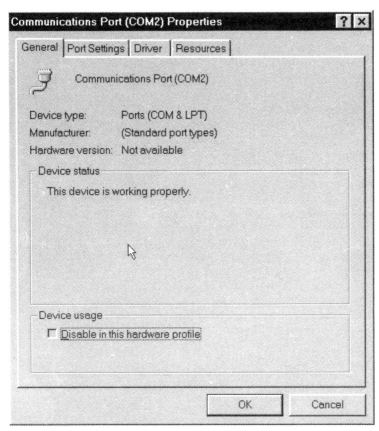

Fig.6.6 This screen in Device Manager gives some basic information

the system will function correctly. It will certainly fail to operate at all if the sending and receiving baud rates are different. Always make sure that both ends of the system are set to the same word format and baud rate. If a serial system fails to transfer data correctly always recheck that the transmitting and receiving circuits are set up correctly.

In Windows 95 and 98 the default baud rate and word format are set via Device Manager. In order to bring up the appropriate control panel, go into Device Manager, double click on the Ports icon, and then double click on the entry for the serial port you wish to check or change. In MS/DOS and Windows terminology the serial ports are COM1, COM2, etc.,

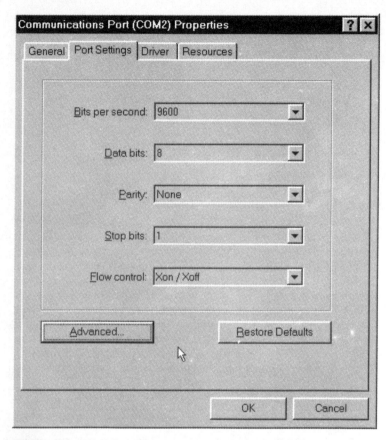

Fig.6.7 The serial port settings can be changed using this screen

and the parallel ports are LPT1, LPT2, etc. To alter the settings for serial port two for example, you would double click on the COM2 entry in Device Manager. This should bring up a screen of the type shown in Figure 6.6, which gives some basic information on the port. Left-click on the Port Settings tab to bring up the control panel of Figure 6.7, where things such as the baud rate and number of stop bits can be set.

It is important to realise that by setting the default parameters you are not necessarily setting the parameters that will be used by applications programs. This is a common cause of serial port woes. Applications software may simply operate with the default serial port settings, and leave it to you to make sure that these are correct for the serial hardware you are using. Quite often though, applications programs set their own defaults and have a control panel where you can alter settings. A few programs, particularly ones, seem to insist that the serial port device is on a certain port and uses a certain word format and baud rate. With unobliging programs of this type you have to use the correct port and set the serial device to suit the program rather than set the program to suit the serial device.

Connections

The normal connector for an RS232C interface is a 25-pin D type, but many PCs have the AT style 9-pin connector. Figures 6.8 and 6.9 respectively provide connection details for 9-pin and 25-pin PC serial ports. It is reasonable to ask why so many connections are required for what is basically just a two-wire method of connection (the signal wire and an earth wire). The first point that has to be made is that an RS232C port provides two-way communications, but it does not use the same wire for communications in each direction. There are separate wires for sending and receiving, and an RS232C port provides full duplex operation. In other words, data can be simultaneously sent and received. However, a full duplex system still only requires three connecting wires (send, receive, and earth). In many practical applications only two or three connecting wires are required, but in others it is essential to implement further connections. These additional connections are mainly concerned with handshaking.

Handshaking is not required in applications where the device receiving data will be able keep up with the flow of

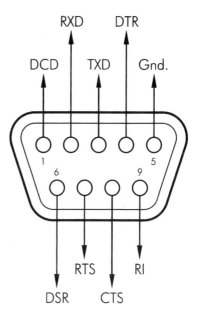

Fig.6.8 The pin functions for a 9-pin serial port

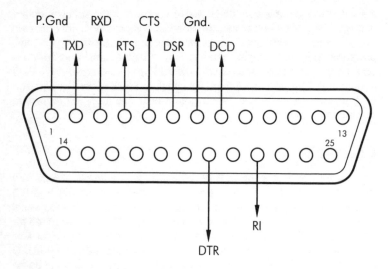

Fig.6.9 The pin functions for a 25-pin serial port

data from PC. Where the receiving device is relatively slow there is a risk that the data will sent faster than the receiving equipment can process it. In order to minimise the risk of data loss it is normal for slow receiving devices to have a large buffer, which is simply some memory in which received data is stored if it can not be processed immediately. In fact most devices that can receive data from an external source have at least a small buffer, and a PC has a small amount of memory set aside for buffering on each of its serial inputs. Actually, there is also a buffer for transmission as well, so that a block of data can be stored for transmission. Under some circumstances this can help the sending software to run more efficiently.

A buffer is not a complete answer where large amounts of data are involved, since it is likely that the buffer would soon become full and data would be lost. Handshaking enables a receiving device to indicate to the sending equipment that it is not able to handle any more data, and that transmission should be halted. Once the backlog of data has been cleared the receiving device indicates that it is ready for more data, and transmission is resumed until the receiving device indicates a further hold-off is required. No matter how slowly the receiving equipment processes the data, the handshaking will ensure that there is a properly controlled flow of data and that no bytes go AWOL. The problem with

RS232C interfaces and handshaking is simply that there is more than one way of implementing this feature. There are two sets of handshake outputs, which are the request to send (RTS) and data terminal ready (DTR) lines. There are also two handshake inputs, which are the clear to send (CTS) and data set ready (DSR) lines.

On the face of it there is no reason for having two sets of handshake lines, since one set is all that is needed to control the flow of data. The usual scheme of things, if both sets are actually implemented, is to have CTS and RTS to control the flow of data, with DTR and DSR indicating whether or not the receiving device is actually operational. If a serial printer is off-line because it is out of paper for example, this would be indicated via DTR and DSR. The CTS and RTS lines would be used to control the flow of data when the printer was on-line. In reality the way in which the handshake lines are used varies somewhat from one serial device to another, and serial links will sometimes only function if they are connected in what is theoretically the wrong manner. It is advisable to avoid hardware handshaking where this is possible. Where it is implemented it often results in a try everything until it works approach!

Unfortunately, there is a possible complication in that some PCs are reluctant to send data unless the handshake inputs are held at the level that indicates the receiving device is ready for action. For some reason this may even "gum up the works" when the PC is set to use software handshaking or no handshaking at all. The root of the problem is that handshake inputs may assume the hold-off state if they are simply left floating. A simple solution that usually works is to cross-couple the serial port's handshake lines. In practice this means connecting the clear to send (CTS) and data set ready (DSR) inputs to the request to send (RTS) and data terminal ready (DTR) outputs respectively.

XON/XOFF

Software handshaking was mentioned previously, but what is software handshaking, or XON/XOFF handshaking, as it is also known? This is where the handshaking is controlled via software codes sent from the receiving device to the transmitting device via a data link. With this type of handshaking you therefore need a full-duplex (two-way) link even though data is only being sent in one direction (half-duplex operation). The ASCII codes 17 and 19 are normally used for XON (switch on) and XOFF (switch off) respectively. In theory it is not necessary to have the handshake lines coupled together, but as already pointed out, the sending device may refuse to send anything unless its handshake inputs are at the "on" voltage. Presumably it decides that the receiving device is off-line and refuses to start transmitting until it gets the appropriate input level on one or both of its handshake inputs.

You might also encounter references to DCE and DTE when dealing with serial interfacing. These respectively stand for data communications equipment and data terminal equipment. In theory a serial link normally consists of a DCE device and a DTE type. A computer is normally the device that controls the system, and is a DTE unit. Something like a printer or modem would normally be the controlled device, or the DCE unit in serial interfacing terminology. The difference between the two types is that DTE units transmit on their "TXD" outputs and receive on their "RXD" inputs. Things are done the other way round with DCE units, which transmit on their "RXD" lines and receive on their "TXD" lines. The handshake lines are also swapped over so that inputs become outputs and vice versa.

This may seem to be pointless and potentially confusing, and I suppose that a good case to this effect could be made. Apparently the reason for having the two categories of equipment is that it enables a so-called "straight" connecting cable to be used. In other words, the cable connects pin one at one end to pin one at the other end, pin two to pin two, and so on. Connecting two DCE units together, or two DTE types, requires the correct method of cross coupling for successful operation. For example, pin two at one end has to connect to pin three at the other in order to provide a data link.

As far as I am aware, PC serial ports are always of the DTE variety, but things are less straightforward with peripherals such as printers and modems. In days gone by it was quite common for printers, etc., to be of the DCE type, as one would expect. These days most units that have a serial interface seem to be of the DTE variety. The only way to be absolutely certain which type of interface you are dealing with is to consult the unit's instruction manual.

Sudden failure

If an existing set-up that uses a serial port suddenly fails to work, the problem is obviously not due to an incorrect cable. On the face of it, the fault is not due to an incorrect setting somewhere either. Even so, it is a good idea to check that no settings in the PC or on the peripheral device have become changed. In theory, one applications program will not make changes to settings that could affect other programs. In practice some programs do seem to alter the default settings for ports, and then fail to put them back again before the program fully shuts down.

A more common problem is that of newly installed software altering settings without asking the user's permission, or informing the user that changes have been made. This can render peripheral devices unusable with other programs. Problems can (and often do) arise when software is uninstalled. If new software has recently been added or old software has been removed from the system, and a peripheral device fails to respond properly, I would definitely start by checking any relevant operating system settings. In the case of something like a printer that has its own settings that can be accessed via the Windows 98 Control Panel, check the settings for the printer as well as the set-up for the appropriate port.

Cables

The situation is very different if you connect a new peripheral to a serial port and the new device fails to respond properly. While the possibility of the port being faulty can not be totally ruled out, it is far more likely that something is not set up correctly or that the serial cable is of the wrong type. When buying serial cables you have to be careful to buy one that has the right type of connectors. Depending on whether the two items are DTE, DCE, or one of each, you will respectively need two female connectors, two male connectors, or one of each type. Matters are further complicated by the fact that many PCs use 9-pin connectors and not the standard 25-pin variety. Where appropriate you must obtain a lead that uses a 9-pin connector at the PC end, or use a 25-pin type with the appropriate adapter. These adapters are readily available, and are often supplied with PCs and peripherals that use a serial interface (Figure 6.10).

When dealing with serial cables you will encounter the terms "straight" and "null modem". A "straight" cable, as explained previously, has pin one connected to pin one, pin two connected to pin two, and so on. This type of cable has a male connector at one end and a female connector at the other, and is used to connect a DTE device to a DCE type. A null modem cable is used to connect two DTE devices together, and has cross coupling of the data and handshake lines. A cable of this type has two female connectors. In order to connect two computers together a null modem cable is required, but a "straight" cable should be needed to connect a PC to a peripheral such as a modem. As pointed out previously, not all peripherals have a DCE style serial interface, so it

Fig.6.10 9 to 25 and 25 to 9-pin serial adapters

is essential to study equipment manuals before ordering a serial cable. Virtually all modern equipment that uses a serial interface will operate using a standard null modem or "straight" serial cable.

In the past serial equipment was much less accommodating, and a fair percentage would not work with any form of standard cable. In order to get things working it was often necessary to resort to a device called a RS232C breakout box, and these are still available. A breakout box is a serial cable having a break in the middle, where a box containing some terminals is fitted. By connecting the terminals using wires it is possible to implement any desired interconnections between the two serial ports. If things end up with the try everything until it works approach, a breakout box enables various methods of connection to be tried quickly and easily. Having found a method of connection that works properly, you then use this information to make up a suitable custom serial cable.

When messing around with serial ports there is a danger of accidentally connecting two outputs together, which is normally courting disaster, but RS232C outputs have current limiting circuits that should prevent any damage occurring. Breakout boxes are perhaps less useful than they once were, and are probably not a worthwhile investment unless you will be dealing with a lot of non-standard serial equipment.

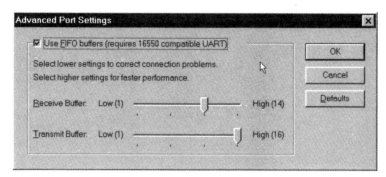

Fig.6.11 The control panel for advanced serial port settings

Sometimes operation via a serial or parallel port seems to be working, but there are odd problems here and there with lost data or error messages appearing on the screen. In the port settings control panel there is a button marked "Advanced", and operating this brings up a window of the type shown in Figure 6.11. The transmitter and receiver buffer sizes can be altered using the slider controls, and by default are normally at high settings to give fast operation. Using lower settings can sometimes clear minor communications problems. Remember that the receiver buffer is only used when the computer receives data via the serial port, and the transmitter buffer is only used when data is sent to a peripheral by way of the serial port. Of course, both are used with a device that supports two-way communications, such as a modem.

The most likely cause of problems is a timeout occurring because the device receiving data provides a long hold-off while it digests a large amount of data. In order to avoid the possibility of a printer error causing the system to hang up, most printer drivers have a timeout facility that produces an error message after a preset amount of time. In theory, a timeout does not matter too much, because the window that appears with the error message usually gives the option of continuing regardless. In practice it can be a bit tedious if you have to keep cancelling the error message, and in my experience the odd glitch can occur in the printing process. For example, I had one system that often lost a page if the dreaded timeout error message occurred.

It should be possible to avoid this message by setting a long timeout value in the control program for the printer driver. To bring up this program go into the control panel, double click on the Printers icon, double click on the icon for the appropriate printer, then select Printer and Properties from the pop-down menu system. This should bring up

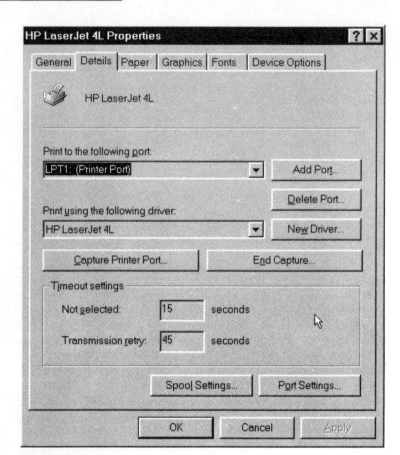

Fig.6.12 An example printer control screen

the control program for the printer, but there could be a number of control and information windows available, so you may have to search for the section that enables the timeout value to be altered.

There may be two timeout settings, as in the example of Figure 6.12. One is the maximum time the computer waits for a response after trying to contact the printer. This is normally a very short time, but with a printer that requires a warm-up period it may indicate to the computer that it is offline for half a minute or more after it is first switched on. The other time is the normal timeout period. This is the maximum time the computer waits after a hold-off handshake signal has been received.

Parallel ports

A modern PC usually has one parallel port included on the motherboard, with any additional ports of this type implemented using an expansion card. Parallel ports are generally easier to deal with than the serial variety because there is only one type of cable to deal with. Actually this is not strictly true, but the only common form of parallel port cable is the standard printer type that has a 25-way male D connector at the computer end, and a 36-way Centronics style connector at the other. There are some parallel port devices that use non-standard cables, but these are usually supplied complete with a suitable cable.

These days parallel ports tend to be used as more than simple printer ports, and are often used for two-way communications. Even when used with printers, a substantial amount of information is often sent from the printer to the computer. This sort of thing enables the printer driver to indicate the amount of ink or toner left in the printer, and other factors that are not accommodated by a basic Centronics style printer link. One practical consequence of this upgrading of the printer port over the years is that some older printer cables do not work properly with modern printers and other gadgets that connect to parallel ports. If you replace an old printer with the last word in modern printer technology it is advisable to replace the printer cable as well.

Port modes

The original PCs did not have various operating modes for the printer port, which operated as a simple eight-bit parallel output port having handshake lines and a few additional lines. These extra lines could be used for such things as the printer indicating to the computer that it was out of paper or offline. Figure 6.13 shows the pin functions for a PC parallel port. Later developments mainly centred on using the printer port for bidirectional operation. In other words, using the eight data lines to read in information as well as sending it. Parallel port scanners, for example, use this ability. Although these enhanced modes have been in existence for many years, it took some time for them to become a standard feature on PCs. Even so, practically every Pentium PC has some enhanced parallel port capability, as do some of the later 80486 based PCs.

If a new device that requires an enhanced parallel port mode fails to work, the obvious first check is to see if the port is set to a suitable operating mode. The operating mode, if any enhanced modes are

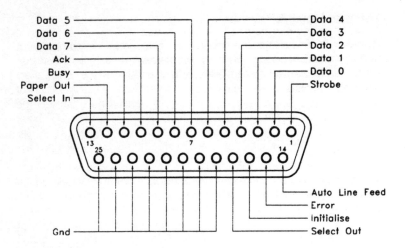

Fig.6.13 Parallel port pin functions

available, is set via the BIOS Setup program. With a modern BIOS there will probably be a page called something like "Integrated Peripherals" that controls the built-in ports, but with older PCs you may have to search through the various pages to locate the right one. If there are no facilities to alter the parallel port modes in the BIOS Setup program it is unlikely that the PC supports any enhanced modes. Figure 6.14 shows a typical page for the control of the integrated peripherals, and there are several entries that are associated with the parallel port. Each port, including the parallel type, can be switched on or off. In the case of the serial and parallel ports it also possible to alter the port addresses and interrupt (IRQ) numbers. This can be useful when trying to avoid conflicts with hardware fitted in the expansion slots.

There will be various parallel port modes available, but with a modern BIOS it is unlikely that there will be a Standard (output only) mode. This option is available on some older PCs. The choices will probably be SPP, EPP, and ECP, which are all bi-directional modes. For most purposes either SPP or EPP will suffice. Only set ECP operation if you use the port with a device that definitely needs this mode.

Like a faulty serial port on the motherboard, a parallel type can be replaced with an expansion card provided the on-board port can be switched off. This should be possible via the BIOS Setup program, as described previously. Having faulty circuitry on the motherboard is undesirable, even it the faulty circuit is disabled, but the alternative is to replace the motherboard, which might also require other items of hardware to be updated. If you use an expansion card to "repair" a faulty port, use the same address and IRQ settings for the card that were used by the port it replaces. This should avoid any problems with hardware conflicts.

Problems with parallel cables are far from rare, and the rather heavy and inflexible cable used does tend to encourage problems with wires pulling away from the connectors if the leads are not given the "kid glove" treatment. Checking this type of lead with a continuity tester is complicated by the fact that the two types of connector are different, with a 25-way connector at one end of the cable and a 36-way type at the other. This table gives a list of the standard interconnections.

PC	Centronics	PC	Centronics
1	1	14	14
2	2	15	32
3	3	16	31
4	4	17	36
5	5	18	33
6	6	19	19
7	7	20	21
8	8	21	23
9	9	22	25
10	10	23	27
11	11	24	29
12	12	25	30
13	13		

There are clearly many more earth connections (also known as ground connections) on the Centronics port than there are on a PC parallel port. The most common solution is to simply leave some of the earth (ground) terminals on the Centronics port unconnected, but with some printer cables each earth connection at the PC port connects to two earth terminals at the Centronics port. Provided the cable carries some earth connections successfully and there are no other problems, it should work well enough. Note that the cable is a screened type, and that the

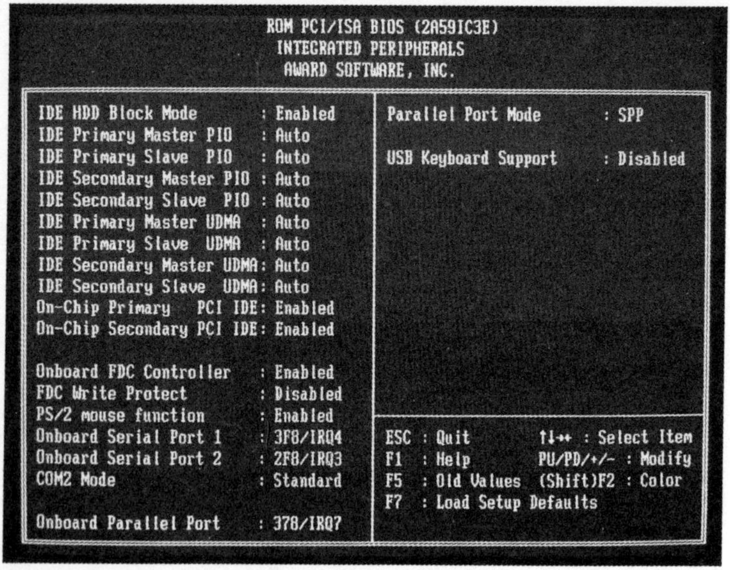

```
                    ROM PCI/ISA BIOS (2A59IC3E)
                       INTEGRATED PERIPHERALS
                        AWARD SOFTWARE, INC.

 IDE HDD Block Mode        : Enabled    Parallel Port Mode      : SPP
 IDE Primary Master PIO    : Auto
 IDE Primary Slave  PIO    : Auto       USB Keyboard Support    : Disabled
 IDE Secondary Master PIO  : Auto
 IDE Secondary Slave  PIO  : Auto
 IDE Primary Master UDMA   : Auto
 IDE Primary Slave  UDMA   : Auto
 IDE Secondary Master UDMA : Auto
 IDE Secondary Slave  UDMA : Auto
 On-Chip Primary   PCI IDE : Enabled
 On-Chip Secondary PCI IDE : Enabled

 Onboard FDC Controller    : Enabled
 FDC Write Protect         : Disabled
 PS/2 mouse function       : Enabled
 Onboard Serial Port 1     : 3F8/IRQ4   ESC : Quit         ↑↓→← : Select Item
 Onboard Serial Port 2     : 2F8/IRQ3   F1  : Help         PU/PD/+/- : Modify
 COM2 Mode                 : Standard   F5  : Old Values   (Shift)F2 : Color
                                        F7  : Load Setup Defaults
 Onboard Parallel Port     : 378/IRQ7
```

Fig.6.14 This BIOS screen provides control over the built-in ports

screen provides a connection between the metal chassis of the two connectors. This connection is not really needed, since there are numerous earth connections carried by the cable. The point of earthing the screen is that it prevents the cable from radiating significant amounts of radio frequency interference (RFI).

Port testing

Most general-purpose PC checking programs have sections that deal with the serial and parallel ports. These can be useful if the problem does not seem to be due to a faulty peripheral or cable, but you require confirmation that the port is faulty. These programs mostly offer two levels of testing. The more superficial tests simply check that the appropriate port registers are present and behave as expected, but make no attempt to read or write data. If a port fails this type of test, or the checking software simply fails to find the port at all, there is certainly a major fault in the port hardware.

The more detailed tests change the states of some output lines and attempt to read the states of these via some input lines. This loopback

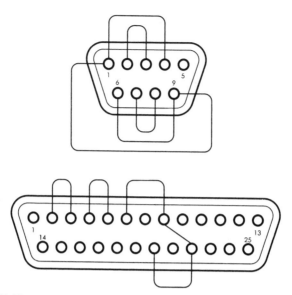

Fig.6.15 The connections for typical loopback serial port testing

testing as it is called requires the appropriate connections across certain pins of the port. In some cases connections are needed from one port to another, but most testing of this type is carried out using just the port under test.

The required connections vary somewhat from one test program to another, and the companies that produce diagnostics software can often supply matching loopback connectors. Details of the required

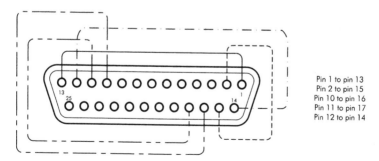

Pin 1 to pin 13
Pin 2 to pin 15
Pin 10 to pin 16
Pin 11 to pin 17
Pin 12 to pin 14

Fig.6.16 Typical connections for parallel loopback testing

interconnections should also be published in the manual for the program, and (or) on the software manufacturer's web site. The loopback plugs illustrated in Figures 6.15 (serial) and 6.16 (parallel) work with the popular

Checkit program and some others. If you have a soldering iron it is easy to make your own low cost loopback plugs. For a serial type you need a 9 or 25-way female D connector, and for a parallel type a 25-way male D connector is needed. The links are easily added using multi-strand insulated connecting wire. Fix the connector to the worktop with Bostik Blu Tack or something similar so that you do not have

Fig.6.17 A 9-pin loopback plug

to chase the connector around the worktop while trying to make the connections! Figure 6.17 shows a completed 9-pin serial loopback connector.

USB

USB (universal serial bus) is intended to replace serial and parallel ports in the fullness of time. Although gaining in popularity, particularly with scanner and digital camera users, it remains less popular than the traditional ports. One reason for this is undoubtedly that is not properly supported by many operating systems, and is therefore unusable on many systems that have the necessary hardware. Many of the problems that occur when using USB ports are probably due to problems with the operating system rather than hardware faults. Users of Windows 95 often find that the entries for the USB ports in Device Manager have the dreaded yellow exclamation marks or question marks to indicate that there is a problem. The motherboard may be supplied with a software fix to remove these problems, but in my relatively limited experience of USB ports the best way around this problem is to upgrade to Windows 98.

USB uses only three connecting wires, which are earth, data, and +5-volt supply. The data line carries data in both directions, and numerous devices can be driven from a single port. Data is sent in serial fashion, but it can be transferred at rates around one hundred times faster than a normal PC serial interface can handle. A USB port is clearly more advanced than a normal serial type, but its standardised three-wire method of interconnection should avoid most of the cabling hassles associated with RS232C ports. The cable should still be checked before concluding that the port itself is at fault. The peripheral device should also be tested with another USB port, preferably on another PC.

Older computers generally lack USB ports for the simple reason that this type of interface did not exist when these PCs were made. If an older PC has USB ports an expansion card will therefore provide them. Most PCs made in the last few years have two of these ports, and they are an integral part of the motherboard. For some reason a fair percentage of PCs that have onboard USB ports have the ports disabled by default. This is particularly common with Socket 7 AT motherboards. It is a good idea to go into the BIOS Setup program and check that the USB ports are enabled prior to using them for the first time.

If a USB expansion card fails there is no great problem. Simply replace it with a new one. Matters are more awkward if the USB hardware is part of the motherboard. As with onboard parallel and serial ports, one option is to go into the BIOS and disable the faulty ports and then replace them with an expansion card. This is less than ideal as it leaves faulty hardware on the motherboard, and there is a very slight risk in operating hardware that is not fully working. On the other hand, with the faulty ports disabled the risk should be absolutely minimal, and the only other way around the problem is to fit a new motherboard.

Hardware conflicts

A hardware conflict is where two or more pieces of hardware try to use the same resources, which means the same address range or IRQ number. Conflicts can occur between practically any two pieces of hardware, but in practice it is when dealing with ports that this problem is most likely to occur. It is a subject that should not really arise when faultfinding, since conflicts should not arise provided everything is installed and set up correctly in the first place. In practice mistakes in the original set-up can go unnoticed until a new peripheral is added to an existing port which fails to work.

It would perhaps be as well to briefly consider what address range and IRQ conflicts actually are. As many readers will no doubt be aware, the computer selects the required memory location by setting the appropriate pattern of high and low voltage on numerous output terminals. These are the address lines, which are known collectively as the address bus. Much the same system is used when the processor accesses a hardware

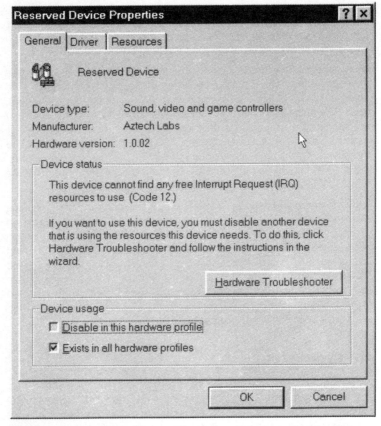

Fig.6.18 The Hardware Troubleshooter can help to resolve conflicts

device, and each piece of hardware is given its own range of addresses. With some processors the hardware and memory share the same address range, but with the 8088 series of processors used in PCs the two are completely separate. An extra output on the processor is used to switch from one to the other, and the same address lines are used for hardware and memory. However, fewer address lines are used for hardware accesses, and PC use a simplified form of hardware addressing that gives even fewer addresses. In fact there are just 1024 hardware addresses available. This should still be enough for even the most feature-rich PC.

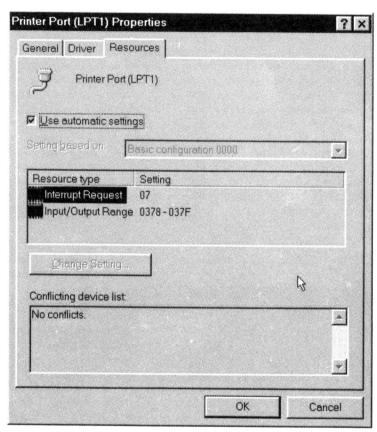

Fig.6.19 Resource settings can be altered manually

IRQ numbers are the more usual source of hardware conflicts. The IRQ (interrupt request) lines are used by many pieces of hardware to indicate to the processor that they need urgent attention. Hardware on the motherboard such as the timers produce a constant stream of interrupts. Expansion cards and even external devices can also generate interrupts. An interrupt is produced each time you operate the mouse for example. The problem with interrupts is that only a limited number of devices can be accommodated by the system used on PCs. Under the right circumstances an IRQ number can be shared by two or more devices, and the PCI bus includes facilities for IRQ sharing, but in general only one device should be used per IRQ number. Note that sharing of addresses is never acceptable, and could cause damage to the hardware.

If a hardware conflict occurs there should be a yellow warning marker in the appropriate Device Manager entry or entries. In Windows 95 and 98 there are built-in facilities that can help you to sort things out in the form of the Hardware Conflict Troubleshooter. If you double-click on the entry for a troublesome piece of hardware in Device Manager a window of the type shown in Figure 6.18 should appear. Simply operate the Hardware Toubleshooter button to launch the program, and then supply any information it requires. With luck, this program will sort things out for you. Note that the Hardware Troubleshooter button will only be present if the device in question has a problem, but it is not really needed if no problems are reported for any of the hardware. However, this program can be launched at any time via the Help system (look up "Hardware - conflicts").

It is possible to manually control the assignment of hardware resources by double clicking on the Device Manager entry for a device to bring up the screen of Figure 6.18, and then operating the Resources tab. This brings up a window of the type shown in Figure 6.19. By default there will be a tick in the box marked "use automatic settings". Left-click on this box to remove the tick, and make the Change Settings button active. Operating this button or double-clicking on an entry in the resource setting table brings up yet another window that

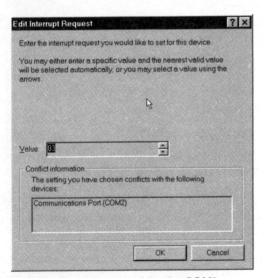

Fig.6.20 This screen enables the COM2 IRQ number to be changed

enables manual changes to be made (Figure 6.20). Unless you really know what you are doing it is definitely not advisable to manually alter the settings. Playing around with the settings for one device could result in another device malfunctioning. In the bottom section of the window you can scroll through various settings, and any conflicts will be indicated here. Remember that you can also use the Windows System Information program to get detailed information on the current assignment of hardware resources.

Something else to bear in mind is that it is no good using settings unless the hardware concerned actually supports them. Also, in cases where the resources of a device are controlled manually by jumpers, DIP-switches, etc., these must be set to agree with the resource assignments used by Windows. For example, if a printer port card is set to a base address of 3BC but in Windows it is assigned a base address of 2F8, when Windows tries to access the device it will not respond. In addition to avoiding conflicts, it is necessary to have the Windows resource assignments and the actual hardware settings agree in order for everything to function properly.

Power supplies

Although early PC power supply units were not the most reliable of devices, modern units seem to be much more dependable. However, like anything else they can and do go wrong occasionally. As pointed out in chapter two, a lack of output from the power supply can be due to a fault in some other part of the PC. A PC power supply is a sophisticated piece of electronics that manages to convert the a.c. mains input into a variety of d.c. output voltages with minimal power wastage. This is achieved using a type of circuit known as a switch mode power supply. Any form of power supply is vulnerable to damage from overloads, transients on the supply input, etc., but switch mode supplies are more vulnerable than most others are. This is probably why many early PC power supply designs were prone to failure. Modern designs are much better, and have comprehensive built-in protection circuits. These circuits will often cause the supply to cut out if there is a problem elsewhere in the PC, such as a disc drive short-circuiting a supply line or one of the motherboard connectors connected incorrectly.

If the supply refuses to supply proper output voltages it will have to be replaced. It is worth emphasising once again that only those having suitable training can only repair a PC power supply, and it is not something that can be serviced by a do-it-yourself repairer. Many parts of the circuit operate at high voltages and some connect direct to the mains supply. Never remove the top cover from a PC power supply unit. The current cost of one of these units is far too low to make repair worth considering, and a faulty unit should be replaced.

Fig.6.21 The power supply is normally retained by four screws

When obtaining a replacement you must be careful to obtain a supply of the right type. If the original supply has one motherboard connector it is an ATX type, but if it has two it is an AT supply. The new supply must have a power rating equal to or higher than that of the original unit. The original supply unit should be marked with a power rating somewhere on its outer casing. Probably the main pitfall when replacing a power supply is that you must obtain one that is a good physical match for the original unit. Otherwise the new supply will work perfectly, but there will be no way of mounting it in the case. This problem is due to the fact that PC power supply units have been produced in a variety of shapes and sizes over the years. Provided the PC is reasonably modern and has a standard type of case there will probably be no problem. An "off the shelf" power supply, whether of the ATX or AT varieties, will probably act as a direct replacement for the original unit. It is still a good idea to make some careful measurements on the old supply unit so that you can compare them with measurements taken from prospective replacements.

Problems are most likely to occur when dealing with an old PC or one that has some unusual form of case, such as a very low-profile desktop type. A standard replacement power supply may not fit into the available space. Even if it will, it is quite likely that its mounting arrangements will be different to those of the original. Unless the PC manufacturer can supply a suitable spare, the only option is to buy a new case and power

Fig.6.22 An ATX power supply removed from the case

supply. The PC is then rebuilt into the new case. Surprisingly perhaps, this will probably cost little more than just replacing the power supply. In terms of the work required it multiplies things by a factor of ten or more, so this course of action is best avoided where possible.

If a replacement power supply will fit in place of the original reasonably well, but only three out of the four mounting bolts can be fitted into place, this should be good enough. It is best not to start drilling new mounting holes in the case as this will inevitably produce small pieces of metal that could find their way into the electronics. This would in turn

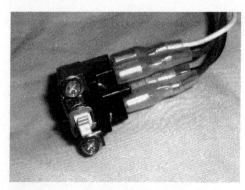

lead to short-circuits that could cause costly damage. Although rebuilding the computer into a new case involves a lot of work, it is safer than drilling and cutting the original case in an attempt to fit "a square peg into a round hole".

Fig.6.23 The on/off switch of an AT power supply has two fixing screws

Assuming the new power supply fits the case accurately, replacing a power supply unit is one of the easier repairs. Start by disconnecting the supply from the mains, and where appropriate also disconnect the mains output lead to the monitor. Next disconnect the power supply from the drives and the motherboard. The supply can be removed from the case by undoing the four fixing bolts that secure it to the rear panel of the case. Figure 6.21 shows an AT power supply, but the mounting arrangement for an ATX power supply is exactly the same. Figure 6.22 shows an ATX power supply that has been removed from the case. There may be other bolts in the case near to the power supply, so look carefully before removing anything.

There is a slight complication with AT supplies in the form of the on/off switch. The new power supply is normally equipped with an on/off switch and lead, so the old switch must be removed and replaced as well. The on/off switch is bolted to the front of the case by two screws (Figure 6.23), but it might be necessary to do some dismantling at the front of the case to get at them. Make sure the insulation on the connections to the new switch is in good condition. It would be dangerous to use the switch if the insulation is not fully effective. Note that although an AT power supply will fit in place of an ATX type, and vice versa, they are not really interchangeable due to the differences in their on/off switches.

With the old supply unit removed the new one can be fitted into place and bolted in position using the four original fixing bolts. Where appropriate, the new on/off switch can also be mounted on the case using the old fixing screws. With all the cabling reconnected the PC is then ready for testing.

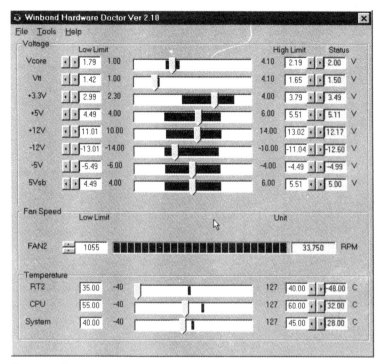

Fig.6.24 Some motherboards have sensors that can be read using suitable software. This is the HW Doctor program in action

Monitoring

It is perhaps worth mentioning that many motherboards are now euipped with sensors that monitor various temperatures and voltages. With a PC that has this facility it is worthwhile using it to check the voltages from a power supply that seems to be giving problems. Figure 6.24 shows the HW Doctor program in action. Some of the monitored voltages might be produced by regulators on the motherboard rather than the power supply itself, so you need to read the documentation for the program to determine what is actually being monitored. An apparent fault in the power supply could actually be a problem with the motherboard.

It is only fair to point out that an apparent problem in another part of a PC can actually be due to a fault in its power supply. It is not unknown for intermittent memory problems to actually be caused by a power supply that has a tendency to glitch occasionally. If a PC has an intermittent fault that is difficult to pin down, some service engineers replace the power supply before trying anything else.

Appendix 1

Useful Web addresses 1

http://www.abit.com.tw	Abit
http://www.aopenusa.com	Aopen
http://www.asus.com.tw	Asustec
http://www.chaintech.com.tw	Chaintech
http://www.ecsusa.com	Elitegroup
http://www.Gigabyte.com	Gigabyte
http://www.gbt_tech.co.uk	Gigabyte (UK)
http://www.iwillusa.com	Iwill
http://www.jetway.com.tw	Jetway
http://www.pcchips.com	PC Chips
http://www.qdigrp.com	QDI
http://www.qdi.nl/english	QDI (UK)
http://www.mycomp-tmc.com	TMC
http://www.supermicro.com	Supermicro
http://www.soyo.com.tw	Soyo
http://www.tyan.com	Tyan
http://www.tekram.com	Tekram

This is a list of the web addresses for a range of motherboard manufacturers. The name of the company concerned is usually apparent from the address, but the manufacturer's name is given anyway. Where two addresses are given for one manufacturer, one is the main site and the other is a UK specific site. If you intend to replace a motherboard it is well worthwhile visiting the web sites of some motherboard manufacturers, where you will find detailed information on their products. In many cases the instruction manuals for the boards are also available, and a great deal can be learned by looking through some of these.

Appendix 2

Useful Web addresses 2

http://www.3com.co.uk	3Com (modems)
http://www.atitech.com	ATI (graphics cards)
http://www.cle.creaf.com	Creative Labs (sound, graphics)
http://www.diamondmm.com	Diamond (sound, graphics)
http://www.fujitsu.computers.com	Fujitsu (hard discs)
http://www.hercules.com	Hercules (graphics)
http://www.uk.ibm.com	IBM (hard discs)
http://www.matrox.com	Matrox (graphics)
http://www.quantum.com	Quantum (hard discs)
http://www.seagate.com	Seagate (hard discs)
http://www.stb.com	STB (sound, graphics)
http://www.wdc.com	Western Digital (hard discs)
http://www.yamaha.co.uk	Yamaha (soundcards)

This is a list of the web sites for some of the main manufacturers of soundcards, graphics cards, hard discs, etc. These sites contain a great deal of useful information in addition to detailed specifications for the products on offer. Instuction manuals for some of the hard disc drives can be downloaded, and a great deal can be learnt from these.

Appendix 3

IRQ assignments

Modern PCs have 16 interrupts available and they are numbered from 0 to 15. These are the (more or less) standard IRQ assignments.

Interrupt	Function
IRQ0	System timer
IRQ1	Keyboard controller
IRQ2	Programmable interrupts
IRQ3	COM2
IRQ4	COM1
IRQ5	Expansion card (usually soundcard or LPT2)
IRQ6	Floppy controller
IRQ7	LPT1
IRQ8	Real-time clock
IRQ9	Expansion card (default for network card)
IRQ10	Expansion card
IRQ11	Expansion card (default for SCSI adapter)
IRQ12	Mouse port
IRQ13	Math coprocessor
IRQ14	IDE1
IRQ15	IDE2

Appendix 4

I/O address assignments

Only the lowest 1024 input/output addresses are used by PC hardware. Originally the lower half was for hardware on the motherboard and the upper half was for expansion cards, but the situation is not as clear-cut as this with modern PCs. As is the convention, the addresses given here are in hexadecimal.

Address	Function
000-01F	DMA controller (master)
020-021	Interrupt controller (master)
022-023	Control register (I/O ports)
040-05F	Timer control registers
060-06F	Keyboard interface
070-07F	Real-time clock and CMOS
080-09F	DMA register
0A0-0BF	Interrupt controller (slave)
0C0-0DF	DMA controller (slave)
0F0-0FF	Math coprocessor
1F0-1F8	Hard disc controller
200-207	Game port
278-27F	LPT2
2B0-2DF	Video card
2E8-2EF	COM4
2F8-2FF	COM2
360-36F	Network ports
378-37F	LPT1
3B0-3BF	Monochrome video card and parallel port

3C0-3CF	EGA adapter
3D0-3DF	CGA adapter
3E8-3EF	COM3
3F0-3F7	Floppy disc controller
3F8-3FF	COM1

Index

Ollscoil na hÉireann, Gaillimh

3 1111 40070 7947